As soon as Darryl got home from the hospital, Dante wanted him to call Deborah in her presence. She demanded he tell his daughter that he would not be paying for the wedding, and when he refused, it led to a knock-down, drag-out fight.

Dante threatened to kill him if he didn't obey. She told him she had a gun, and all at once, there was something in her voice that scared him. It was like she was a different person. At first she ranted, then her tone moved to this incredible calm.

"I've done this before," she said, smiling, "and I've always gotten away with it. . . ."

Praise for Aphrodite Jones's *All She Wanted*

"The book sizzles . . . a gripping read."
—*The Herald* (Lake Worth, FL)

"This fragile family background has been compellingly and encyclopedically documented by the true-crime writer Aphrodite Jones. . . ."
—*The New Yorker*

"Riveting, well-researched."
—*Fort Lauderdale Sun-Sentinel*

Attention: Schools and Corporations have 10 or more copies for special promotions [?] premiums. For details please write to the Vice President of Special Markets, Pocket Books, 1230 Avenue of the Americas, New York, NY 10020-1586. [?]

For information on how to use [?] legal resources to place orders please write to Mail Order, Department Orders, Pocket Books, 1230 Avenue of the Americas, New York, NY 10020.

Books by Aphrodite Jones

Cruel Sacrifice
The FBI Killer
All She Wanted*
Della's Web*

*Published by POCKET BOOKS

DELLA'S WEB

A TRUE STORY OF MARRIAGE AND MURDER

APHRODITE JONES

POCKET **STAR** BOOKS

New York   London   Toronto   Sydney   Tokyo   Singapore

An *Original* Publication of POCKET BOOKS

A Pocket Star Book published by
POCKET BOOKS, a division of Simon & Schuster Inc.
1230 Avenue of the Americas, New York, NY 10020

ISBN: 0-671-01379-3

First Pocket Books printing March 1998

10 9 8 7 6 5

POCKET STAR BOOKS and colophon are registered trademarks of Simon & Schuster Inc.

Cover photo courtesy of Shawn Craig

Printed in the U.S.A.

For Janet

Acknowledgments

This book would not have been possible without the support of so many Cincinnatians, many of whom appear on the pages you read here, others whose silent voices helped to add texture to this timeless story. In particular, I want to thank the men who were brave enough to talk about the domestic violence they suffered. This was not something they did lightly or easily. For them, it was a necessary evil, something they talked about in order to bring this subject to light.

Through the years, I've been fortunate enough to have cooperation from judges, prosecutors, and other lawmen and officials essential to the telling of a true story. None have helped me more, however, than prosecutors Tom Longano, Steve Tolbert, and Jerry Kunkel. I hope I did justice to these three men in my portrayal of them, though I know that is almost impossible—the sweat and anxiety these guys lived through was greater than anything they would ever allow to be seen in a court of law.

I also need to thank Judge Richard Neihaus, Sergeant Thomas Boeing, Hamilton County Coroner Carl L. Parrott, Tom Gould and Jerry Kosta of the Hamilton County Clerk of Courts, and Lois Gorrasi, the reception-

ACKNOWLEDGMENTS

ist for the office of Hamilton County Prosecution Attorney Joseph T. Deters. Additionally, many thanks to Guy Hild, of Katz, Teller, Brant & Hild, who spent countless hours talking about his friend and client, Darryl Sutorius; and Michael Florez, attorney-at-law, who allowed me to gain access to his client Olga Mello.

There are other people who cooperated with me whose names I did not use in the text—mainly doctors and nurses—whose details about Dr. Darryl Sutorius and his reputation in the medical community were key to my understanding of this man's life. I thank them for their generosity of time, and of spirit.

To my phone buddies—Beth Evans, Cheryl Sullivan, Scott Mello, and Shawn Craig; my best buddy, Annette Ross; and my sweetheart, Jeff Myhre—for being there, for listening, and for keeping me straight and sane. Without realizing it, you are the people who influenced my style and my storytelling voice in the pages that follow.

Then there's Jeff Hilliard, who first told me about Della Dante Sutorius, and John and Sue Aber, who rented me a place to live—thank you for making this endeavor feasible. In addition, I thank my assistants, Louis Flores and Pamela Wilfinger, who dealt with my demands for perfection and my need for things in a *rush*. In a work such as this, their timely contributions are absolutely critical, and without them, this book would not exist.

As always, I'm grateful for the support and trust of members of the media—specifically, Linda Vaccariello, senior editor of *Cincinnati* magazine, and TV reporters Ann Alexander and Hagit Limor, who showed me news clips and shared intimate details of their coverage of the breaking Sutorius saga.

To my agent, Matt Bialer of the William Morris Agency, a big huge kiss. Again, Matt, I thank you for your wisdom and care, for guidance in leading me through the ordeal of writing a real-life crime story. You will always be my friend.

ACKNOWLEDGMENTS

To my editor, Jane Cavolina, I thank you for your enthusiasm, and for the significant structural suggestions. You helped me more than you know.

Of all those who helped me, however, no one took greater interest than Deborah Sutorius. To me, she has become a true friend; I never expected it. In return, she has asked people to write to petition the State of Ohio to keep Della in jail forever. I certainly encourage that, and hope people will remember to do so when Della comes up for parole. Although—at first—Deborah didn't want this book written, she came to see its potential value to all the men and women out there who marry for the wrong reasons. Maybe this story will cause *someone* out there to think—to prevent future marriage vows from becoming fatal. FYI, here's the address:

To Whom It May Concern
Ohio Department of Rehabilitation and Correction
1050 Freeway Drive North
Columbus, Ohio 43229
Re: Prisoner # W038992

"It is a trap for a man to dedicate something rashly and only later to consider his vows."

Proverbs 20:25

To the Reader

This book is nonfiction. The story is true, the people are real, the dialogue comes from recollections of the participants and has been cross-checked. I have used pseudonyms for three of Della's boyfriends whose names appear with asterisks as follows: Sid Davis,* Jeff Freeman,* Brian Powell.* I did this to protect the innocent.

My narrative is based on interviews with dozens of subjects who were kind enough to share their stories. It is through their remembrances and thoughts that I have been able to imagine Della, and re-create events as they actually happened. I did manage, on more than one occasion, to interview Della face-to-face. I believe I have remained faithful to the essence of her being. It is worthwhile to note that she continues to deny her guilt regarding the death of Darryl Sutorius. She did not speak about the threats she is said to have made to her former husbands and lovers.

Though this is a work of nonfiction, I have taken certain storytelling liberties, mostly having to do with the timing of events. I mention this even though the alterations I have made are quite minor. As always, my books are based on thousands of pages of court transcripts, police interviews, and newspaper accounts.

While I'm on the subject of things being authentic, let me state for the record that my name was given to me at birth. Aphrodite was the name of my mother's mother. I'm half Greek descent, half English. At times, I've had to bring out my driver's license to prove that, yes, I am for real. It's not a stage name, not a pen name, and I tell you this because people always ask.

PART ONE | The Triangle

CHAPTER | 1

*H*E WAS GIANT, CERTAINLY OVERWEIGHT, AND HE SAT ordering lunch like it was his last supper. Darryl was like that; he had to make a big deal about the menu. It was important to have the right wine, to be familiar with the house specialties, to know the waiters by name. He frequented Primavista, an Italian bistro crowning Price Hill, but this afternoon he wasn't really enjoying the view, nor was he paying much attention to Dick Brunsman, his friend of twenty-five years who sat across the table talking about a new private golf club community in Hilton Head.

Darryl and Dick shared a passion for the game. The two of them had just come back from a trip to Dick's oceanfront condominium, and Dick already missed it so much he was talking about buying a larger time-share. Darryl loved it down there; it was where he spent his happiest days with his first wife and kids. Yet at lunch he seemed to be indifferent. By the time the food arrived, Darryl was sullen. He was avoiding conversation. His eyes became fixed on the floor-to-ceiling windows. It was unlike him to let his food sit, getting cold, and he brooded with an uncanny faraway look on his face. He stared at the slopes of Cincinnati as though they were

3

the Seven Hills of Rome. He was only fifty-five, but in that moment he looked absolutely ancient.

When he finished studying the city skyline, finished examining the shadows cast by the Carew Tower, where his new wife was having her hair done, Dr. Darryl Sutorius became so preoccupied with carving his veal chop—Dick couldn't help making the parallel—the guy could have been dissecting an artery. Being an insurance salesman, Dick had no notion of what might really be running through a surgeon's mind, but Darryl seemed so acutely focused on his entrée, it was as if the artichoke hearts and mushrooms were part of a delicate bypass operation.

"You sure don't make it easy to be your friend," Dick finally muttered.

"I've got problems with Deborah," Darryl confessed. "She just announced she's getting married."

"Well, that's great!"

"I don't know. I'm not so sure about this wedding she's planning."

"Where's she getting married?"

"Hasn't decided yet, but she and Bill came to the house last night and it looks like she's planning the wedding of the century. For starters, she wants the service beamed up on satellite to Columbus."

"Hey, better open up the old wallet, buddy boy!"

"And Dante's having a fit."

"Well, she's *your* wife, Darryl, but I don't think she should have any say about what you spend on your kid."

"I know that, Dick."

"I mean, you're a heart surgeon, for God's sake. It's not like you don't have the dough."

"Well, I'm not so sure."

"Oh, come on, Darryl. Cut the poor-mouth routine."

As their conversation faded, Darryl became totally engrossed with slicing his thick portion of veal. Then, after a few bites, he suddenly laid the utensils down. For some reason, the big guy wasn't eating, he was just pouring down the cabernet.

4

Sure, Darryl was sometimes moody. But he was being particularly gloomy and quiet. It just didn't make sense. It was near Christmas, it was the holiday season, yet Darryl was finding every reason to be unhappy. Dick noticed it the minute the two of them met—they had just gone to buy the wives their presents, a regular ritual for which they both ended the workday early. It was supposed to be celebration time, but Darryl was acting weird.

Dick kidded Darryl about his golf game, reminding him that after lunch they were headed to the country club. It was an unusually warm day for December in Ohio, and Dick planned to whip Darryl in a quick round of golf at Beckett Ridge.

Dick had wondered about Darryl's behavior earlier at the jeweler's. For a while his friend had been all smiles, elated about the Mediterranean cruise he had just booked on *Renaissance,* which he bragged was one of the top cruise lines in the world. Darryl said Dante was half expecting the cruise as a gift—she had hinted about it so many times—but she would never be expecting another fur jacket. He thought it was a knockout mink, and he bought it for her—just on a whim.

But then Darryl showed little happiness when he picked out a diamond tennis bracelet for Dante. It was more money than he had anticipated. Of course, Dick had approved. The bracelet was elegant, not flashy; it matched Dante's personality to the letter. Darryl wanted his wife to wear diamonds of the finest quality; he could just picture it dripping off her exquisite porcelain wrist. He hoped it would please her, yet he didn't seem sure.

When the two men ordered coffee, the surgeon passed on dessert, his attention fixed on the multiple downtown structures, the high-rises that preside over the Ohio River. Dick cracked some father-of-the-bride jokes but Darryl seemed not to care. The surgeon's eyes were droopy. One would think Darryl had some serious form of depression, but Dick didn't really suspect that. Still, he was bothered by his friend's flip-flop demeanor, especially when Darryl's pager went off and he used it as an excuse to cancel their golf plans.

As usual, Dante had changed her hair appointment at the Paragon, driving her stylist crazy with her new demands for additional services and specialized color. Now she was paging Darryl to shift their dinner plans. She wanted to eat downtown at La Normandie and intended to coax him into buying tickets to see *The Nutcracker*.

When she hung up with her husband, Dante got on the phone again with the Paragon Salon receptionist, saying she was aware she had originally been set up for partial foil highlights, but now she wanted just a retouched tinting. A few minutes later she called back, requesting glossing with full foil highlights, switching the appointment time by an hour. The receptionist at the Paragon became slightly annoyed, but Dante was good at getting people to do things her way. If her usual girl Cindy wasn't available, that was fine. She didn't care who worked on her. Within the past few months, Dante's head had been coiffed by just about every stylist in the place. Dante had such an erratic schedule, it was no wonder that Paragon workers speculated about her keeping a room at the Omni Netherland Plaza, the ritzy hotel nestled in the Tower up above.

As the beauticians stood in their uniform smocks huddled around the reception desk, laughing about her having a secret afternoon rendezvous, Dante Sutorius moved through the foyer of the hotel lobby, floating down the impressive stairway carved of Italian marble, then taking a separate elevator to the street floor. When she emerged in her beige Armani suit, long mink coat, and Ferragamo shoes, everyone turned their heads. The angular shape of her face seemed diffused under the salon lights and the girls at the Paragon kept their chuckles to themselves, greeting the soft-spoken fortysomething woman like she was royalty.

One thing about Dante—she commanded attention.

CHAPTER | 2

Mrs. Sutorius never talked much about her private life, especially not to beauty service people. Her stylist, Cindy, couldn't believe it. Dante spent so many hours at the salon, yet all she ever mentioned were things like vacations or what kind of treatments she'd had at an exclusive resort. Pleasantries like that. About the only time Dante revealed any part of herself was the day she came in, just furious, because she'd been robbed of a Louis Vuitton trunk. Otherwise, she was totally closemouthed about her money, her past lovers, her girlfriends, and even her husband.

Cindy knew that Dante lived in Symmes Township, only because of the address on her checks. It irked her that this woman would bother to come all the way to a downtown location, a good half hour south of her plush neighborhood, demand all this special treatment, and then fail to leave a decent tip. When she was pressed for time, Dante sometimes patronized any number of salons near her home, but none of them were good enough, she said. One day, just out of curiosity, Cindy checked with some friends up in Montgomery, but nobody seemed to recognize Dante's name.

It's true, Dante kept a low profile. She often used her given name to keep people at a distance; sometimes she just made something up.

In Symmes Township, Dante was a phantom who whisked past the red bricks and white shutters of her subdivision, hiding behind her trademark Gucci sun-

7

glasses, driving leisurely in her dark Jaguar or white Lexus, every golden hair on her head in place. She made sure she looked like she just stepped off the pages of *Vogue*. Her neighbors would see her at various social committee meetings, just brief informal settings, little chitchats around warm fireplaces where the topics of discussion revolved largely around the weather or local news or media events, and she would sit, quiet and demure, like she was nobility.

Often she had no real opinion, but she had a lot to say about O.J. and the horrible way he treated Nicole. She enjoyed putting O.J. down and in general seemed to be a bit of a male-basher. Still, she had very little to say about herself. Nobody really knew Dante.

But, of course, she was relatively new to the area. She and the surgeon had only been wed a few months. They had just barely moved in. Slowly, she was trying to become a part of them, and people needed to give her a chance. Surely, there was a good soul behind all those designer labels.

The place on Symmesridge was just a starter house for the newlywed couple, and it was obvious she didn't think too much of the pristine ranch, because the minute they got there, she was busy interviewing every decorator and contractor in town to renovate it. Even though it was a showplace, it was simply not up to her standards.

One close neighbor, Kathy Bowen, the owner of a title company, had managed to linger at Dante's house after a committee meeting, working out details regarding the annual subdivision picnic. Dante didn't have much time to spend organizing the event. She was on her way to the Doral Spa in Miami—where she was headed without her husband—but she offered her input, for the neighborhood's sake.

Actually, Kathy was surprised that Dante took any interest in a picnic whatsoever. When the elegant lady brought up a plan to incorporate a hayride and square dancing and make it an *event,* offering to check on the

8

availability of a house in the Seven Gables subdivision across the way, Kathy was impressed. Dante had no children of her own, so it seemed strange that this midaged woman with a propensity for travel would concern herself with such child-oriented fun.

Dante apparently knew the people in Seven Gables, a much pricier tract where the houses look almost like mansions. The stately manor Dante was referring to, the place with the large circular driveway, was a home Kathy knew well. She had gawked at it countless times.

Dante offered use of the property for the benefit of the neighborhood children, either for picnics or local Girl Scout meetings, and Kathy thought that was gracious. Dante said she would check on it. She was sure it would be no problem. For her part, Kathy Bowen had never been on a hayride; in fact, she had never even considered it. Suddenly Mrs. Sutorius seemed more down-to-earth.

Here she was, standing beside her baby grand piano, her large chandelier in the backdrop, her ornate mirrors and gold moldings lining every inch of the home, serving tea and biscuits from a sterling silver tea set, talking about *hay*. It was all so amusing, Kathy thought, as she focused on the portrait of Dante that hung prominently in the dining hall. The artist hadn't done a very good job, Kathy decided; the piece didn't really look like her hostess.

Dante was much more beautiful in person. Her makeup, for instance, was near perfect, not nearly as overdone as it appeared in the painting. Kathy was transfixed by Dante's bewitching hazel eyes, by her soft, pouty lips. Everything about Dante was delicate; her features were model-perfect. Everything about her was refined; even her skin was flawless. And there was something about her mannerisms, about the way she carried herself: She seemed *above* everyone else. Dante was someone Kathy could honestly picture on a movie screen. She looked like a cross between Faye Dunaway and Mia Farrow, only younger.

The people who handled Dante's beauty treatments up in that area were located in Olde Montgomery, an exclusive township that caters to Cincinnati's ultra-rich in Indian Hill. On the rare occasions when Mrs. Sutorius did socialize, she visited her husband's colleagues in that posh setting, where stone mansions line rolling hills and the majority of homes are serviced by some type of domestic staff. Kathy and other social committee members decided Dante carried herself like Jackie Onassis; she was in total command of any room she was in, she was imposing and self-assured. She talked a lot about Indian Hill, and it made perfect sense that she preferred it; as she was a top surgeon's wife, she deserved the best. The yuppie professional set of the Symmes Creek subdivision was no match for her.

Of course, without even trying, Dante intimidated most of the social committee members. The only person who wasn't unnerved was Beth Evans, and that was partially because Beth worked for Bethesda North Hospital and was familiar with Dr. Sutorius's reputation. On some level, Beth had a hunch that Dante was putting up a front.

Beth knew Symmes Creek was a respectable upscale community and a beautiful place to raise kids. She was proud, even thrilled, to live there. Her home was well appointed, with its great room and fireplace and multiple rooms of antiques. And so what if she couldn't compete with the posh living of Indian Hill? She had no dreams of living in a palace—ever. Beth was comfortable with herself, with her role as mom and wife, with her upwardly mobile clique in a subdivision where an occasional basketball hoop was a welcome addition to a driveway. She saw no reason for Dante to act uppity.

Beth could see through Dante. For starters, Beth was personally aware of just how verbally abusive Dr. Sutorius was to hospital staffers. Beth was determined to find out if Dante was subject to the surgeon's tirades at home. She instinctively felt sorry for Dante. No amount of fur coats, no amount of trips or diamonds, would be worth *her* having to put up with his nonsense.

When Dante tried to make herself appear like the dutiful wife, acting like all she cared about was Darryl's career, Beth didn't buy it. Dante said they had chosen Symmes Creek because it was near Bethesda North, but Beth had heard a lot about Sutorius and his high-end ways, so it really didn't add up. If he could afford to live someplace better, he would.

Dante boasted about how much she appreciated her husband's sense of responsibility to his patients and the elevated reputation he had, but Beth knew otherwise. Darryl Sutorius was honestly hated in the medical community. Those who didn't fear him seemed to steer clear. Dante had to be aware of that. Beth wondered if maybe the doctor's practice was failing. Through the grapevine at the hospital, she knew the number of his referrals had been steadily dropping off.

Of course, Sutorius was affiliated with other hospitals in the city, so she really had no way of knowing what his circumstances were. Beth wanted the real scoop.

A few facts plagued her. Dante seemed to be rolling in dough. Beth didn't believe it was inherited money, but it was possible that Dante had been married previously, that she had been married to money. Beth wondered who was choosing all the Palm Beach antiques that were arriving at the Sutorius home.

At the very least—whoever this Dante was—she hadn't been born rich. She was working at it too hard, Beth determined; her movements were practiced, not natural. It was obvious the doctor had married her because he wanted a beautiful, well-behaved wife draped on his arm; he wanted to outshine everybody. Mrs. Sutorius tried to exude the impression that she had come from old money, very well-heeled money. She bragged that she had never worked a day in her life. But to Beth, it all seemed phony. The woman was a bit of a fake.

When Dante offered to take over as chair of the social committee, Beth happily offered to help. It was an easy job anyway, and a perfect excuse for the two of them to spend time together. Beth did medical transcribing out of her home, so she could effortlessly schedule her time to be there when Darryl wasn't home, assisting Dante with flyers and purchase lists. For Beth, the connection to Dante was a feather in her cap, particularly since no one else seemed to be able to penetrate the Sutorius household. She thought it would be great to hobnob with this woman, if for no other reason than to learn some interesting tidbits about the notorious surgeon.

Beth was curious about Dante's wardrobe. Why was she always dressed in starched white blouses and expensive suits? She couldn't understand why Dante never let her hair down, why she wore mink coats to shop at places like Thriftway and Kenwood Mall. Even when she went for a simple stroll, the surgeon's wife strutted in some kind of casual designer apparel, never in jeans. She was the fastidious type. So particular, in fact, that she had a plastic bubble carrying case for her little white pooch, which Beth thought absurd.

Next-door neighbors loved to gossip about Dante's detached air, about her Laura Ashley prints and her genteel ways. She was the complete opposite of Darryl, who always seemed to be on the job, like he had an imaginary stethoscope hanging from one of his pockets at all times. One of her neighbors, Gail, always remembers the image of Darryl in sweatpants, groveling in wood chips and mulch, sweating bullets over a flowering plant, while his wife was seated nearby under the shaded porch, her white cotton outfit looking fresh as a daisy. Dante's tall glass of iced tea with a lemon wedge seemed more like an accessory than a drink, and she sipped it cautiously, watching her husband stumble through the yard with a grimace on her face.

"When they first moved in, Beth and I walked down there with a plate of cookies and stayed for about fifteen minutes and the doctor was happy about being with her," one neighbor, Trish Bird, reflected. "She was like his little pet. I could just tell, he looked at her lovingly.

"She gave me the impression that she was from blue-blood stock, so to speak," Trish insisted. "I thought she was terribly dressed up for a Saturday afternoon, for just hanging around the house. I thought she had possibly just been somewhere. They sure weren't *my* typical lounging-around clothes."

CHAPTER 3

IN THE SAME WEEK THAT DARRYL WAS CHOOSING Christmas gifts for his wife and kids, Dante found an afternoon available to take Beth to lunch. They ate at Fridays, the TGIF place that is forever multiplying in Ohio suburbs, and on her way back from the ladies' room a guy slipped Dante his business card, on the back of which he had written, "Call me." Dante laughed about the gentleman, who was now beckoning to her from the bar, and Beth thought it was funny. That Dante could take the card and act so interested, however, was a surprise.

"He's not fat like Darryl," she joked, "so if I slept with him, at least I wouldn't feel like I would be suffocated in bed."

Weeks later Dante confided that she got bored and actually met the guy for lunch. It wasn't the first time Beth heard Dante make references to cheating on Darryl. A God-fearing Catholic, Beth didn't like what she was hearing, even if it was all just innocent flirtation.

At their first lunch, Dante hardly ate at all, which was typical for her. She ordered a bunch of appetizers, then let the food rot. Beth, on the other hand, was an eater. Always on a diet, struggling with her weight, she ate her sandwich and had a hard time refusing the appetizers, but did.

Anyone looking over at them would have thought these women were an unlikely pair of friends. For one thing, Beth towered over Dante, and she wasn't the dainty type, she had no use for frills. She looked much more grounded, more real. She wore casual slacks and a matching wool sweater in subdued tones, while Dante seemed to be screaming for attention in her white silk Emanuel Ungaro dress, more befitting an afternoon tea in New York's Plaza Hotel.

Dante insisted that they order a drink. It was obvious that she needed some encouragement to vent, so Beth made an exception and had a glass of Chablis. At first Dante started with some vague complaints about Darryl being cheap, about her husband spending too much money on his kids and their exorbitant college educations, the usual second-marriage issues. But inside the scope of the hour, Dante had gotten extremely personal. When she mentioned something about Darryl being no good in bed, Beth pretended she didn't hear it.

As they stared across the red and white stripes of the plastic tablecloth, Dante fidgeted with the special dessert menu. Without realizing it, Dante had retreated into her past. She was mesmerizing; eerie to watch, Beth thought. It was like she had gone into a trance. Dante seemed changed, she looked frightened and suddenly much younger. When she spoke, it was almost as if she were referring to some other little girl who had been emotionally abused by her mom. Dante said her mother kept dark secrets. She insinuated that her mom was sinister. Beth learned that Dante's dad had died when she was a toddler, that Dante felt she had nobody. As soon as she was old enough, she had run away from home, and hadn't even bothered to finish at her private high school. Dante had barely spoken to her mother since.

She described her childhood like it was a bad dream, asking Beth to never repeat anything; she didn't want neighbors to talk behind her back. Dante's sad story ended with her insistence that her mother never loved her, never kissed or touched her. Dante's only memory of being held was the day of her father's funeral.

"Oh, you poor thing," Beth said, patting her on the shoulder.

Dante was reduced to tears.

"You're such a good mom to your boys. I wish you had been my mother," Dante blurted.

"Oh, I'm not the perfect mom," Beth assured her. "I'm too much of a pushover."

"No, you are, you're exactly the kind of mother I wish I had. You love your children. If you only knew my mother's way of showing me love. It was to pour boiling water over my hands!"

"What? Why would she do a thing like that?"

"I had to go to school and I was eating cream of wheat and I wasn't eating fast enough. It was hot and I was waiting for it to cool down."

Dante's eyes started to well up again as she tried to hold back the tears.

"And she poured boiling water on my hands to show me what hot *really* was."

"Oh, my God!"

"You have no idea, Beth, how cruel she was. That's why I hardly ever talk about her. When I saw you with your boys it struck me that I wish I had a mother. But I mean, to me, my mother is dead."

"But she's alive, right?"

"Well, yes, but I just won't have anything to do with her."

"Does she know you're married to Darryl?"

"Of course, Beth, the woman has nothing better to do than check up on me all my life. My sisters tell her everything, which I don't really care, as long as they know not to give her my phone number. I just don't want her around me, and if she ever does have the nerve to call, I've forbidden Darryl to talk to her."

"You've forbidden Darryl?"

"Beth, she's jealous of me, she always has been. Whenever I've let her into my life, she has deliberately tried to *ruin* me."

"What do you mean?"

"It's just not worth wasting my breath. But I'll tell you one thing. I'll be damned if she's ever going to get that chance again."

"But she's your mother, Dante. Why don't you think about—"

"You just don't understand what I'm dealing with."

After lunch, Beth hooked up with her friend Pat and they invited Dante to come along to take the kids to see *Toy Story.* Dante was just livid on the ride home in the car, moaning about Darryl's spoiled daughter. As she got more detailed, they noticed that the soft-spoken woman had become quite animated. She began to lose her composure.

Apparently the fact that Debbie was getting married and expected some big lavish event was really eating at her. Dante didn't feel she should have to pay for it, and, according to her, Darryl didn't seem too keen on a big wedding production, either. He was being railroaded by this self-centered girl, Dante said, describing Darryl as being happy about his daughter's engagement one minute, then angry and nasty the next. Dante was of the opinion that Deborah was pushing him over the edge. She joked that Darryl might need to see a shrink before it was all over.

Pat just listened without saying much.

While Dante raged on about how unloving Darryl's kids were, insisting that they only understood dollar

16

signs, Pat was unmoved. Dante complained about Darryl paying out all this alimony plus child support and his kids had been given everything in the world. She thought Deborah should come down off her high horse and be happy with just a simple wedding. She wanted Darryl to put his foot down.

When they dropped her off, Pat mentioned how inappropriate it was for Dante to characterize the doctor as some kind of manic-depressive. She didn't think it was fair to fault Darryl for having mixed emotions about his eldest child's wedding—it was only natural. She told Beth she didn't care for Dante. In Pat's eyes, this snooty woman was more trouble than she was worth, and the more Beth defended her, the more Pat didn't want her around.

For some reason, Dante gave her the creeps.

Of course, Beth didn't see Dante that way. She argued that the woman needed to confide in *somebody,* and Beth wanted to be there to help.

CHAPTER | 4

*E*VEN THOUGH HE EARNED A HANDSOME ANNUAL SALary, Darryl Sutorius did have financial troubles. He resented paying his first wife all that money every month, and further resented the kids coming to him for extras all the time. With three of them in college and the fourth about to enter, he was looking at a $250,000 tab over the next twelve years, and that was a conservative estimate. It wasn't that he minded spending the money so much as he felt it wasn't being appreciated.

Money had gotten Darryl into trouble through the years. He used it as a tool to control his kids, and that landed him in stalemate position with his daughter Becky, because he was insisting that she attend an Ivy League school or he wouldn't fund her college education. When she had managed to earn an athletic scholarship and had run off to a university in North Carolina, a school he didn't approve of, the two of them no longer spoke. Partially it was because Darryl refused to supply her with any money for books.

Then there was Deborah, who had completed a four-year degree and was now at Xavier doing graduate work, but with no particular career goal in mind. Darryl felt it was a shame. He kept quiet about it until it came time to pay the tuition, then he'd just blow up. He hated wasting his money, and tried desperately to give her some direction, but Deborah wasn't ready.

When it came to throwing away money, however, his son John was the greatest of them all. John was his only boy, and Darryl had dreams of him following in his footsteps, of him becoming a doctor and taking his place among the medical community in Cincinnati. Instead, John had recently dropped out of the University of Pennsylvania, and was blowing the tuition-money refund on girls and ski trips. With a base tuition of $21,000 a year, Darryl was furious about it. More than on any of his kids, he had put the most money behind John, yet his son was floundering.

As a compromise, John had taken a job as a muffler mechanic. He was considering matriculation for the following semester, but Darryl was just crushed that his son had rejected the Ivy League. Of course, there was still his daughter Chrissy, but from what he gathered, the girl didn't seem at all interested in the likes of Harvard or Yale.

Much more devastating to his pocketbook, however, was the whole managed health care business and the problems that HMOs had recently posed to doctors.

With the old fee-for-service system no longer in place, managed care was interfering with Darryl's net income big-time. HMO providers were now calling the shots.

Of course, netting over $300,000 wasn't anything to sneeze at, but to Darryl it didn't feel like very much money, especially when he had grown accustomed to driving around in Porsches and Mercedes sports cars and flying everywhere first class. Darryl wished for the good old days, when Blue Cross was supreme. But with Clinton in the White House, that didn't seem too realistic.

More than ever, Darryl was living above his means. By the time he married Dante, he found himself refinancing his homes and borrowing far too much money. Suddenly he was drowning in credit card bills, membership dues, and tax payments.

Regarding the HMO issue, it wasn't just about profits—although that was the main thing—it was also about decent patient care and the fact that patients were being shortchanged medically because HMOs were determining it was better, economically. It seemed to Sutorius that managed-care firms were busy beefing up their own profits by denying patients the care they needed and deserved. He discussed this repeatedly with his colleagues. It disturbed him.

If he was nothing else, Sutorius was a sincere man of medicine. He was the best at what he did. And he was of the old school, before there were specialists for everything, so he personally had seen it all, done it all. He was a surgeon's surgeon. And he cared.

Beyond the HMO backlash, Sutorius had a problem within his own specialty. Darryl did thoracic and cardiac work—he operated on the heart and lungs—but the field had changed drastically from the days when he had first started twenty-five years earlier. For one thing, Sutorius had not been trained specifically in open-heart surgery. What little of that he performed was at Christ Hospital, but by and large, he was being squeezed out by younger surgeons with top-flight medical training. Some years before, Sutorius had traveled to Houston to brush up on his specialty, he had taken a few courses, but it still didn't make him competitive in the open-heart field.

Although Sutorius was certainly considered among the top heart surgeons in the city, although he still performed a lot of cardiac and vascular procedures like bypass operations and the cleaning out of clogged arteries, lately he had been relying on more thoracic work, which frustrated him.

To his way of thinking, he had been spending too much time reading sonograms of carotid arteries and interpreting vascular studies, which was anything but glamorous work. He needed to be in the operating room. And Sutorius was the type to make mountains out of molehills. If things weren't going precisely his way, if he wasn't the top dog, he felt his world coming to an end.

In his view, his career had gone into a downward spiral.

Dante was naturally concerned. Her husband wasn't the same happy guy she had married a few months before. Without knowing who to turn to, she decided to call an old friend of Darryl's, David Selzer, who had known Sutorius since their days as surgical residents, when the two of them had rotated through surgery at Cincinnati's VA Hospital.

Dante was straightforward with Dr. Selzer, explaining that her husband was extremely depressed, that he was angry and embarrassed about needing help. Since Darryl performed surgery at Christ Hospital, Dante was unsure whether he would agree to see anybody affiliated there, but she wanted to set up the appointment with Selzer regardless. She was trying her best to get Darryl some kind of psychiatric treatment.

When Dante called and canceled the appointment a few days later, she assured Selzer she had something tentatively scheduled with someone in a psychoanalytic group over on Highland, so he needn't worry. She felt Darryl would be more amenable to that, and she was sorry for having taken the doctor's time.

Selzer's professional relationship with Sutorius was tangential. They would see each other every now and then at the doctors' lounge at Christ, would exchange a few pleasantries, and that was about it. They didn't really work together. So up until that point Selzer never viewed Sutorius as a man with psychological problems. He was confused to hear about his colleague's deteriorated mental state. That wasn't the Darryl he knew. Sutorius was either quiet and preoccupied with work or was throwing a temper tantrum about someone's professional inadequacies. Sutorius was temperamental, but never despondent.

Yes, Sutorius demanded perfection and could sometimes take himself too seriously, but still, the surgeon seemed quite capable of enjoying life's frivolities. In Selzer's eyes, his old med-school chum never lost his sense of humor; Sutorius was always up for a good punch line.

By coincidence, Selzer had bumped into Sutorius just days before he received the call from Dante, but as far as he could tell, there wasn't anything in the surgeon's demeanor that waved any flags. Chatting in the doctors' lounge, Sutorius seemed his usual self.

CHAPTER | 5

THE MORE DEBORAH FOUND HERSELF FIGHTING TO HAVE a decent wedding, the more she felt like a pressure cooker about to explode. What infuriated her was that she couldn't seem to get near her father. He was so overly attached to Dante, he even refused to have a quick sandwich without his other half. Deborah was at a loss. Her dad had never treated her this way before. She was his firstborn, his favorite; he made time for her. Alone time.

Deborah prayed for answers, but the situation wasn't changing. Her temper was flaring; it was interfering with the joy of picking out a wedding dress and a cake. Though her fiancé offered to elope, to pay for everything himself, this was between Deborah and her father. She wanted his blessing and approval. She wanted him to be involved.

Two years earlier, when her mom and dad first decided to divorce, Deborah had been the one to hold her dad's hand. Darryl was like a lost sheep back then. He was in a panic, not knowing how to run a household by himself, not knowing how to make do in a cramped condo. Now she felt she was of no use to him.

"It was a weird time to be his daughter," Deborah confided. "Before he met Dante, Dad was so scared of being alone his whole life. I felt like I was the parent and he was the teenager. He would cry and tell me that no one would ever love him, that he was going to be a lonely old man."

Back then, Deborah had felt sorry for him. Even though she had been vehemently opposed to the divorce, even though deep down she thought her father was getting what he deserved for splitting up the family, she hated to see him so depressed. A sensitive girl and an artist, she and her father had spent many hours together painting portraits in his condo basement. It was a way for them to pass the time without having to focus on problems. Deborah wanted those days again.

Of course, what Deborah *really* wanted was to see her parents get back together, but in the interim, she was willing to offer her dad a shoulder to cry on. She was supportive up until the time he started dating Lisa Johnson, someone twenty years his junior, whom she initially pegged as a gold digger.

The thought of Lisa with her dad didn't sit well with

Deborah, especially since he actually seemed serious about this girl. She had a hard time dealing with the two of them *living* together, much less in a fancy townhouse in Blue Ash, where they had set up an instant family. The whole situation was annoying, and whenever Deborah was around, Lisa would be so overly demonstrative, so sexual, it added insult to injury. Lisa couldn't really be in love with him, Deborah decided.

For months, Lisa caused a rift in Deborah's relationship with her dad, but ultimately Deborah realized it wasn't worth it. She decided to be mature about it and did her best to accept Lisa as a friend. She needed her father.

Deborah's mom, Janet, however, was coming at it from a different perspective. She had been the conscientious wife for thirty years, had been the devoted one, tolerating Darryl's God-like ways, enabling his temper tantrums, and after all that she had to suffer the humiliation of *him* leaving her. Understandably, Jan was venomous. If she could have had things her way, she would have had all four kids reject Darryl. Nothing would have made her happier, but the more she encouraged her children to stay away from their father, the more they didn't.

In the early days of the divorce, the Sutorius kids still had a special relationship with Darryl. He was the voice of reason to them, the person they turned to in times of need. He was best under pressure, never blamed them for things like having a car wreck or failing something in school, and they trusted his judgment. He had a gruff exterior but he was a cream puff inside; they all knew how much he cared and how miserable he was about not being around after the marital split. Of course, none of the kids were comfortable about their dad dating, but they felt enough sense of loyalty to put up with it.

When he started showing up at Becky's ball games with Lisa draped on his arm, the Sutorius girls would smile and be polite. John didn't show emotion one way or the other. The only person who would cringe was Jan. She would get flustered. She loathed seeing her ex-husband marching a woman around who looked like his daughter, especially to high school events where the whole community would talk.

But local community gossip was the least of Darryl's concerns. Darryl was already having problems with Lisa; she was pressuring him for a ring, threatening to walk out, and he didn't know what to do. Lisa had two children of her own—preteenagers—which was about the last thing Darryl needed. If she hadn't been so sexy, he never would had considered the prospect. But she was vivacious and loving, she was everything he thought Jan was not, so when Lisa asked him to marry her, to be a pseudo-dad to Michelle and Jonathan, Darryl decided he would give it a shot. He wasn't entirely opposed to starting a new family. He was hopeful this might work out, even if the kids did eat pizza on his new white couch.

When Jan Sutorius learned about this, nothing could have irked her more. Darryl was complaining about money, yet making precious little time for his own family and suddenly playing daddy for his new fiancée. Jan never believed it would happen, but it didn't take long for Lisa and her brood to become entrenched in Darryl's townhouse in Blue Ash, for the kids to be part of the school system and the roots to be planted. All at once Darryl was perfectly set up, living right near his good buddies Alan and Sue Browning, enjoying the home life that he had felt cheated out of with Jan.

Darryl's world seemed to be just peachy, which made Jan wonder what kind of justice there really was in the universe. Here she was struggling on a paltry divorce settlement, while he was busy socializing, parading his fiancée to every country club event in town. Through her kids, Jan would hear about how Darryl whisked Lisa away on a Caribbean vacation, about how he lavished her with expensive clothing and jewelry.

Whatever the cost, when it came to Lisa, Darryl didn't seem to care. He worshiped the ground she walked on. Surely Lisa wasn't affording new diamond earrings on her own, yet that's what she was prancing around in, while Becky was struggling in college. Becky's first-semester book money was supposed to come out of Jan's alimony payments, but Jan's budget was too tight. As it was, she was scrimping wherever she could, and could hardly make ends meet.

Darryl made it clear that any costs above his child support were entirely Jan's concern, and he wanted Jan to stop complaining. He wasn't an endless money pit. He was moving on with his life.

Deborah found herself in the middle of her parents' squabbles, but she had no real knowledge of who was paying for what at her dad's place, and she really didn't feel it was her business. As far as the finances went, Deborah worked, she had a good job, and didn't need support money. She was aware that Lisa worked as an office manager, and was almost positive Lisa was paying for her own needs and those of her kids. Lisa seemed to have control of her life, so in that respect Deborah found her acceptable. But the money concerns were just a side issue. Lisa was still a thorn in Deborah's side.

For starters, Deborah didn't feel Lisa was sincere. She didn't like the way Lisa acted; she seemed plastic, just too doll-like. Deborah hated the way Lisa and her dad carried on, the way they'd turn on music and dance around the townhouse. They looked ridiculous, and Lisa was obviously too young, too *pretty* for her father. Besides, Deborah thought Lisa's overly affectionate ways were classless. The girl was all over him, kissing and hugging him in front of everyone.

While she pretended to be happy for her dad, it made her sick to see him acting so needy and codependent around his girlfriend. Her mom sure didn't act that way. Her mom didn't feel the need to act like a goofy *teenager*.

When things between Darryl and Lisa got shaky and it turned out that she refused to sign a prenuptial agreement, the Sutorius kids were ecstatic, especially Deborah, who felt a real sense of relief. She felt, perhaps, that all along this woman was out for only one thing—a meal ticket.

In fact, the day Lisa returned the engagement ring, when Darryl met with his daughter to cry to her about it, to get a female perspective, Deborah could barely hide her glee. Her dad said he thought Lisa was seeing someone else, a twenty-five-year-old guy she used to date, and on a whim, Deborah suggested they hop in the car and take a ride, just to check things out.

With hesitation, Darryl drove his daughter through his Blue Ash neighborhood and, bingo, there was Lisa's car, parked at her old boyfriend's house. It was a place Lisa had pointed out during one of her threatening tirades. She had told Darryl all about this guy, about how much he loved her and wanted her back.

For Darryl, spotting Lisa's car was the last straw.

He ordered her out of the townhouse but she refused to leave. Darryl was gentleman enough to stay with some friends in Indian Hill until things could be worked out, but Lisa wasn't being reasonable. Before she moved, she threatened to file a palimony suit. Darryl had to offer her a settlement to get Lisa out of his home. Some weeks later, when she started calling, trying to win back his heart, Darryl had already been introduced to Dante Britteon. Immediately there had been chemistry. This new woman was more his type, more sophisticated, and closer to his age.

Darryl knew he wasn't the handsomest guy in the world—his hair was graying, his gut was getting big, but somehow Dante made him forget about all that. With her encouragement, he stopped eating so much; he was playing more golf and getting exercise, just feeling good about life.

From their first date, Dante raved about how impressive he was—his tall frame, his massive hands, his sapphire eyes—she thought he was more than attractive, that he was the sweetest guy in the world, and a terrific catch.

Initially, Darryl didn't introduce her to his kids at all; he wanted to wait on that. But he described her to Deborah over the phone, and his daughter liked what she heard. She was ready to meet Dante with an open mind. From what her father said, Dante was exactly the kind of woman he needed—someone educated, independent, and financially well off.

CHAPTER | 6

DANTE AND DARRYL TOOK POSSESSION OF THE HOUSE on Symmesridge just months after they met. It was no mansion, really, but the main entranceway had a sixteen-foot ceiling with a graceful stairway rising toward an arched window, which Dante would descend as though she were the mistress of a Beverly Hills estate.

Just days before they moved in, she and Darryl were wed by a justice of the peace across the river in Covington, Kentucky, an unglamorous occasion for which Dante wore a full-length white silk coat dress. Darryl had agreed to don a double-breasted black suit; it was something Dante had selected as a gift for Darryl, and he wore it with gratitude, even if it did make him look a bit like a gangster.

The two of them honeymooned in Hilton Head, where they drank too much champagne and swallowed a lot of coffee in the mornings. They ate too many meals, and they both enjoyed the getaway, for the most part, but were happy to come home to Ohio, to settle into an existence where they intended to keep largely to themselves. They liked creating their own private bubble.

The dining hall and main living room of the house were overproportioned spaces, which suited them just fine, having absolutely no need for play areas or family rooms. They preferred more formal settings, particularly Dante, whose sense of importance and grandeur dictated that she live like an aristocrat, even if she wasn't one. In her previous marriage, she told Darryl, she'd had all the trappings of aristocracy—the furniture, the paintings, the jewelry—and she griped about how much she missed that life. She was angry that she had gotten rid of everything, that she had been reduced to pawning her most precious items for cash. Dante always complained that her alimony just wasn't enough. She bitterly hated David Britteon, her ex, who she said had robbed her of a decent property settlement.

Indeed, Dante seemed to have none of the mementos of old money—though she spoke with fondness about some antique pieces. They were things she had stupidly given away to previous boyfriends in more frivolous times, when her funds seemed endless. Darryl, being a homespun kid from Columbus suburbs, seemed not to care about all that. He assured Dante it wouldn't have mattered if she had a whole truckload of important paintings and fine furniture, but in truth he wished she had managed to hold on to some of her wealth. Darryl was definitely nouveau riche; even though it cost him dearly at times, he liked to be flashy with money.

After his divorce, Darryl was always trying to buy girlfriends, then later he'd become angry, thinking all women were bimbos, just out to get whatever they could. Just months after he and Dante first started dating, he actually pulled into her driveway with a brand-new Lexus. If she would consider his hand in marriage, the keys to the car were hers. Of course, since Dante really had no real feelings for the man, she just laughed him off.

During the weeks of their engagement, the two of them agreed to purchase all new furnishings, to start fresh. They went to a major home show together, scouting diligently for thick-wood cabinetry, designer wallpaper, and distinctive carpet. The house wasn't really to Dante's taste. She preferred the vaulting and pointed arches of gothic architecture, but with enough dollars spent, it would become more acceptable. Even if it seemed a bit of a hodgepodge, Dante was determined to insert English style into the contemporary ranch, to mix wing chairs with the sharp angular ceilings. She was of English descent, after all, and anything else in her home wouldn't be civilized.

The gourmet kitchen, the televisions and appliances, were all Darryl's domain. He had brought some furniture along from his first marriage, and most of it was relegated to the basement. Dante had no use for any of his junk, with the exception, maybe, of the exercise bike, which she used exactly once.

For her part, she came to Symmeridge with an elegantly curving Queen Anne bedroom set, which landed in one of the guest bedrooms upstairs. That was to be her own bedroom, she informed Darryl, because she needed her privacy. She had to have a place where she could smoke cigarettes and light candles and sip Royal Crown in peace.

Deborah didn't remember when the tension between her father and stepmother started. It might have been just weeks after they married, but she knew she hated going over there, to their house on Symmesridge. She'd see her dad sitting across the table with his arm wrapped around Dante's shoulder, Dante always seeming aloof, always pulling away whenever she could. It made Deborah sick to see her dad fawning all over this irritating little woman.

Dante was the stuffy and conceited type; she wasn't very easy to like. She was good at making others feel inferior. Certainly Deborah didn't have a wardrobe to compare to *hers*. Of course, in Dante's view, no one did.

Deborah thought Dante's laugh had a hollow ring to it. When Dante would brag about the places she'd been, about the important people she knew, her tone was condescending. Dante was just so hard to take.

"You know, I'm one of the most intelligent women in the world," she had announced the day they met.

"Oh, I can see that," Deborah said, trying to be polite.

"I can read people like a book," Dante boasted, "so you don't have to pretend to be worldly with me. I can see right through you. You're a sweet girl, and if you play your cards right, I just might be able to teach you a thing or two."

Over the summer, Deborah set up a studio in their greenhouse so she could paint, thinking that was one way she'd get to see her dad alone, but that plan backfired. Dante immediately set up a third easel alongside them, and with Darryl constantly being paged to the hospital, Deborah and Dante were often left to themselves.

If Darryl was gone and Dante didn't feel like painting, she'd just stand around asking questions about Deborah's private life. When Deborah would become evasive, Dante would hang around inspecting the floor for paint spots, finding new ways to squeeze Deborah for details. She could really get on the girl's nerves.

Deborah tried to talk and be civil, but Dante was increasingly confrontational. She wanted to know why John and Chrissy didn't come around to see their dad. She wanted to play an active role in the Sutorius family as a stepmom.

Darryl would later hear angry reports about Deborah being a bitch. Dante had tried everything, but she just couldn't break through the girl's barriers. She offered advice, tried to take her to expensive trendy lunch spots, but Deborah just wasn't interested. Nothing could entice her.

When Darryl finally felt compelled to call his daughter, pleading that she find a way to be nice to his wife, his request fell on deaf ears. Deborah was hurt, still resentful about the divorce. She had no intention of befriending Dante.

"Are we alone, Dad?" Deborah whispered into the phone.

"No, Debbie, I don't think so," Darryl said. "Why don't you call me at the office tomorrow?"

Deborah didn't understand. When she finally pried it out of him that Dante was listening in on their calls, she dialed Dante, just furious. "I called her up and bitched her up one side and down the other," she boasted. "I told her what I thought of her from the very beginning. I told her everyone hated her."

"I hope you know you're not getting one penny for your wedding," Dante shrieked, "because your father will do what I ask him to!"

"Well, you have some nerve! Let me talk to my dad."

"He can't talk to you right now, and I don't think you should call this house back ever again."

CHAPTER | 7

"**W**HY WOULD YOU DO THIS? YOU'VE GOT DARRYL," that's what you wanted, and now you've got him, so why would you come between him and his daughter?" Cheryl asked for the umpteenth time. It was one of the constant conversations Dante had with her sister during the Christmas holidays that year. Instead of focusing on the big Christmas dinner party she was throwing, Dante had become obsessed with Darryl's daughter, and Cheryl just couldn't understand why.

It was bizarre.

Dante was ruining the Christmas holiday spirit, incessantly calling with new updates about Deborah's exorbitant wedding dress, about Deborah's notion that the bridesmaids' dresses should be custom designed. Cheryl was so sick of hearing about how furious Dante was. It was the same complaint over and over. Darryl was planning to meet Deborah's demands and Dante wasn't going to stand for it.

Desperate to get Dante off her back, Cheryl finally suggested her sister go for psychological counseling.

"I'm not the one who's crazy," she snapped. "Darryl's the one who needs help!"

"But you're making a big deal over this wedding, and I think you need to get a perspective on it. The wedding date hasn't even been set and I just think, you know, maybe if you talked to a professional ..."

"It's Darryl who's got problems, Cheryl. You don't know the half of it. He's the one who has this twisted relationship with his daughter. He's the one who can't handle the fact that she's getting married even though she's a twenty-four-year-old woman!"

"What do you mean?"

Dante just couldn't discuss it.

"She's his *daughter,* Dante. Why are you starting trouble?"

"Because we don't have that much money, that's why," Dante insisted.

But they both knew that wasn't true.

"I'm his wife, Cheryl. I should come first in his life."

"Why can't you just leave him alone, Dante? Why can't he spent his money on his daughter if he wants to?"

"Because he wants to give all his money away, just throw it away on his ex-wife and his parents and treat Deborah like a little queen when she's done nothing to deserve it. He's already talking about making some big donation to the church!"

"But—"

"Why can't you ever see things my way?" Dante snapped. "Why are you always turning against me, Cheryl? What have I done to make you hate me so much?"

Cheryl gave up. She knew her sister always had to be right, that she would always find people to take her side. With a household of four kids to raise, Cheryl had her hands full; she had no time to waste trying to convince Dante. She'd been through the same routine with her sister all her life. Cheryl was one of the suburban dwellers who was satisfied with places like McDonald's and Wal-Mart, everything that Dante despised. The two just didn't see eye to eye.

Cheryl's happy marriage to Gary and her brand-new home in Butler County didn't impress Dante one bit. In fact, to her friends, Dante made fun of her sister every chance she got. She thought Cheryl's house was too small, that it was poorly constructed. And the *location*—

stuck way out in the middle of nowhere, in the farmlands—that was no place for decent human beings to live.

Without coming out and saying it, Dante let people know that Cheryl's life just wasn't upscale enough to be meaningful. Unfortunately, her sister had settled for a commoner, and since her wedding she had never been abroad, had never even been to The Maisonette, the five-star restaurant downtown.

CHAPTER 8

"**Y**OU MARRIED HIM, SO YOU BETTER FIGURE OUT A way to have sex with him," Cheryl advised her sister.

"Well, our marriage has never really been about that."

"What?"

"Never mind, Cheryl. Listen, you just have to come over and see this coat Darryl bought me."

"Well, I'm not too thrilled about fur." Cheryl balked. "Lots of animals were killed for that coat."

"Oh, don't be so petty, Cheryl. It's an early Christmas present."

"Why is Darryl buying you extra presents if the two of you aren't even speaking?"

"We're just going through a rough time with Deborah. Listen, you still haven't seen the new chandelier. I'm telling you, it's tremendous. You know, it took five engineers to hang it."

Cheryl wasn't impressed.

"I'd really like you to stop by and see it. Don't tell anyone, but it came from Victoria's Secret. Maybe you can pop over when you go shopping with Nikki and Carla. I want them to see the house anyway."

"Victoria's Secret?"

"Yeah, it's from one of their stores that closed. Darryl and I bid on it."

"What'd it cost?"

"Oh, don't be crass, Cheryl. You don't ask people how much things cost. Didn't *Mother* ever teach you that?"

Over the phone, Dante would eventually confess that things weren't going so great for her, that, even though they were spending all this money, she and Darryl were actually talking about getting a divorce. The situation with Deborah had heated up because Dante, admittedly, had listened in on a few of Darryl's conversations. He had confronted her about it, and Dante didn't understand his anger. What was the big deal?

Dante felt she had a right to know what was going on behind her back, especially when it involved her pocketbook. Cheryl listened, but she wasn't about to get involved. She told her sister she'd see her on Christmas, and rushed to end the conversation.

In search of a sympathetic ear, Dante dialed her kid sisters, Nikki and Carla, looking for someone she could more easily persuade. She called Nikki incessantly, leaving an incredible amount of messages on her machine, and in hopes of gaining an alliance, Dante had arranged to take Nikki down to the posh Aronoff Center to see *The Nutcracker*. Afterward, she insisted that Nikki join her for a holiday party in Indian Hill.

"Well, I'm not really dressed up enough," Nikki protested.

"Don't be silly. You look fabulous. Your dress can pass for something expensive, and look, we're even wearing the same shoes. But, of course, mine are Ferragamo, yours are probably from Payless, but don't worry, no one will be able to tell the difference."

The people in Indian Hill were really Darryl's friends,

Nikki realized, and it was obvious her sister was uncomfortable around them. In fact, she started acting strange the minute she walked through the door, putting on a phony voice and an upper-class accent.

"She was drinking wine, she had over five glasses," Nikki recalled. "She was drunk, and she was very touchy-feely with Darryl. When he was talking to a female colleague of his, she made the woman move over. My sister was practically sitting on his lap, and she's normally not like that."

From what Nikki could see, Dante was too possessive and jealous of Darryl. Nikki thought her sister's world revolved around the surgeon in an unhealthy way. Still, Nikki didn't argue with her explanation about why she needed to monitor Darryl's secret calls. Dante made it clear that she was only trying to save her marriage. She had taken drastic measures because her husband was becoming irrational. If Darryl didn't change, if he didn't seek some kind of help, Dante said she wanted out.

"Do you have any idea how I can tape-record Darryl's phone conversations?" Dante asked in a whisper, her eye focused on Darryl's movements at the bar.

"No, I don't know how to do it," Nikki told her, "but I know it can be done."

Nikki muttered something about a guy she once dated who used to tape his mom's conversations and Dante whispered she was thinking about putting a small recorder in Darryl's glove compartment.

In their subsequent talks, when Dante tried to make it seem like Deborah was out to sabotage their marriage, Nikki didn't know what to believe. She had never even met Deborah. Maybe there was ample cause for Dante to eavesdrop on her husband's conversations. Of course she herself would never have done such a thing—it was just so sneaky—but Nikki didn't have the nerve to say it.

Darryl, meanwhile, felt forced to tell Deborah not to call the house. He instructed her to call him strictly at his office or on his beeper, without explaining why.

While his wife was busy arranging a Christmas dinner for her siblings, the Sutorius kids were told to stay away from Symmesridge, told they'd have to wait until after the holiday to retrieve their gifts from under the tree.

Darryl couldn't understand how everything had become so insane, why he couldn't enjoy the sanctity of Christmas under his own roof. He complained to his buddy, Dick, that Dante was so pushy, yet he still loved her. He had spoken to his attorney once and had mentioned the problems in the marriage, but he really didn't want another divorce. He wasn't prepared for that.

When the day came that Darryl learned that his wife was rifling through the files and phone numbers at his office, quizzing his secretary for names and numbers, he couldn't believe his ears. He wanted to think his secretary was exaggerating, but what business did Dante have at his office? At one point, she had acted like she wanted to work there. In any event, he thought his wife was too concerned with discovering his amount of take-home pay. To a number of people, Darryl confessed that Dante had been badgering him to see his books.

"What the hell were you doing snooping around my office?" he boomed as he walked through the door on Christmas Eve.

"Calm down, sweetheart. Whoever told you a thing like that?"

"Well, my secretary said you were checking my appointment book and—"

"Sweetheart, I went to your office and talked to her about a surprise Christmas present for you. Why would she try to spoil everything? I know she doesn't like me, honey. I think she's jealous of me."

"Well, what could be her reason?"

"I don't know. But do you know what your problem is, Darryl? You never socialize. You need to get out more. Come on, sweetheart, we're invited to Beth's."

But Darryl already had a twenty-pound turkey sitting in the refrigerator. He was cooking the Christmas meal the next day, preparing everything from the pearled onions to the mashed potatoes, so he really didn't feel like going out.

As Dante watched him staring out the window at the evergreens, her heart just sank. She called and explained things to Beth, apologizing for Darryl, confiding that she was seriously concerned about him, that he seemed angry at her over nothing. She told Beth she was trying to surprise Darryl with a vacation, that she had gone to his office to figure out when he'd be free for a weekend trip. Now the whole thing was blowing up in her face.

Beth refused to take no for an answer. She didn't think it was right for them to sit around and be unhappy on Christmas Eve. She insisted they show up for at least one drink. Before Darryl knew it, Dante had sweet-talked him into breaking out a bottle of champagne to bring over to the Evans's place. His wife had promised him a good time. She said she wanted him to turn over a new leaf.

On the way over, the two of them became playful. Dante was carrying a battery-operated stuffed dog with a bright red bow around its neck, and she was making the thing bark and chomp at Darryl's neck. When they arrived, the stuffed doggy was a hit. Beth's young sons just adored it.

All at once, it seemed Dante and Darryl had put their monumental worries behind them, and after a couple of scotches, the moody surgeon became the life of the party. Beth thought Darryl actually looked cute with Dante on his arm. He had a mischievous smile; it was the first time she'd ever seen him that way.

Dante had a feeling that Darryl's gift was going to be a Mediterranean cruise, but Darryl kept it a secret. All night, she had been trying to pry it out of him, but Darryl just kept smiling and saying, "You have to wait." It was ironic that Darryl's gift might be a vacation, when apparently Dante had been unable to arrange the surprise getaway weekend she'd spoken of.

When Beth handed him a gift of Mondavi chardonnay, Darryl was truly gracious about it, promising to have Beth and her husband over to share one of his rare vintage bottles. Watching him sit around her Christmas tree, Beth was shocked by Darryl's demeanor. He was almost jolly, telling her all about his painting, his golf, his extensive wine collection. When he admitted that he secretly loved to read trashy novels, that he loved Patricia Cornwell, the two of them became engrossed in a chat about their favorite murder mysteries.

Within an hour, Darryl had relaxed, and he was ready to forgive Dante for everything. But as he talked about how much he enjoyed being in solo practice, about how he loved being his own boss, hinting that he was about to embark on a new field of surgery, his wife was growing increasingly jealous of his time spent with Beth. Most of the evening, she sat with her feet up on the couch, complaining to Beth's husband, John. Dante's back was bothering her, and even after Beth propped her up with a few pillows, she couldn't be appeased.

By ten that night, Mrs. Sutorius had lost her Christmas spirit. She just wanted to leave. Apparently she didn't want Beth to like Darryl, because that seemed to be the reason for her foul mood when they left. "She was just jealous about not being the center of attention," Beth confided.

"I talked to her Christmas morning and she had received a tennis bracelet and a trip to the Mediterranean and Dante was so very, very happy that his entire family was coming over to be with her," Beth recalled. "But then I spoke to her later and apparently her mother had called and had hung up on her."

Dante had hoped for a Rockwell moment. The unexpected phone call had ruined the whole event.

CHAPTER | 9

*T*HE NEXT DAY, DANTE CONFIDED TO BETH ABOUT HOW disappointed she was with the tennis bracelet. It was only three carats, when she thought it should have been a minimum of five. She wanted to return it to the jeweler's somehow without hurting Darryl's feelings. She also mentioned something about needing a new couch for her bedroom, which Darryl refused to buy. Beth suggested if it was so important, Dante should spend her own money for the couch. But that wasn't the point; Dante told her it was the principle of the thing. Darryl was paying his daughter $200 a week from his office payroll when Deborah did absolutely zilch to earn the money, and yet he was refusing her a stupid couch.

When Beth hung up the phone, she sighed a big sigh of relief that her own marriage wasn't manacled by financial troubles. If Dante's marriage wasn't hellish, it certainly was dispiriting. She and Darryl just seemed to get on each other's nerves all the time, and it was just so sad. They were still newlyweds.

Even though she was busy preparing for New Year's, Beth agreed to let Dante stop by for coffee later that day. She always had a fresh pot brewing and she invited her for a piece of home-baked carrot cake. When her friend got to the door, Beth automatically inspected the tennis bracelet, telling Dante she thought she was being rather unreasonable. Any woman would be proud to have such an expensive trinket, Beth said, but Dante just tweaked her nose.

"Did you know that my daughter lives in a house without a furnace?" Dante remarked.

Beth didn't even know Dante had a daughter.

"Shawn's the exact same age as Deborah and Darryl's paying thousands of dollars for his daughter's wedding but he won't help my daughter get a furnace."

Beth was shocked. It was the first she had heard of it. Dante didn't seem the motherly type. The fact that she had a grown daughter and grandchildren, even, was something Beth never even fathomed. Beth thought Dante's body was too picture-perfect for her to be a mom.

Dante briefly explained the history of Shawn, how she had given birth when she was just nineteen and then married Shawn's father, Joe, but things with them didn't work out. Joe had a wandering eye and they were both too young to be serious about a commitment.

Shawn was eventually put into foster care and it wasn't until recent years that Dante and Shawn had reunited. Her daughter was now married and lived almost two hours away, in some small town in Indiana. Dante had been there once, but she just couldn't bear to go back. She couldn't stand to see her child living that way.

Shawn and her kids had been to Symmesridge to meet Darryl, but mostly they kept in touch long distance, and Dante had asked Darryl never to tell anyone that she was a grandmother. Dante didn't like to think of herself that way, and besides, Shawn had adopted a new set of parents many years prior. Dante was her biological mother only, nothing more.

But recently Shawn had been calling a lot, crying about money problems, and Dante just couldn't deal with it. She told her daughter that since she had chosen to marry a man who couldn't support her, she had no one to blame but herself. Dante really didn't approve of the guy Shawn was hooked up with. She had tried her best to get Shawn to have an abortion when she was pregnant the first time.

41

Now, in recapping things to Beth, Dante felt bad that Shawn was stuck eating macaroni and cheese four times a week. Shawn was pregnant with number three, and since her husband was a housepainter, Dante wanted to offer him some odd work at her place on Symmesridge, but Darryl wasn't crazy about the idea.

Beth thought it would be worth a shot to ask Darryl one more time, but to herself she wondered why Dante wasn't sending any cash to her only child. Her friend was spending large amounts of money at art galleries and antique shops, was a regular at Kotsovos Furs in Montgomery, and was considering a membership at The Club at Harper's Point, yet Dante let her daughter and grandchildren freeze all winter. It was outrageous, and what made it worse was Dante's attitude. She was obviously embarrassed to even discuss Shawn.

All Dante wanted to talk about was how unhappy she was. She said she was miserable with Darryl, she could hardly stand the sight of him, much less going away on the cruise he'd come up with. She didn't know what to do; she had already checked with the travel agent about a refund, but the Mediterranean trip was nonnegotiable. She thought of asking her sister Nikki to join her instead; her husband was just too depressing to be around.

Dante wanted to help him through his depression; she wanted him to consider marriage counseling, but she was having a hard time convincing him. She wasn't sure Darryl loved her anymore. She told Beth she thought he might be having an affair.

Dante confided that they had been having fights over Darryl's strange work hours, and that recently she was growing afraid of him. She was having nightmares where his large hands and fingers would be grasping at her neck. During one of their tiffs, she said, Darryl had grabbed her and almost choked her.

"Well, you should have called the police," Beth said, filling their coffee cups. "If it was me, that's exactly what I would do."

"I could never do that." Dante hesitated. "It would ruin his reputation."

"You're always cowering behind Darryl," Beth scolded, "and I think if you took up some volunteer work, you know, if you had something to feel good about, you'd focus on yourself more and wouldn't let Darryl control you so much."

"Well, it's hard for me to work with my bad back, and anyway, it wouldn't matter what job I did. It's Darryl. He has a terrible temper and he just yells at me for no reason. Last night, I accidentally spilled a Coke on the coffee table and Darryl actually called me a slob. He acted like I totally disgusted him."

"For knocking over a Coke?"

"That's when I got so mad that I swiped my hand across the table and knocked his beeper, his keys, glasses, everything on the floor."

"Well, you probably shouldn't have done that, but be proud that you stood up to him."

"Well, that's not all. He was drinking scotch out of this Waterford glass and it shattered when I knocked everything over, and Darryl picked up a piece of the jagged glass and threatened to slit my throat!"

"What'd you do?"

"I ran up and locked myself in the bedroom," she said flatly. "And I'm considering buying a gun."

Beth glared at her and stood absolutely still.

"I just think maybe I should protect myself."

Her friend was appalled. She reminded Dante that most times, people get hurt by the very guns they purchase. Under no circumstances would a gun be acceptable. She suggested Dante call a battered women's hotline.

Dante said her six-foot-four-inch, 280-pound husband was becoming a real threat, and that she had an appointment set up for January 6 with Dr. Louis Spitz, one of the top psychiatrists in town. Even though he wasn't a marriage counselor, Dr. Spitz had agreed to see both of them together—just for the first session—as a way to ensure that Darryl would show up.

Before the matter was dropped, Dante promised Beth she wouldn't think any more about guns, and decided she needed to hire a locksmith to place some extra dead-bolts on her bedroom door. When Darryl got home that night, she spent the evening locked away in her room. Dante found it funny that when she did go downstairs, Darryl had locked himself in his bedroom. She wondered why he was stonewalling her.

CHAPTER | 10

In THE MORNING, WHEN DARRYL LEFT LATE FOR WORK, he noticed the lights turn on in the house, and he sat in the driveway a minute, spying Dante in a black negligee floating down their long staircase. She was all dolled up. When she paged him later that morning, he agreed to accompany her to Spitz's office. He wanted to work things out. He had been irreparably altered, haunted by his first divorce. The thought of separating his assets again, and the relentless quarreling it would cause, was nightmarish. And he was still drawn to Dante, even if she wasn't the person he thought he'd married. Apart from her looks and her gentle voice, she had a freedom of spirit that was contagious. He needed her.

Yes, they talked less and less, but Darryl was really holding back his feelings, which he knew was causing problems. To his colleagues, he would enumerate Dante's finer points, yet at home, all he ever seemed to do was pick on her. Dante had a vast number of desirable traits, things that were missing in his previous wife. He thought she was the sexiest woman he had ever known, yet lately he'd become emotionally unavailable. Perhaps he had been too hard on her. Certainly there had to be some reason the two of them hadn't slept together since their trip to the Bahamas back in November.

Before Darryl met Dante, he was included in a local newspaper list as "one of the most eligible bachelors in town," so when the nurses on the fifth floor at Bethesda North first found out he had a serious girlfriend, they all teased him about it for weeks. Of course, Darryl was all smiles, showing around a studio portrait of Dante, bragging to everyone about how great she looked in a bathing suit.

Just weeks before they wed, when Dante eventually stopped by the hospital, she was somewhat of a disappointment to them. She certainly wasn't as friendly as they had anticipated. It was right around Valentine's Day, and even though she was immaculately dressed, none of them thought Dante was all that pretty in person. She had good features, but her face didn't glow, especially under all that makeup, and she looked annoyed that Darryl had bought the nurses a bouquet of expensive roses. After all the good things they had heard about this woman, Dante was a big let-down. They thought she was a snob.

Some of the nurses were surprised that Dante seemed so intimidated by Darryl's generosity. Dr. Sutorius was just like that—he'd buy pizzas and flowers and bring in home-baked pies for the nurses; it was just something that was a part of him. They knew it was his way of balancing out his gruff exterior, because sometimes, when he walked through the hospital on one of his rampages, the walls would seem to shake around him. Everyone knew he could be extremely demanding, even imposing. Whenever one of his patients had been left unattended, he would really chew people out. He was tougher than nails, and on many occasions a nurse would be reduced to tears in the wake of his rage.

But for all the harsh reputation that preceded him, Darryl was a kindhearted man, and the nurses who worked with him closely never lost sight of that. He was the guy who spent his own pocket money to buy them a microwave when their requests went unanswered by hospital administrators. It was unheard of for a surgeon to do that. Most surgeons wouldn't dream of going that extra mile for a nurse, and really, it wasn't their place. So even though he could be very God-like and condescending in the operating room, he more than made up for it.

Recently, however, his little kindnesses had decreased somewhat.

"Since you've gotten married, you never cook for us anymore," Pat Purdy casually mentioned on one of her late-night shifts over the holidays. A veteran nurse of twenty-one years, she and Darryl had a special working friendship, and it was her way of making sure everything was okay with him. Around Christmas, it was especially unusual for him to forget to bring in home-baked cookies or some type of dessert for the nurses.

"Well, I don't cook as much anymore," he told her. "Dante won't touch anything I cook. She has a germ phobia."

"What does that mean?"

"It means I bring her Boston Market chicken or White Castle burgers most of the time. She's got a thing about food left in the refrigerator. She's always questioning me about any meat dish I prepare, refusing to eat it until she checks the expiration dates on the packaging."

"That's a little extreme, but I've heard of people like that," the RN said.

"Well, she won't touch a spoon that's been put on the table. She's very peculiar about food. Every night, I have to go home and clean the kitchen before I can cook anything."

"You clean the kitchen?"

"My wife insists I clean the kitchen and scrub down the sink because she's afraid of germs. If I don't, she refuses to eat with me."

"Well, I understand you've got a lovely home," Purdy said, changing the subject. "And one of the social workers at the nurses' station mentioned that you've bought a lot of antique furniture. I'm sure it's just beautiful."

"Yeah, sure, we went into an antique store looking for a purse for Dante, and we came out with thousands of dollars' worth of furniture."

"Oh, is your wife a big collector?"

"No, she's just a big spender."

Nurse Purdy thought it was funny—Dr. Sutorius was always making jokes—and even though he seemed half angry about his expenditures, she knew that was just the surgeon's general demeanor. In the fourteen years she had known him, he never seemed happy about spending money. He was a natural-born complainer and always acted as though he'd been forced into spending by his first wife. It seemed fitting that he'd have a similar game going with Dante.

But the tone of his complaints had changed notably in the days after Christmas; her prized heart surgeon wasn't smiling anymore, Purdy realized. When she'd stop him in the hallway, he seemed so removed. She just couldn't get a laugh out of him. Not even her old jokes about his big belly seemed to work.

Just after the New Year, when she asked him how his holidays were, he just shook his head. "You don't want to know," he said as he rushed off to surgery.

CHAPTER 11

"**D**AD, YOU SOUND LIKE YOU'VE BEEN BRAIN-washed," Deborah told her father when she finally got through at his office number.

"What did you say to Dante on the phone? You weren't cursing at her, were you?"

"I told her that we don't like her—yeah, I was cursing. That's why Chrissy won't have dinner with you anymore, Dad. It's because she can't be alone with you."

"What exactly did you say to her?"

"I told her that she's separating you from us, and it makes us mad. She's not family, Dad. She's your wife, but she's not my family, and I don't need to like her."

"Well, don't call Dante, don't talk to Dante, please, Deborah. Just try to understand. I've got to live with her. She's my partner."

When Dr. and Mrs. Sutorius showed up at Louis Spitz's office, they were battling. At the outset, Dr. Spitz thought Dante was being very harsh in the way she described her husband, but there seemed to be truth in what she was saying. Darryl admitted he was sometimes rude to people at the hospital, and Dante said her husband was irritable. He didn't care about anybody, not even himself. Dante complained that he wasn't even bathing or showering anymore, and in fact Dr. Spitz noticed that Darryl looked disheveled, that he had some body odor.

When Dante started to discuss Deborah's upcoming

wedding, Dr. Spitz thought it was inappropriate that she should be so jealous and argumentative, especially when it was obvious that Darryl was going to help his daughter anyway. The psychiatrist wrote notations about Darryl being very depressed and sad-looking. As he spoke, the surgeon had tears just beneath the surface of each word.

In that first session, Darryl admitted that he had been suicidal during his previous divorce. Dante seemed somewhat concerned about him, but they were both expressing so much anger, Darryl's comment went practically unnoticed. After the forty-five-minute session was over, Dr. Spitz made an appointment to see Darryl alone and told Dante that she had accomplished her goal, that her husband now realized he needed to be seen for individual work, which was a step in the right direction. He recommended they both consider marriage counseling, and referred them to Miriam Warschauer.

Within the course of the next few weeks, Dante and Darryl did manage to have a few sessions with Warschauer but it didn't go very well. When Dante learned that Darryl had secretly been calling Warschauer on his own, she thought the medical community was ganging up on her. They were protecting Darryl, she felt. In particular, she thought this female counselor was taking Darryl's side completely, and Dante decided it was time for her to see a separate counselor. She couldn't handle the burden of living with Darryl on her own. She made an appointment with Jack Neihaus, a counselor Dr. Spitz had recommended.

Throughout January and into February, Darryl continued his sessions with Dr. Spitz, and slowly disclosed that he was feeling pain over prior lost loves. As it turned out, Darryl had regretted breaking up with Lisa, and in fact he still had doubts about his first divorce. He thought he might have made a mistake. To complicate matters, he was hurt by the rejection he suffered from his children, and just devastated about his broken relationship with his son, John.

Darryl also confessed that he had been experiencing certain problems with impotence and was embarrassed to sleep with Dante. When they had threatened each other with divorce, Dante once hinted she would expose him to his colleagues. He was afraid about what she might say about his finances, about his drinking, and his sexual prowess. They had agreed that they both wanted out—and Dante was willing to take somewhere between $2,000 and $3,000 a month in alimony—but now Darryl didn't really want to leave the marriage.

At times he seemed like a scared child. He claimed he loved his wife, loved his house. He didn't want to lose everything, and hated to go through the expense of lawyers again. The last divorce had cost Sutorius $68,000 in legal fees, which he was still making payments on.

"I want you to think about an antidepressant," Dr. Spitz suggested. "I can see you're depressed, and you're tearful."

Darryl said no. He wasn't amenable to that. He didn't want medication interfering with his practice. But then, after a huge fight with Dante that left him shaking in the hallway outside the OR at Bethesda, the surgeon decided he would start on a low dose of Effexor. He realized his personal stress and tensions were adding to the marital problems, and Dr. Spitz had convinced him that this newest form of chemical antidepressant would help.

In the interim, Darryl's unease with his wife had become worse. He was living in a state of utter paranoia, telling people he thought Dante might kill him. He had become desperate, walking around the hospital in a bulletproof vest and locking himself in his bedroom at night. When he felt he had no other choice, he called Guy Hild, his divorce attorney, and set up an initial interview. Guy was already aware that Dante hadn't signed a prenuptial, and Darryl made it abundantly clear that he did not want to lose his house, so things were going to be sticky.

CHAPTER | 12

"**I**T WAS A BAD SITUATION THAT HE COULDN'T CONTROL. If he could have controlled it, he would have changed it," Darryl's attorney reflected. "I don't believe Darryl knew how to verbally express himself over disappointment. I don't believe he knew how to fairly approach a problem. Darryl understood how to fix things medically. He was at the very top of his profession. However, life is more than being accomplished in one field. I don't think Darryl was able to see the bigger picture."

On Super Bowl Saturday, Darryl told his wife he was headed to his sister Carlene's, just outside of Columbus. When she saw him throw a golf shirt and trousers into a suitcase, she pulled out her overnight bag, wondering what the big attraction was, since Darryl wasn't really into football.

"Why are we going to your sister's?"

Darryl didn't answer.

"I *am* going with you, aren't I, Darryl?"

As Dante started to pack, pressing Darryl about what she should wear, the surgeon finally let his wife have it, telling her that he couldn't stand the sight of her, that he had no intention of dragging her along. Dante was beyond crushed. She felt she didn't deserve that kind of nastiness.

She called Beth and related the whole incident. She suspected Darryl was lying about going to his sister's. "Dante told me she and Darryl had intercourse a grand

51

total of four times since they were married," Beth reluctantly confided. "I was surprised, because she was much younger than him, and I thought there was a strong lust between them."

Dante was positive Darryl had a girlfriend, but Beth didn't believe that. There just wasn't any proof. Later that day, however, when Dante placed a quick call to Carlene to confirm that Darryl was there, her brother-in-law, Gus, said he hadn't heard from him. Dante started to give Gus a rundown on the problems in her marriage, but Gus didn't want to hear it.

"You two are adults," Gus said, "so why don't you work your problems out as adults."

Frightened that Darryl might be lurking in the neighborhood, Dante placed a call to the police, requesting extra patrol. She informed Officer Rich Limle that she was afraid of her husband, that they were having domestic problems. He wasn't home, she told the officer, but she thought he might return and do something crazy.

To take her mind off things, she rented a movie and brought it over to Beth's. They had a pizza and joked around with the kids, but as soon as the boys went off to bed, Dante showed Beth a letter from Darryl. She read it aloud with an inflection of complete disbelief, and Beth was at a loss about how to respond. Darryl seemed to enjoy being miserable and appeared unwilling to compromise about anything. Dante confessed she didn't know if they could stay married.

"Do you love him?" Beth wanted to know.

"I care about him."

"Why on earth did you marry him so fast?"

But Dante just stared at her, her lips quivering. Dante wasn't sure why she had married someone who made her so unhappy. He had few friends, fewer hobbies, and she was getting tired of being his support system.

"Darryl felt he was a failure in all respects, partly because his relationship with Dante was far gone at that point," Beth recalled. "Dante told me about how he

came home crying one day because he had no friends.
He had seen this intern at the hospital who was successful, attractive, who was loved by his children. It was
someone about whom Darryl was jealous."

Dante and Beth made plans to be together for the
Super Bowl, and they joined a crowd over at McLevy's
Pub in Montgomery, a cozy bar hidden in the Duffy
Square shopping plaza, strictly a local hangout. Beth's
husband, John, was pretty much a regular at the place,
and Dante felt welcomed—so much so that in the weeks
following, it would become the spot where she spent
most of her evenings. She could easily hide from her
husband there, because it was a modest tavern, not the
kind of bar Darryl would ever patronize.

She was running late on Super Bowl Sunday, so by
the time they arrived people were already in a party
swing, slugging imported beer and stuffing their faces
with nachos, chicken wings, and pizza rolls. Dante insisted on ordering a cold-cut sandwich from the menu,
checking around the edges of the plate for germs, and
much to Beth's dismay, she treated everyone and everything in the establishment like it was beneath her.

But by the time the big game started, Dante had loos-
ened up a bit, and she was giggling and using her little
girl's voice to flirt with a twenty-five-year-old blue-collar
worker at the bar. "You know, I've never had trouble
picking up guys," she whispered to Beth, flashing her
cute dimple and winking an eye.

After halftime, Beth and Dante weren't really paying
attention to the game anymore. However, at one point
an interracial couple flashed on the screen—a shot of a
football player with his wife—and Beth remarked that
she thought women threw themselves at athletes because
of all their money.

"What? Do you have a problem with that?" Dante
snapped.

"Well, no, it's just—" Beth began.

"It sounds like you're prejudiced."

"Not at all, but I don't agree with interracial marriages, because I feel sorry for mixed-race kids. You know, they're not sure what their heritage is."

"Because I'm *black,* you know," Dante blurted. "Did you realize that? It's true I'm from England on one side, but one of my grandparents is black."

Beth thought she wasn't hearing right. Dante was pretty drunk, and she was acting so dramatic about being African-American.

"Can't you tell my hair is *kinky?"* she asked, twisting a strand of soft golden hair around her finger.

"Well, I'm Welsh and English," Beth teased. "From what I can see, I think *my* hair is kinkier than yours, Dante."

"Oh, I don't think so!"

"Really? Come on, you've got to be kidding."

Beth and her sons left the tavern early, but Dante hung around awhile, flirting with a couple of men, playing it real cool. She figured everything with Darryl would blow over by Monday, but she wanted some backup if his bizarre behavior continued. She always liked to keep a few guys in the wings.

When Darryl came home the next evening, the two of them stayed up fighting all night. Apparently he had been talking to somebody about Dante's past, and he quizzed her about things that went on with her previous husbands. She was simply outraged about the rumors. She suspected one of her sisters was involved, but Darryl flat out denied it. Dante had no idea where he was getting such information. She knew her siblings were jealous; they were always working against her, and she figured he probably contacted one of them over the weekend. She couldn't wait to get her hands on Cheryl, the most likely of the bunch. She was sure Darryl was out sleeping around, yet, because of someone's vicious lies, he had managed to turn the tables and put her on the defensive.

Just before dawn, Dante began to have such severe

chest pains that she drove herself to the emergency room at Bethesda. Even when she paged him over and over, Darryl refused to come to her aid. A physician in the ER told Dante she was just overly stressed and needed some counseling. By 8:00 that morning, she appeared at Beth's front door unannounced, wearing a dingy jogging suit under her full-length mink.

Through her tears, Dante was rubbing her forearm, showing Beth the red marks where Darryl had hurt her. She told Beth about two nurses who had come over to extend their condolences about her being married to Darryl. The fact that Darryl never showed up to check on her, though, really broke her heart.

Later that afternoon Beth decided to give her friend a buzz, and Dante started crying the minute she answered the phone. More worried than angry that Darryl wasn't returning her calls, she was concerned that something might have happened to him.

Through the grapevine, Beth discovered that Darryl *had* shown up in the emergency room that day, supposedly with scratches across his face.

CHAPTER | 13

DARRYL HAD RUSHED TO SEE GUY HILD, ONCE, BACK in early January, and they had talked about the paperwork for a divorce, but the surgeon became hesitant about going through with anything. While at Guy's office, Dante had paged him, and Guy noticed how much Darryl seemed to jump.

"She has caller ID and she knows I'm here," Darryl mumbled when he hung up the phone.

"Why should that be a concern to you?" the attorney asked. "You've made her aware that you were coming to see me, right?"

"Yeah, but you don't understand. If she wants something, you have to do it. Guy, I don't know what's going on in my life. Things are out of control."

"You've been discussing a settlement, correct?"

Yes, they had. But Guy could see his client was backing down. Perhaps he was still in love with his wife.

"When he met with me, it became clear that he didn't have a small marital problem where they were sexually incompatible or she couldn't cook," Guy recalled. "It was clear to me that this was a bizarre relationship at best. She wasn't sleeping in the same bed or even on the same floor level with him. Then he started to relate to me some of the matters he was finding out."

When Darryl detailed the portrait of his life with Dante, Guy thought to himself, *Give me a break.* He was shocked at the things the surgeon had let her get away with. The woman obviously had some kind of psychopathic hold over him.

Even after the incident on Super Bowl weekend, even though he was faxing more documents to Guy, he didn't truly seem more open to a divorce. Darryl was afraid that Dante would destroy his property, might damage his reputation, yet he wanted this marriage to work out.

"Darryl and I had a whole host of topics we were talking about, with no real understanding of who Dante was or what she wanted," Guy confided. "We were learning new things every day. He wasn't sure he wanted to divorce her. He really wanted to know what his options were."

In and around that time, Darryl called Guy from his car phone in an absolute panic. During a fight earlier that day, Darryl learned his wife was keeping a gun in the house. She had threatened him.

"I think I believe her." Darryl's voice trembled. "She's told me she's got a loaded gun locked in her bedroom."

"Go back into the home, Darryl, and get the gun."

"Her doors are locked with deadbolts."

"Jimmy it, get the door off the hinges somehow," Guy advised. "Call a locksmith. There's a lot of ways to get into a bedroom. Just get the gun and take it to the first available police station and make a full police report."

"Then what do I do when she gets home?"

"Don't hide the facts from her. Tell her you don't want guns in the house. Tell her you're afraid of guns, and say if she ever has a gun again, you're going to consider it an act of domestic violence and you'll have her arrested."

Guy's suggestion was the only thing that made sense, unless Darryl wanted to move out. Before he went home and broke her bedroom door down, the surgeon stopped at Chester's Roadhouse and downed two double scotches, so he wasn't as shaky when he located a .22 under her bed. He immediately brought it to the Loveland Police Station and spent a few moments with people from the Hamilton County Sheriff's Department.

He discovered that the gun had a broken firing pin, and he did not want to file any charges against his wife.

February 12, 1996
Guy Hild
255 E 5th Street
Cincinnati, OH
Dear Guy,

After reviewing in my mind our recent conversation, I was in error when I told you that at the time of the filling out of the marriage license I was unaware Dante had children. She did tell me about her daughter early on and about her initial marriage and most recent marriage. I was under the impression that she had been married twice, once to Joe

Hoeffer and once to David Britteon. She had told me she had one daughter, Shawn, and that Shawn was married, however, she hid from me the fact that she had grandchildren because she does not like to be associated with that stage of life. I eventually found out about the grandchildren but this was something that she held back initially rather than the fact that she had children.

The other inconsistencies in her background I have already enumerated for you in our initial interview. I again this week tried to impress upon her the fact that it would be financially advantageous for her to sit down with you and work out a settlement. She still resists this and apparently is receiving advice from two friends of hers who are attorneys.

I would like to proceed to file suit as soon as possible and would very much like to have the temporary restraining order I mentioned put into effect as well would love to see an eviction notice and a temporary restraining order keeping her away from my house as well as from me.

As we have discussed, I don't know whether I have any grounds to support these requests or not. I certainly do continue to feel threatened, although she has changed her tack at the moment and is very patronizing whenever I am at home or talking to her on the phone. Please let me know if there is anything further I need to complete.

Thank you very much for your consideration,

Darryl J. Sutorius, M.D.

CHAPTER | 14

DISPATCHER: This is 911 emergency.

CALLER: I work for Darryl Sutorius and he's a doctor and I've been paging him. And, umm, I'm afraid something has happened to him 'cause it isn't like him not to answer his page.

DISPATCHER: Have you tried him at home?

CALLER: No, there's personal things going on at home.

DISPATCHER: Where does he live?

CALLER: 9014 Symmescreek Road, Loveland, Ohio. He didn't answer his page from the hospital last night and it was an emergency. It was on the answering machine this morning.

DISPATCHER: Okay, 9014 Symmescreek, there's no such address. Do you have a better address for him?

CALLER: That's his address. Umm, I can give you his phone number, it's 538–5556.

DISPATCHER: When's the last time somebody talked to him?

CALLER: I'm not sure. I saw him Friday. I don't know if anybody saw him over the weekend or not. I know he didn't answer any emergency pages, and I consider this a real emergency. It's not normal for him not to answer a page. He had emergency pages.

PART TWO | The Scandal

THERE WAS A TERRIBLE SLEET AND ICE STORM IN CINCINNATI the weekend of February 16, and by Monday morning, Presidents' Day, Dante was completely holed up in her room, feeling isolated and sick. She had drugged herself with heavy prescription medication for two days and sounded light-headed when she spoke, almost out of touch with reality. On Saturday, she had plans with Nikki to go to a Mardi Gras party up in Mt. Adams, but she phoned and canceled, telling Nikki she needed to hang around for Darryl's call. On Sunday, she was so sleepy and groggy all day, she didn't even make it around the corner to see Beth.

It was exactly 9:38 A.M., February 19, 1996, when Corporal Greg Huber received a radio message from Dr. Darryl Sutorius's office manager. Huber called and spoke to a frantic employee, who could not come up with the doctor's correct address. The police officer ran a license tag number on his mobile data terminal, which indicated that the black four-door Jaguar registered to Darryl Sutorius was listed under his office address. Huber had to drive throughout the labyrinth Symmes Creek division before he was able to put two and two together. He finally spotted a black Jaguar sitting in a driveway at 9014 Symmesridge, one of the many nearly identical streets starting with the prefix "Symmes." It was a rather slow day in this picture-postcard neighborhood, so Huber happened to have his supervisor, Sergeant Zoellner, following him.

As the two men approached the residence, Corporal Huber looked around briefly to see if there were any signs of life outside, but there weren't. No broken windows, nothing out of the ordinary to catch his attention. When Sergeant Zoellner greeted Dante at the front door, the woman seemed a bit confused about his reason for being there. She was just peering around the corner at the officers, not opening the door all the way, holding on tightly to her small dog, Teddy.

"Are you Mrs. Sutorius?" Huber asked.

"Yes."

"Is Dr. Sutorius at home?"

"No."

"Are you sure?" Huber wanted to know. "Are you sure that he didn't come in sometime late in the evening? Is it possible that he may have come in and you didn't hear him?"

"No, I didn't hear him. I know he's not here; I would have heard him come in."

"Well, could you just double-check and make sure he's not home? Because we got a call this morning. His office is concerned that he didn't return any of his pages, and he hasn't shown up for work today."

"Well, I don't think he's here. I've been paging him myself."

"Would you mind just checking the garage to see if his car's in there?"

Dante nodded her head and stepped away from the door, letting the cold wind blow into the house while the officers stood by. After a few moments, she came back to report that Darryl's car *was* in the garage. She didn't understand what it could mean.

"Did you look in the car at all?" Zoellner asked. "Or feel to see if the car was warm?"

"No."

"Would you like us to check the car to see if it's warm?" Huber offered. "To see if he used it recently? He may have just got a ride to work with somebody else."

Dante hesitated for a moment. She seemed baffled, in a fog, as if she had been woken up out of her sleep. Now she wanted to know where her husband was, telling the officers to come in, leading them through the foyer, beyond the laundry room, and into the garage.

As the police were climbing over a bunch of boxes and golf clubs to get to the doctor's Lexus, Dante had run through the house in search of Darryl. Within seconds they heard a faint scream coming from somewhere, and both men flew back into the house, yelling for her, but Mrs. Sutorius wasn't answering.

At the top of the basement stairway, the two longtime veterans were confronted with something unpleasant. It was an odor they had smelled before, like rotting meat. They knew they had someone deceased down there, someone who had been dead quite a while. And as they turned the corner of the stairwell, they saw Darryl Sutorius lying on the couch with a stainless steel revolver on the floor close to his head. It was a bloody scene.

Mrs. Sutorius was standing over the body at that point, with her hands crossed over her chest as though she were praying. She was bending over Darryl slightly and was exceedingly upset with her husband.

"What's wrong with him?" she was yelling. "Tell him to wake up!"

Then everything seemed to happen in slow motion. The officers pulled Dante away from the body. She didn't seem to understand that her husband was lying in a pool of blood; she thought he had vomited on himself. She thought Darryl was terribly sick and kept screaming for her husband to wake up.

"Are you mad at me, Darryl?" she wanted to know. "Why won't you answer me?"

Dante was led upstairs, where she promptly dialed Beth, shrieking, "Help me, somebody help me," but she hung up too quickly. It took a while for Beth to realize it was Dante, but when she did, she ran over in sub-zero temperatures without even bothering to throw her shoes on.

As Huber contacted the dispatcher to report that Sutorius had been found dead, that there was a gun involved, Dante paced the kitchen floor, clinging to Teddy for dear life. By the time Beth arrived, Dante was crying so hard, refusing to let go of her pet, that Beth couldn't seem to get her friend's attention.

"What happened, Dante? What happened?" she kept asking.

But Dante wouldn't focus. She sat there, flanked by two police officers, and had nothing to say. She was just shaking. The only remnants of her composure were her little tweed skirt and her cashmere sweater.

"Are you hurt?" Beth asked. "Did Darryl hurt you?"

"The doctor is dead," Officer Huber reported blankly, and of course Beth was stunned. She asked if Darryl had a heart attack, but Dante was in a daze. Beth had no idea Darryl's body was in the house until she saw a crime unit arrive. When the basement door was opened, however, she could smell it.

As the investigative team began their work, tagging and blocking off areas, they proceeded as if they had a possible suicide on their hands. They had been given consent by Dante to search the house, so Huber walked upstairs and to the bedroom that was deadbolted, noticing that the doorframe had been broken and then repaired. Suddenly he remembered where he had seen this white Lexus before; it was all coming back to him. Huber had met Dr. Sutorius on January 24. He had run into him at a gas station, and at the time the surgeon was driving around with a .22-caliber pistol wrapped in a towel, requesting directions to the nearest police station.

In the kitchen, meanwhile, Beth was trying to help Dante. Her friend was unable to remember her own date of birth or Social Security number. She couldn't tell police the names or numbers of Darryl's children. She was fumbling in her purse for a phone book, but she couldn't find anything.

"What happened?" Beth was still asking.

"I want to see my husband," Dante insisted. "Why don't you let me go down there?" she asked Huber. "What are they doing down there? What kind of tests?"

The police officer led Dante away from the basement door, but she kept circling around. Beth finally put her arm around Dante and walked her to Darryl's bedroom. She thought Dante needed some rest and tried to pry Teddy away from her so the poor dog could be fed. Dante wanted a priest there so Darryl would be read the last rites, and Beth called her buddy, Father Robisch, who rushed over and said some prayers at the top of the stairwell, since no one was permitted in the basement.

The scene was now secured by the coroner of Hamilton County, Dr. Carl Parrott. He was in control downstairs, investigating the death, busy trying to make a determination. Wearing the obligatory white rubber gloves, the coroner was making notes about blood and other findings.

It was an atypical suicide. There had been two shots fired: one into the doctor's head and the other into the couch. Parrott took samples of the blood that had caked on the right side of the doctor's head; made note of a small defect in the skin behind the forehead, where a trickle of blood had run out; and had a discussion with the detectives about DNA testing. There was blood spattered on the face and on the sofa pillow. Some had reached the corner of the coffee table.

It struck the coroner as somewhat peculiar to find a smear of blood across the front of the white couch.

* * *

Beth spent most of the day with Dante, who was generally crying and incoherent the whole time. While the cops treaded lightly, trying not to upset her with too many questions, Dante kept rotating Darryl's wedding ring around her thumb, as if somehow that was going to bring her husband back.

Early that morning, Beth had noticed how immaculate Darryl's room was, almost sterile; so by afternoon, when Dante asked Beth to accompany her upstairs so she could change clothes, Beth was quite shocked to see Dante's room. For the first time, Beth finally understood just how incompatible these two people were. Dante's dirty laundry was strewn around, a lot of her clothes hadn't been taken out of the moving boxes, and there were Dr Pepper cans and candy wrappers left on the floor. It was messy, to say the least, especially the makeup area, with countless beauty products spilled on the vanity and clumps of fake hair everywhere.

Upstairs alone with Beth, Dante seemed to become more upset, and she finally spilled her guts, crying on her friend's shoulder about how Darryl had wanted to continue marriage counseling, but she had refused. She confided that Darryl had changed his mind about the divorce, yet all she could do was tell him to leave her alone. She had made him so unhappy.

"He found the yellow piece of paper," Dante blurted. "The yellow paper in my coat!"

"What piece of paper, Dante? What are you talking about?"

"From Target."

"What are you talking about? What's Target?"

"The gun!" she yelped. "The gun!"

"What gun?"

"The gun. Darryl took the first one and I was scared!"

As they came down the steps, Dante was just wailing. She said something about Darryl wanting counseling, and then her voice trailed off.

CHAPTER 16

"MRS. SUTORIUS WOULD CONTINUOUSLY WANT TO GO down and see the doctor's body," one of the officers later recalled, "and we tried to explain to her that it was sealed evidence and she couldn't see it. She wanted to see him before he was taken away, so we let her see the body bag as they brought it around the outside of the house."

"You told me I could see him," Dante was yelling as the body was being lifted into the mobile unit. "I want to see him!"

Detective John Hinrichs felt sorry for Dante, so he yelled outside and asked the officers to hold up a minute.

At the roadside, Dante asked them to open the body bag, but her request was refused. She just stood there a second, staring at this large plastic mass that was once Darryl.

As soon as she walked back in the house, Detective Hinrichs wanted to take her to the police station to talk. It was time to get some information from Dante. But she was worn out; she just wanted to get some sleep.

"We'd really like to talk to you while the weekend is still fresh in your mind," Hinrichs said.

"Well, okay," Dante told him, "but does it have to be at the police station? Can't we just talk here?"

"Well, the police officers are still going to be here, and I thought it might be easier to do it at the station.

You would be much more comfortable there, rather than being in the house with all that's going on."

But Dante wasn't sure. She was exhausted, and she had nothing to really offer the police. When Beth finally agreed to accompany her, Dante grabbed her purse. But on the way down in the unmarked car, Dante had a brief change of heart; luckily Beth reassured her that she was doing the right thing. It was just a formality, Beth said, and Dante owed it to Darryl.

When they got to the Symmes Township Police Station, Beth and Dante were put into an interrogation room, and they sat staring blankly at each other, each minute hanging like hours.

"What are these straps for?" Dante asked nervously.

"I think it's for lie detectors," Beth said.

"Well, I'm not taking any lie detector," she declared, her nose stuck up in the air.

During the six and a half hours that Dante was questioned at the Symmes Township station, she made a number of calls to Beth, who had long since been escorted home. Beth couldn't understand why Dante was still there. She offered to come pick her up, but Dante said not to, she'd decided she should let them ask all the questions they wanted.

The officers discovered that Dante's name was Della, that she preferred to be called Dante even though some people still called her Della. She was very charming while talking about herself; of course she broke down in tears a lot, but she had become less incoherent once they gave her a Diet Pepsi and a Big Mac to munch on. The officers were careful to be delicate with the bereaved widow; they offered her as much courtesy as possible. They wanted to accommodate her. They were keeping things informal.

Della Dante Sutorius stated that on Saturday, February 17, she was running late for her 8:30 A.M. appointment at Target World, where she had a shooting lesson.

Afterward, she returned home and called her friend Beth, and in the afternoon, she and Beth visited one of their neighbors, then went to dinner at McLevy's Pub. It was still daylight when she got home, somewhere around 6:00 P.M., and she paged her husband at his office and at the hospital. When he didn't respond, she drove over and checked the hospital parking lot, but she couldn't find his car.

Dante told police that shortly after she returned from her drive to Bethesda North, Darryl had come walking through the front door. That was Saturday night. Apparently his son had been involved in a hit-and-run accident that morning, and Darryl was upset about it. Dante had felt sorry for him, seeing him so sad and lonely in the basement. She sat down there and talked with him. He was quite upset. Darryl felt John was always in trouble and was irresponsible. She then sat on his lap and asked, "Do you love me?" and Darryl asked her why she had canceled the appointment with the marriage counselor. She told him that nothing had changed, that she wanted to move on with her life.

Dante told authorities about how thoughtful Darryl had been through their courtship, about what a great guy he was. When she had been sick, she happily recalled, the man personally delivered a sandwich to her place in Covington. But her tone changed drastically when she explained how Darryl had recently become rude and hateful toward everyone. She conveyed that she wanted him to see a psychiatrist, but when it didn't seem to help, she told her husband she wanted a separation. She said that got Darryl "pissed and ticked off," and in his anger he kicked their puppy, Teddy, off the couch.

"I yelled at him about that," Dante recalled. "I told him that dog was the only thing that really loved him."

Back to Saturday night, Dante said she left Darryl in the basement and got into her car to go to a Mardi Gras party in Mt. Adams. After a few minutes of driving, she didn't feel very well, and she turned the car around, taking sleeping pills the minute she got home. Before she nodded out, she called and canceled her plans with her sister Nikki, and, realizing that Darryl was no longer home, she tried to page him.

On Sunday the eighteenth, Dante said she got up late in the morning and went to Wal-Mart, but other than that, she stayed home. She told authorities that she didn't see Darryl Sunday, that she paged him again and left messages at work and on his voice mail, but he never called. At around 9:30 P.M. she was tired of waiting for Darryl, so she went to White Castle for burgers, then started to drive the Norwood Lateral to head for Nikki's, but felt too groggy and returned home. The doctor's bedroom door was closed when she got there, she said, so she went up and knocked on it, but there was no answer.

When she woke on Monday, she noticed Darryl's door was still closed. She told police she recalled hearing a loud noise, like a door close, somewhere around 3:00 A.M. and stated that when she heard the noise, she had gone downstairs to check the security alarm, but she didn't see anything suspicious, so she went back upstairs and fell asleep. She said Monday had been a weird day.

Dante recounted the events that occurred when the two patrol officers appeared at her door, explaining that she tried to wake her husband when she found him in the basement, but his head was stuck to the pillow. She realized that her dog, Teddy, was licking the floor right by the gun, so she picked up the dog, and then the two officers reappeared.

When police asked Dante how her husband came to possess the gun, she said that when Darryl had found a yellow ticket from the Target gun shop in her coat pocket Saturday night, he had become irate because she had purchased another gun. He then insisted that she march upstairs and turn it over to him, which she did.

"Was the gun loaded?" a detective asked.

"I think it was loaded. I loaded it a lot," she said, "for protection."

Dante told police that she was taking a gun lesson for safety reasons. She had become frightened about prowlers because the doctor had left her alone quite a bit. That was why she had locks put on her bedroom door.

Police asked Dante about her medical history, and she automatically began grasping at her chest, saying she had a hole in her heart, carrying on about her poor health, which included back problems. Apparently she'd had a metal rod surgically implanted in her back, which caused a lot of discomfort, and she was taking a number of prescriptions—pain medication and tranquilizers.

By this time in the interview, it was already after dark and Dante was feeling tired. She asked to use the phone to call her friend John Spalding, a prominent attorney in Covington, and left a message on Spalding's machine. She also dialed Beth, complaining that the police weren't letting her go home and her back was killing her.

In continuing her conversation with police, Dante detailed her marital problems, including the fights with Deborah over the wedding, but maintained that she and Darryl had decided to make the marriage work. After harping on the subject of Deborah, Dante became so upset she started to hyperventilate, and the Colerain Township Life Squad was called. She was clutching her heart, yet to paramedics, Mrs. Sutorius denied having chest pains. She absolutely refused to go to the hospital for treatment, and quickly signed a medical release form, anxious to resume the interview and get it over with.

"Do you have a small brown box in your room?" Detective Hinrichs inquired.

"Yes, and I haven't seen it for years," she said. "I don't know what's in it."

"Are you in any way involved in the death of your husband?" he asked.

"No."

"Did you kill your husband, Dr. Sutorius?"

"No," Dante whispered, "and I really think I need an attorney at this time."

When Dante turned her head away from the man, she placed her hands over her ears and became melodramatic about it, refusing to listen to anything else the cops had to say.

"This is just like the movies," she was saying to herself. "I don't understand what's happening."

The time was approximately 9:30 P.M. and apparently she was no longer going to cooperate. At that moment an officer informed her that some cocaine was found in her small metal box during the house search. Della Dante Sutorius was read her rights and was told she'd be spending the night at the Justice Center. When she tried to stand up, her knees buckled.

"They're accusing me of *killing* him," she cried to Beth over the phone. "You better get me a lawyer."

"But I don't know anyone I can call this late," her friend said.

"Well, try to think, Beth. I need to get bailed out. I can't stay in the Justice Center; it's filled with bugs."

"But it's almost ten at night, Dante, I just don't know—"

"All I need is someone to come down to the Justice Center with twenty-five hundred dollars. They're holding me on a drug charge for cocaine that isn't even mine. I didn't know they could do that. It's stuff I saved from one of my old boyfriends."

CHAPTER | 17

*T*HOUGH SHE HESITATED TO CALL HIM AT HOME, IT ONLY took a few minutes for Beth to get her attorney friend Shannon Smith to agree to represent Dante Sutorius. At 10:20 P.M. the lawyer called Detective Hinrichs and said he did not want Mrs. Sutorius to make any type of statement. Hinrichs advised Smith that Dante would be brought downtown and detained for approximately two to three hours.

When Hinrichs hung up the phone, Dante started hyperventilating, saying that she was ill and unable to walk. He practically had to carry her over to Police Officer Cindy Isaac, who searched the frail woman and delivered her to the Criminal Justice Center, a temporary holding facility next to the courthouse downtown.

As Dante was being processed, authorities confiscated her purse, a large leather sack filled with everything but cash. She had papers on an upcoming Society of Bacchus trip to Chicago; receipts from Kroger's, Wal-Mart, and Radio Shack; receipts from the Doral Spa and used airline tickets to Miami; stubs from the bank, various bank statements, and travel statements; a number of unfilled prescriptions and doctors' phone numbers; and a passport identifying her as Della Faye Britteon. Apparently she used quite a few names: Della Dante Sutorius, Della Dante Bassett, Della Dante Hall, Della F. Britteon, Ms. Dante Britteon, D. (Britteon) Sutorius, and then there was just plain Della.

*   *   *

By the following afternoon, Della Dante Sutorius and her surgeon husband were the top story on all Cincinnati television and radio programs. Already the media was turning the bereaved widow into the prime suspect. They had the luxury of speculating without any burden of proof.

Of course, her phone was ringing off the hook, and while she was thoroughly insulted by the idea that people could think she might have done such a terrible thing, she understood the process, which to her meant that she would be a suspect until the autopsy results came in. In her view, everything would calm down once the police finished their investigation, and in the meantime she had lots of support in the neighborhood, which made life bearable. People were standing behind her, letting her know if she needed anything, they'd be there. Neighbors felt sorry for her, especially since the media was hounding her day and night. There were TV vans and reporters camped out all over Symmesridge, and people were offering to sneak Dante in and out of their garages and through their backyards.

But as nice as everyone was, bringing her food and sympathy cards and flowers and all, for Della this was all still a bad nightmare. Her reputation was on the line, and the drug rap wasn't making her look very good.

"This is like a bad nightmare for me, too, because they called me and talked to me," Cheryl complained when she finally got hold of Della that afternoon. Della agreed. She was sick of seeing her face plastered all over the news. Della was becoming a household name.

"The drug thing is silly," she told Cheryl. "I didn't know it was there. I don't even know how much it was. I don't think it was a lot. It couldn't have been very much."

"It's a felony, so it had to be a lot," Cheryl said, "felony drug possession is what the man told me this morning. That means it had to be a certain amount."

"Well, I just told them no comment. That's what the attorney said."

For some strange reason, it occurred to Cheryl that she could easily turn on the recording device of her answering machine, and she decided to run a tape throughout her conversation with Della. She wasn't sure why she felt tempted to do it. Maybe it was because Cheryl never trusted her. Deep down, she didn't actually believe her sister was capable of murder, but she could see how Della might easily drive someone to suicide. She wanted it all down on tape for posterity.

"I just don't know what happened, I really don't know." Della said. "I need to find out myself first. Obviously I can't tell you anything. I don't know."

"And so they absolutely ruled out somebody coming in and breaking in or something?"

"I don't know, I guess they didn't rule it out. Obviously you can't rule it out. They're doing everything; they were here all day Monday."

"And what made the police come there anyway?" Cheryl asked.

"He wasn't answering his page. Sunday night, late at night I was paging him. Then I called the office and he didn't answer at the office."

"Okay, but you're paging him from *home*, Della, and he was at your house?"

"Well, I didn't know that. God. Cheryl, you know, I knew he was . . ."

"Well, I mean, I'm sorry. I just can't believe it. You're paging him and he was *right there?* Didn't his beeper go off? Didn't you hear it?"

"No, I don't even know where the beeper is," she explained. "Sometimes he puts it on vibrate, so he must not have had it on. Although, you know, I was in the kitchen upstairs. I always call him from either the kitchen or my room, so if he's down in the basement, I might not have heard the beeper. Probably he just had it on vibrate, which is what he does a lot of times at home or while we're in the movies or something like that."

As Cheryl and Della continued to chat, she flipped the microcassette over to side B and kept prodding. Cheryl wanted to know how on earth her sister never noticed Darryl's car in the garage. Della said she hadn't taken out the trash all weekend, so she hadn't gone in there.

Della commented bitterly about the night before and the way the police had treated her like a criminal. She was in shock, she was upset, her back was giving her shooting pains, yet they wouldn't let her lie down, wouldn't let her go home or do anything. She said she was so shaken up by the whole ordeal she couldn't sleep all night. She was in tremendous pain, and her medication wasn't helping.

As they spoke, Della seemed confused about the times and dates of the weekend. She thought Darryl killed himself Saturday morning, then realized she saw him Saturday night. She wasn't sure when he might have done it. Cheryl informed her that the news reports said Darryl's suicide happened on Sunday morning around 2:00 A.M. and she couldn't understand how Della didn't hear the shot go off.

"I'm sorry, you're just going to have to bear with me for a while," she told Cheryl as she clicked back from another call. "I'm not thinking clearly or rationally. My mind is just numb. I haven't had a chance to brush my teeth today. They don't let you take a shower and they don't let you brush your teeth."

Cheryl just let her sister talk on, her answering machine tape running.

"When I was on the news," she complained, "when you saw me on the news this morning, I hadn't brushed my teeth, hadn't washed my face or combed my hair in over a day and a half, so that's why I looked like that. I need a really hot shower and some sleep. I feel like I could sleep for a week."

"So, how are things around your home?"

"My home? They've been calling all day," she said, her voice picking up. "The lady down the street's going to bring dinner over in a little while, and you know, she doesn't even know me very well, but Darryl was really mean to her. She signed up for the social committee and when I wound up being the head of the social committee, she wouldn't come over because of Darryl. She hated Darryl."

"Really?"

"She was a nurse at his hospital, and he would just snap her head off right in front of the patients and everything else. He was just rude and insulting to her, you know. That's humiliating, with other nurses around and patients around."

As Della went on about how rude and nasty Darryl was, Cheryl wondered about the funeral arrangements. The subject hadn't come up yet. All her sister seemed to care about was herself.

"You know, all the neighbors have talked, and they thought I was abused because I always walked around looking sad," she said. "There were rumors that I was abused. Now, this is great. I'm finding out the neighbors think he's been beating me up or something."

"Did the police tell you they already talked to all the neighbors?"

"Well, they talked to Beth because Beth knew more than anyone what was going on and what kind of person he was," she said. "Beth knew about his suicide attempts. She just knew all along, you know, she knew him long before me. She used to work at the hospital and she'd see him every day and he was always mean and nasty to her and hateful. She told the police to just ask around the hospital. No one liked him."

There was a long pause, but Cheryl remained silent.

"Cheryl, he didn't have one friend in the whole world," she complained. "Not one person liked him. He didn't have a best buddy, you know, he didn't have anyone to call. Sometimes he'd get teary-eyed about it, but he just didn't have any friends."

"Yeah, but Della, you know we're talking about a man that's *dead* right now, just like it's *nothing.*"

"I know, but it's just as though he's not really dead. I just can't, I don't know what's wrong with me," she whimpered. "It's like I'm gonna hear the garage door go up and he's gonna come home, you know what I mean? I just keep thinking any minute now, the garage door is going to go up because that's the way it always is."

When their conversation jumped back to the problems with the press, Della asked about her brothers, Gene and Scott, wondering if they had anything to say, and Cheryl reported that their brothers wanted nothing to do with the radio and TV people who were calling. They were both just furious, in fact. They wanted no part of the Sutorius mess. When Della heard that, she acted like it didn't matter, and talked about how nice it was to have so many friends, so many neighbors who cared about her.

"Wouldn't you know the people who are against me are my *family,*" she whined, "that the only people that are going for my jugular, that I have to think about twice are my family? Is that just the saddest thing?"

Cheryl didn't answer.

"My mother, she called up to the police station. Did you know that? She called the police station and started bad-mouthing me, telling them all these awful—"

"When? When did Mother call?"

"Yesterday evening. She called the police station and she's trying to hang me. *Why?* She's my *mother.* Why would she do it, Cheryl?"

Cheryl had no answer.

"You know, the detective told me this, he said my mother had been telling him things about me, and I asked him why he called my mother, and he said he didn't. *She* called *him.* Can you believe it?"

"Well . . ."

"And I sat, and that's when I got hysterical. That's

when I hyperventilated. I mean, I just, after all these years, I just couldn't believe how she could have such deep hatred for me that she wants them to arrest me for murder or for hiring a hit man or something. You know what I mean? She wants to put me in such a bad, bad light."

"Maybe she knew more than we thought she knew."

"About what?"

"About the whole situation."

"She didn't know anything about Darryl and me. I never talk to her. Unless Nikki or Carla told her stuff. But I didn't tell Nikki anything terribly serious, just that he was so weird all the time, but everyone knew that. That isn't anything Mother could use against me. *Why,* Cheryl, why would she make a point of calling the police?"

"I don't know. I can't tell you. It's just so strange."

Just at that moment, their mother, Olga, broke into Cheryl's call waiting. She was anxious to hear what Della had to say, and she wanted Cheryl to call back the minute she hung up. When Cheryl clicked over, Della just wanted to get off the line. She was tired, she said, and very sad. Her stomach was all knotted up.

"I just can't believe it, Cheryl. I just can't believe all this. It's like I'm in a movie and it won't stop. It's like watching a movie, only it's me."

"I know. We all feel the same way."

"Man, I'm going through my own little hell here," she wailed.

"Well, you know, at least you're alive to go through it. I sure do feel sorry for Darryl. He's the one that's dead."

"You just have no idea what's happened to me in the last two days."

"I don't?"

"How would you feel? Just think of it for one moment. Put yourself in my shoes. What if you really needed your family's support, and Mother called and tried to get you in more trouble. How would you feel?"

"If my husband was gone, my mind would be on my husband. I couldn't give a damn about my mother."

But Della went on a tirade about Olga, complaining that her mother hurt her feelings, that she was flabbergasted by her mother's actions. Olga was trying to get her into serious trouble this time, and Della felt she was an unfit mom and a monster of a person. No matter how much Cheryl reminded her that her poor husband should be her utmost concern, Della just couldn't let it go.

When they ended their talk, she seemed to be in total denial that Darryl was dead. Della was still waiting for the garage door to open.

CHAPTER 18

"**T**HEY'RE MAKING ME OUT LIKE SOME CRIMINAL, LIKE I'm some Bonnie and Clyde," Della said in a phone interview from her home Tuesday night. Della was publicly responding to claims by Darryl's kids that she had threatened to harm the surgeon. She declined any further comment.

"It's really up in the air," Captain Don Coyle told the *Cincinnati Post.* "We're still looking into it and talking to everybody we can. We have no reason to arrest anyone at this point."

"We were in complete shock," one neighbor told the press. "They were a lovely family." Another neighbor told reporters, "They seemed to be the perfect thing."

"We're not really sure if we have a crime," Captain Coyle admitted. "We don't know if it's suicide or foul play." Coyle remarked that the police didn't yet know the significance of the two bullets, explaining that the gun could have been test-fired. "It's happened before in suicides," he said.

"Mrs. Sutorius has been cooperative with us," Coyle stated. "She has been married and divorced several times, and we're checking into her background."

Colleagues of Darryl's told the media they were quite puzzled by the news.

Dr. Jim Mills recalled a conversation with Darryl in the locker room of the operating suite just five days before his death, stating that his friend seemed no different than usual. He certainly didn't seem like a man who was pondering suicide.

"From what I could gain, he obviously was not happy with his situation with his wife," Jim Mills told the *Post*, "but Darryl seemed like Darryl. He was an individual who was a very kind person, but he was gruff. People around him would be a little bit scared of him, but that was just Darryl."

At 11:30 Thursday night, February 22, a frightened Dante Sutorius called the Symmes Township police and asked that a patrol car stop by. When officer Ron Packwood responded, Dante was shaken, saying she had seen someone out around the deck area. She thought he was trying to break into her kitchen door, but then fled when her dog started barking. She thought it was a male, but all she could really see was a white jacket.

The next morning, Friday, February 23, Dante had an appointment with a new attorney, Scott Croswell, who wanted a $100,000 retainer to take her case. On the phone with Beth later that afternoon, Dante seemed desperate. She was nervous about the media pointing fingers. Moreover, she was having problems with the Sutorius kids; she wanted to cremate Darryl's body and have a simple memorial service, but that was turning into a fiasco.

"She was talking to me on the phone and thanked me for being her friend and hoped I would always remember her as a good person," Beth recalled. "She said she was going to make some phone calls and say good-bye to some people. She had some unfinished business to take care of with her mother. She had a few things to say to her."

The more Beth listened, the more this was sounding like another suicide. Dante seemed pretty drugged already, her voice drowsy, lethargic, and Beth started panicking.

She asked Dante to hold on, and dialed 911 on the other line. Then she told Dante she'd be right over, jumping in her car and dropping her kids off at a neighbor's house on the way.

As Beth turned the corner to Dante's place, she spotted a police cruiser and yelled out that he was headed the wrong way. But the officer just gave her a strange look. Then Beth looked down the block and realized something bizarre was happening all over again. Cop cars were everywhere at the Manoocheri residence, and it looked like quite an emergency.

Over at Dante's, Beth dealt with her screaming friend, who had a vial of tranquilizers in her hand and declined to turn them over. When a white-haired police officer appeared at the door, urging Dante to go to a psychiatric unit for help, she wouldn't hear of it. Dante signed a pink slip, refused medical treatment, and politely sent the officer away.

Just as Beth was leaving, the phone rang, and she and Dante listened while the answering machine picked up.

It was Scott Croswell returning Dante's call.

"We'll work out the money situation somehow," he promised. "Now, you've got some assets, and you told me you didn't do this and I believe you. I will get you out of this. Just calm down."

* * *

As Beth drove home, dying to find out what was happening at the Manoocheri residence, she was waved away by police officers. For some reason there was another media camp in her affluent subdivision; there were camera crews setting up, and everywhere she looked there were antennas, cords, microphones, cables, and lights.

She tried to stop in the middle of it all, figuring there had been a robbery, that she could find out from a reporter, but she couldn't get anywhere with them.

Through one of her connections with the Cincinnati police, Beth learned that Mrs. Manoocheri's mother had been killed in the basement of their home. Beth found it very hard to believe, since Mrs. Alavi was an eighty-two-year-old Iranian woman, in the United States for just a few weeks, paying a visit to her daughter and grandchildren. The woman had been brutally murdered, Beth found out, and the word was that it had been a professional hit.

News reports stated that the elderly lady had been bound, gagged, and then had her throat slashed, all during an alleged robbery. Police had recovered the Manoocheris' 1992 tan Lexus from Enyart Square, a shopping center directly linked to the subdivision, but oddly enough, nothing else had been stolen from the Manoocheri place.

Beth knew Mrs. Alavi because the woman walked through the neighborhood daily. Even though she hardly spoke a word of English, she seemed to be a friendly old lady, who liked to smile and wave at passersby. Now her face was flashing all over the 6:00 P.M. news, and people in the neighborhood started to feel their little world shatter. A Neighborhood Watch meeting was called for the following week, and a number of housewives decided to have security alarm systems installed.

To the press, Symmes Creek residents expressed sympathy for the families of the victims, but they refused to talk to reporters about the deaths. They just felt they didn't need any more negative publicity. For years their subdivision had always been one of those places where nothing ever happened. Now they were coping with two mysterious deaths inside of a week.

CHAPTER | 19

"*I* TOLD NIKKI THAT NO MATTER WHAT ANYONE SAYS** bad about me, don't think of me that way. Don't think of me as a bad person," Della was insisting to Cheryl. It was the second of their taped phone conversations, and the last.

"I just told her that I loved her when she was a little baby," Della went on. "I loved her so much. And I told her I wanted her to call and thank Mother for me. I wanted Nikki to tell her, I want to thank her for doing this to me, for being such a good mother."

"Oh," Cheryl said. She was eating up the sarcasm.

Della seemed annoyed that Beth had shown up with the police the day before, but all Cheryl wanted to discuss was the Iranian woman who had been murdered down the street. She couldn't understand why someone would want to hurt an eighty-two-year-old woman, but Della moved the conversation back to herself and her suicide attempt. She was deep in self-pity, freaking out about her negative portrait on the news, angry that she had no way to defend herself.

"They're taking this little grain of sand out of my past, you know, something I did in my past that wasn't all that horrible, and making it into something else," she moaned. "You know, yes, I've been married a lot, but do you have to make me look like Mata Hari for that?"

"Well, they went back and spoke to—"

"And all this was because of Mother. I found out that she called long-distance to all the TV stations and bad-mouthed me on all three of our TV stations. What kind of a person is she? Can you imagine, Cheryl? Doing that to one of your kids?"

"Nope."

"Well, you're not believing everything you read in the paper and on the news, are you? They said I was married eight times."

"They did?"

"One of them did."

Cheryl was surprised to hear that. Apparently the TV station Cheryl watched had gotten all the information correct, listing each person Della had been married to, going directly by court records. As they lingered on the phone, the sisters eventually moved away from the topic of unpleasant ex-husbands, and Della began to repeat herself, especially when it came to Olga calling the police. At one point, she started a fight with Cheryl about their mother, thinking Cheryl was taking Olga's side. Della became so irate about it, Cheryl could practically see her foaming at the mouth.

"I just want to tell you something quickly," she warned Cheryl. "If something happens to me, I want Shawn to have everything I own. Everything I own down to the smallest picture is to go to Shawn, okay?"

"All right."

"And you have to be tough on one other thing," she requested. "I do not want Mother at my funeral. She's not allowed to walk in the door. She's not allowed to have anything to do with my funeral and she is not allowed to have my ashes, do you hear?"

"Yeah, but who says you would be cremated? That's a disgusting thought." Cheryl recoiled.

"No, I want to be cremated. I don't want to be in the ground where bugs are going to get me."

"This is disgusting," Cheryl told her. "Why are we talking about this?"

But Della went on about her funeral arrangements and requests. She wanted to be placed in a mausoleum, on the other side of a little wall, where people could come and talk to her whenever they wanted to. As much as Cheryl tried to get her off the subject, Della wanted to be morbid. She seemed to be having fun with it.

"It was Mother who brought it all on," Della ranted. "She got it going."

"She didn't—"

"She has never told me why she hates me," she continued, her voice all choked up. "In my whole life she never told me why. Why do you hate a little girl? I was only seven years old when she put my hands in boiling water. I was *seven*. What had I done to her? I was so little and cute. That little girl had pigtails and was so teeny-tiny. Why did she do that to her? Why beat her up, punch her in the nose, and give her a bloody nose? Why did she do all that?"

"What in the heck are you talking about?" Cheryl wanted to know. "Are you talking about you?"

"Mother's doing this to that little girl."

"What little girl? *You?*"

"That little girl, Della," she said. "You don't hurt little kids like that. And, now, why does she do it still? Why does she want them to arrest me? Why does she want them to put me in prison? Does she want them to kill me, too?"

"I don't know, Della."

"Cheryl, it was from day one. As long as I can remember, I got beat more days than I didn't get beat. Water spots on that piece of tile that I missed. She would look for reasons to beat me."

Cheryl told her sister to calm down, to take some tranquilizers, but Della wouldn't stop. She raved about her mother, and she still wanted answers. Cheryl suggested she just try to get some rest, but Della insisted that just wouldn't happen. The sleeping pills no longer worked.

When Della started saying that she was too tired to live anymore, Cheryl told her to just cut it out.

"Don't let her hurt me anymore," Della whined. "Don't let her near the coffin. Don't let her in there. Don't let her touch me. You promise?"

"Della, you need to settle down. Try and eat something."

"I'm really not a horrible person. You know that, right?"

"Yeah."

CHAPTER 20

As soon as she hung up with Cheryl, Della called Beth, crying that she was lonely. She wanted to borrow some videos, which was obviously an excuse, since the Sutorius house had a satellite dish with access to practically every movie channel going.

Beth happened to be in the middle of preparing a big birthday party, so the house was full of goodies and she invited her friend over for a snack. When Della got there, Beth couldn't help but notice how poorly she looked, wearing what appeared to be the same white sweatsuit and Farragamo shoes. Beth invited her to stay for the party, but Della refused. She ate a toasted bagel with cream cheese and quietly excused herself before the guests arrived.

That evening, Beth brought over a plate of food, but Della wouldn't let her in. She was too exhausted for company. In some ways, Beth was relieved to hear that. Since everyone in her family was giving her a hard time about it, she had begun to feel torn about her friendship with Dante, or Della; her name made no difference. In her heart Beth felt Darryl did kill himself, but still, Della bought the gun, which crossed a line for Beth. Besides, she was tired of all the newspeople in the area, and now her kids were asking questions. It was getting to be too much.

"One day, I had her in my car, and unfortunately the Channel 5 News Team saw us," Beth recalled, "and they followed me through Symmes Township in their white Bronco. We cut through the GE and McDonald's parking lots, then we went through Montgomery Trace and Calumet, and I finally lost them. I drove her home as close as I could, and she ran in and slammed the door."

Evidently the newspeople had special days for camping out at Della's—Wednesdays were particularly big because that was garbage day, and they would hover at the far end of the double garage. When she realized this, Della started driving her trash out of the neighborhood. The last thing she needed was a piece of her garbage making it onto the six o'clock news.

Of course, Della wasn't the only person fighting off the media. Darryl's first wife, Janet Sutorius, had been contacted so often she found it necessary to get an unlisted number. And the Sutorius children were being hounded, especially Deborah. To add to their grief, Della was in control of the body and she wouldn't allow them to give Darryl a proper funeral. In desperation, they held a family conference to decide how to get around her. Of course, Deborah had already made public statements about Della's threats against her father, so she was out of the loop.

The decision was made to have Becky, the least

threatening of the kids, call her. They gave her a script that went something like: Hello, I'm really sorry. This is Becky. I've never met you, but we understand that the body's going to be released to you and we'd like to have some say in the arrangement.

"Think about it and call me," Becky told her. "Or if we don't hear from you, I'll get back to you tomorrow."

Two days passed without a return call from Della.

Becky didn't want to call again, so Jan took the job and determined she would just keep calling the house and leave messages. Della did actually answer the phone sometimes, and when she did, Jan would be very friendly and polite, asking Della if she needed something, if she could bring her over some soup or anything.

"Well, what about if you say where you want him buried and we'll say what funeral home we want?" Jan asked in one of their brief talks.

"That sounds like a good idea."

But the next thing Jan knew, the director of Gilligan Funeral Home was calling to inform her that Della had given him instructions to handle the body. She wanted Darryl cremated.

Jan knew that ultimately Della held the cards, but for the sake of the children, the people at Gilligan were trying to be accommodating. Now it was up to her to somehow get Darryl's body.

On Thursday, February 22, Jan and her three kids were at the funeral home anxiously waiting for Della to walk through the door.

"When she came up the stairs, you should have seen the look," Jan said. "I will remember the look on her face forever."

It was clear Della disliked the Sutorius children and was quite unhappy to face them.

"When she started crying," Jan recalled, "I put my arms around her."

Inside the lobby of the funeral home, Jan continued to comfort Della, telling her how sorry she was. Della let Jan know that she felt no one else had been so sincere. Jan seemed to be the only person who really cared. Della wanted Jan to write the obituary, and that was fine with Jan. Then, after a brief grieving session, all of them agreed to ride together. The driver brought them to Spring Grove Cemetery on the north side of town.

On the way there, Della talked about how difficult Darryl was to live with, and Jan had to agree. They eventually had a pleasant conversation about Darryl's love of art, about his hobby of painting and drawing, and before they knew it, the car stopped at a picturesque spot under a big oak tree at Spring Grove, where the children thought Darryl would like to be buried. Up until then, the kids had been pretty quiet with Della, hardly opening their mouths except to sigh.

"I tried to get him to a psychiatrist," Della blurted.

"I know he had troubles with depression," Jan commiserated. "He was seeing a psychiatrist when he left me."

"He just seemed so unappreciative of what he had," Della explained. "We'd go to the hospital and he'd see a resident with his family and he just didn't understand how someone could be that happy. He was a man who had everything, but he didn't know it."

The two of them discussed how much Darryl loved his kids, yet seemed to be unable to appreciate his family. Throughout the trip back, Della was wonderful at complimenting Jan, at making her and the children feel important. Yet after the cemetery ride, a few days went by and none of them heard from her. When Jan left more messages, she found Della was hard to pin down.

"You're not going to believe this," Della said when she finally returned one of Jan's calls. "I've just come home from my neighbors', and there must be somebody loose in the neighborhood. My neighbor down the street has just been *murdered*."

"Well, there must be something going on," Jan said.

"I'm sorry this happened in your neighborhood. Do you think it could, in any way, be linked to Darryl?"

"Well, I don't know. I'm really frightened. There was a prowler here the other night and I just think, you know, isn't it funny that it happened so close? I'm getting scared to stay here."

"Well, you're probably safe, but it sure is crazy."

Of course, Jan had already heard the particulars about the Iranian woman on the news, but she let Della describe the death in vivid detail. Apparently the rumor in Symmes Creek was that the woman had been killed by a drug gang. People were saying her tongue had been cut out.

"Let me ask you," Jan said. "Have you decided about Darryl? Have you made any arrangements?"

"Not yet."

"Well, do you have any ideas?"

"I want him cremated."

"He's not going to be cremated," Jan insisted. "The kids don't want that and Darryl's father just won't allow it."

"Well, I'm thinking of having him cremated and having his ashes thrown either at Gate of Heaven or Hilton Head. We used to walk around the beach a lot, and I think Darryl would like to have his ashes there. He always loved it on the beach."

CHAPTER 21

WHILE THE FOUR CHILDREN PREPARED FOR A MEMO-
rial service, their mother was relentlessly calling Della.
It was already Tuesday, February 27, and Della had yet
to make a decision about what to do with the body. Jan
finally reached her that afternoon. Della was just about
to shower and dress, she said, and planned to make it
to the Lutheran Church of the Good Shepard on time.
She was quite annoyed that she had to read about the
memorial service in the paper. Jan realized they couldn't
keep Della away from the church, and she cringed at
the thought of Della's arrival. She felt certain that her
kids would want their stepmother escorted out, that
there was going to be a scene.

"We couldn't depend on you, Dante, so we had to
take matters in our own hands," Jan said flatly. "You've
not been very cooperative, and this is very important to
the children."

"Well, it's not right that you've left me out of everything. I'm his wife," Della protested.

"You know, I'm sorry it had to come to this, but we
just can't work with you any longer because we just can't
trust you."

And Jan hung up the phone.

Within minutes, Jan's phone rang. It was one of the
detectives. He was calling to tell her that lawmen were
on their way to arrest Della, that Dr. Carl Parrott had
officially ruled the death a homicide. The detective refused to talk about the evidence against Della, but said

the charge would be aggravated murder—apparently they suspected the killing was premeditated.

At 4:45 P.M., as the Good Shepard Church was filling with mourners, TV crews captured Della's arrest for their late-breaking reports. On the 6:00 and 11:00 news, the forty-five-year-old blonde was seen being led from her home, wearing nothing but handcuffs and a white bathrobe.

A couple of people at the service had already heard the news on the radio, and two or three print reporters had actually shown up at the church, one of whom caught Jan just outside the vestibule before the service began.

"This period of not knowing, that's the worst," Jan confided. "Just to have some closure, it's a relief that all this has come together."

But it really hadn't ended. Not at all. Della Dante was proclaiming her innocence, and she had the best defense attorney in town standing by her.

"I picked this church because it's where Dad was supposed to walk me down the aisle," Deborah told mourners. "I just want everyone to go home and hug the ones you love. You never know if it's going to be you. You never know if you'll see tomorrow."

As Deborah stood behind the church's pulpit, addressing a crowd of over three hundred people, she shared a paragraph she had written in a journal years before: "I decided today, I love my dad, even though sometimes he does things I don't always agree with. He taught me unconditional love . . . and that was a beautiful lesson."

Delivered with a quavering voice, Deborah's message came across loud and clear. People were moved to tears. Della's sisters, Nikki and Cheryl, who were in the back row, especially felt the weight of her sorrow. Then John spoke very briefly, calling his father a great healer, followed by Becky, who was almost as brief, being very stoic as she quoted lines from her dad's favorite song: "When you walk through a storm, hold your head up high."

"Faith was a very important part of my father's life," youngest daughter, Chrissy, told the congregation with an emotional voice. "He chose to serve God. Before surgery, he always prayed to God to direct him."

"How many lives will not be saved by Darryl's hand?" the pastor of Good Shepard asked. "Darryl was a family man and a friend," he told mourners, "and death has robbed Darryl's children of their father. It has robbed them of future words of love, forgiveness, and support. It has robbed them of talking with their dad about life and all its twists and turns."

Out in the church lobby, the children stood composed, greeting friends, family, and long-lost acquaintances. People came up and wanted to say how thankful they were that Darryl saved their lives, reminding the kids about how intelligent and conscientious their father was. The family suggested any memorials be sent to the University of Cincinnati College of Medicine, where Darryl Sutorius was an associate professor until the time of his death. Together with their mom, the children thanked everyone for all the sympathy and prayers, having received more cards and gift offerings than they could ever have fathomed.

"We're relieved to hear something," John told a reporter when asked about the arrest of his stepmother. "It's been a long week. I'm going to miss him. I wish he was here."

If convicted of aggravated murder, Della Dante Sutorius would possibly be facing the death penalty. She was being held without bond in the Justice Center, pending an appearance in Hamilton County Municipal Court in the morning. Sheriff Simon Leis, the man responsible for going after Larry Flint in decades past, held a press conference that night, but refused to discuss motive. He told the news media he could "not speak to any of the facts of the case" other than that an arrest had been made based on "police calculations and designs."

Ironically, the following day, as the news of Deborah's engagement to Bill hit local papers—their photo captioned with their plans for an October wedding—a portrait of Della Sutorius was splashed across the front pages.

She had appeared in court that Wednesday morning to answer to the charge in the slaying of her husband, and her bond was set at $225,000, an amount she couldn't afford to pay. Her attorney declined to discuss the case, except to call the evidence circumstantial, insisting that the claims that Mrs. Sutorius bought a .38-caliber pistol days before the death were irrelevant.

"There are no eyewitnesses, there are no statements," Croswell told the media. "The state has made an allegation and they'll have an opportunity to try to prove it."

Della covered her face throughout the hearing, often trembling as she stood next to her large-framed attorney. She never spoke at all. "She is anxious to face these charges and have them resolved," Croswell said as he stepped outside the courtroom.

A number of sources informed local newspapers that Darryl Sutorius had expressed fears about his wife killing him, but these sources refused to give further details and would not allow their names to be listed. Cincinnati papers printed the story anyway, reporting that the surgeon's fears were so great, Darryl was staying with friends and family, and sometimes in hotels, just to keep at a distance from his wife.

Some people wrote in and complained publicly about the county sheriff's "gestapo" and berated the harsh treatment Della received at the hands of the sheriff's deputies. "You should be hanged on Fountain Square," Beth Bowan of Northside wrote to the *Cincinnati Post.* She was one of many whose emotions had run high because the lawmen had hauled Della out of her house barefoot, shocked that she was yanked from her home, absolutely *nude* under her terrycloth robe.

Documents filed in Hamilton County courts estimated Darryl Sutorius's estate at $450,000, most of which would be distributed among his children, according to his will. That sum did not include the surgeon's million-dollar pension and retirement fund, nor his hefty life insurance policy.

Further court records showed that Mrs. Sutorius, who was born Della Faye Hall on August 8, 1950, had been married five times since 1969. Her former husbands included a computer consultant, a commercial photographer, a sewer worker, and an engineer, none of whom wished to be quoted or even identified by the press.

Further news accounts revealed that Della Sutorius had a criminal record—a misdemeanor menacing conviction—for threatening a former boyfriend with a gun at his stock-brokerage firm in September 1991.

The former boyfriend, however, was unavailable for comment.

CHAPTER | 22

As THE MEDIA ATTENTION SWELLED, PEOPLE INVARIABLY came out of the woodwork, one of whom was Robin Zygmont, a woman with a chip on her shoulder. Having worked at Bethesda North as a lab technician, she was all too familiar with Dr. Sutorius and his harsh ways. What's more, Robin was unhappily married to a doctor herself; she knew how tough living with a medical expert could be. Outraged by the way Della was being treated by the press, she sent a note to her at the Justice Center to offer sympathy and support.

"When you're married to a doctor, they believe that they have free rank to do whatever they want because they make money, they have pull . . ." Robin wrote.

Della decided that she would become Robin's friend. In her first collect call, she thanked Robin for the $25 money order she had sent along with the note—it bought a lot of Snickers bars. It turned out Robin was offering to become a character witness against Darryl, and Della asked her to drop by and visit her in jail.

"Darryl had a borderline God complex," Robin told her.

"He was rough around the edges," Della admitted.

"I don't want to hurt your feelings, but he was a miserable human being."

"Well, he wasn't *always* that way."

"When I think back to that period of time, we all hated him. We were all equally afraid of him. I'll always remember the day when I was trying to get my lunch and he just grabbed my Tupperware out of the refrigerator and threw it at me."

"Sounds like Darryl."

"The thing was *airborne.* It hit me right in the stomach and I was pregnant."

Robin was referring back to a time when Darryl was involved in divorce proceedings and was particularly unpleasant to be around. Even though she hadn't worked at Bethesda in years, Robin felt like she still knew him.

As Robin spoke through an in-house phone at the Justice Center, Della sat staring at the attractive young blonde on the other side of the glass wall. The young woman had beautiful long hair, good taste in clothes, and a killer figure. Della asked her why she wanted to get involved, but Robin didn't really have a straight answer.

"He hated women, you know."

"He hated people, period," Della told her.

"Look, I just want to help you through this, that's all."

"Yeah?"

"I know Darryl abused you. I know he did."

But Della couldn't talk about that at the moment; she was sure the phones were bugged and she had a suppression hearing coming up. Tears streamed down her face as the phone disconnected and she was signaled by guards to move out of the visiting zone. For Della, their time seemed too rushed. It had lasted only thirty minutes, but Robin promised she'd be back. Initially they mostly talked about trivia—things like jewelry, favorite restaurants, and historic hotels in Cincinnati.

"There was an element of trust there," Robin confided. "I liked her. She made me laugh. After we met, she would call and she would talk to me. She felt helplessness about losing her dog and about Beth abandoning her. There was a lot of frustration."

"My whole life is upside down because of Darryl Sutorius," Della finally blurted in one of their talks. "I'm going to lose everything. They run stories on me on Channel 12 that don't even resemble the facts. That son of a bitch blew his head off and now they're trying to blame me. I *never* wanted him dead."

PART THREE | The Good Wife

CHAPTER | 23

JANET NEVER WANTED TO DIVORCE DARRYL; IT WAS SOME-thing he brought upon himself. She always loved him, even when she hated him, and she wore his wedding ring even beyond his death. When she heard about his body being discovered in the basement, that didn't surprise her. Darryl had always lived in the basement. He had constantly accused her of exiling him to the lower level of the house, when in fact that had been his place of choice.

"You were the one that chose to separate yourself from this family," Jan would tell him. "You were the one that didn't want to hear about what happened in our day."

Jan didn't want to be hard on Darryl—she knew he'd come home exhausted after surgery—but his behavior seemed to require it. All Darryl wanted to do was rest on his couch and watch television, and that was no problem, but when he would try to make her out to be the bad guy, as if she sent him downstairs as a punishment, Jan couldn't let him get away with that.

As much as she tried to excuse him, for thirty years Darryl always had to lay blame elsewhere and somehow

103

put her down in the process. He acted like he was a genius who couldn't be questioned or argued with, so for Jan, the hardest part of their marriage was putting him in his place. He suffered from daily arrogance.

Of course, she realized Darryl didn't make it to the top of his medical class without having an edge to him, but he seemed to never let up. Even when she ventured into a subject about which Darryl knew nothing, he had to be argumentative. That was just part of his personality. He had been that way all his life. He had to outsmart everyone, especially his wife.

"For thirty years he convinced me that I was stupid," Jan confessed. "He challenged me on everything I said or did. It was a continual struggle for survival."

Jan met Darryl at the University of Cincinnati in the early 1960s, where she was a nursing student and he was a junior in the College of Medicine. Once he had graduated—he was number two in his class—Darryl spent his surgical residency and thoracic and cardiac fellowship at Cincinnati General Hospital, where Jan was already on the staff. The two of them worked together every day, but Darryl was too large-framed, too big for her. Jan wasn't initially attracted.

Jan was twenty-one at the time and dating a handsome Phi Delta Theta man. She was wearing the guy's fraternity pin, her version of a preengagement ring, but by the time Darryl asked her out, she'd had second thoughts about her boyfriend. She gave the pin back.

For Jan, working in Cincinnati General was very much like a soap opera, with clandestine romances everywhere. But still, it was a harsh existence, particularly because the hospital catered to indigent people, which meant staffers were dealing with a lot of victims of crimes on the street.

"I grew up very quickly," Jan recalled. "Between age eighteen to twenty-two, I had dealt with dead people, had seen babies born, I readily had to come to grips with things working in an emergency room. People were stabbed to death, shot to death. During my nurses' training, I had to go to a public health district. I really saw what it was like to have no money, no heat, and no food."

As part of the grueling program, Jan was also required to spend time at Long View—a nearby insane asylum that has since been torn down—and, for a fresh-faced girl coming straight off a farm outside Cleveland, that was a rude awakening. "I walked around with my mouth open," Jan remembered. "There were people locked up without any clothes on, people roped in chairs. There were people rocking on the floor, curled up in a fetal position. And this is where I worked."

Back then, Jan tooled around in a red convertible Renault. She was breezy and cool, and Darryl was just crazy about her. She had exotic eyes, perfect posture, and a preppy wardrobe. She was just what he dreamed of, and he seemed anxious to fight for her time. Of course, she gave him a run for his money. Although she found him to be more and more her type, she never offered much of a hint. In the beginning, Darryl was extremely giving and generous; he liked to put her on a pedestal, so that was great. Except sometimes she'd notice that his cruel side would come out, and that troubled her. Around Jan's mom, for instance, Darryl seemed like Dr. Jekyll and Mr. Hyde.

Nonetheless, the young intern seemed to have every intention of acquiring Jan, even if she wasn't so sure about him, and it wasn't long before the two of them fell into a sort of codependent relationship. Darryl made it very clear that he needed her. He catered to her every whim, and he finally melted her down. The beautiful dark-haired nurse became putty in his hands, willing to give up everything for him.

Jan was the type of person who was great at taking care of others, as long as she had someone taking care of *her,* and Darryl seemed willing to offer her that. He was her male energy, she felt. He was the masculine part of her that was missing.

She started thinking that all she wanted in life was to fall in love, get married, and have a family. It was in the middle of their first kiss on the tennis courts that she realized that.

"I couldn't imagine I had found somebody to love me, because I thought I never would," Jan admitted. "I thought I was the luckiest person in the world, and I would give up anything to have that. I mean, all I wanted to do was be Darryl's wife and make him happy."

CHAPTER | 24

JAN AND DARRYL SPENT EVERY DAY TOGETHER. HE lived in a horrible green apartment with a roommate. It was a bachelor hell, with roaches crawling on the shelves, and at first Jan had no intention of ever spending the night, but she finally gave in. It was only their courtship, and Darryl was already calling all the shots.

Within a few months, he had moved to a new apartment, a more acceptable place, right across from Cincinnati General, and Jan found herself increasingly surrendering to Darryl's will. Back then he was studying a lot, and she just wanted to support him any way she could. Darryl was the biggest brain she knew, destined for greatness. He was determined to surpass everyone in his field, and Jan had an image of how successful he would be. She tried to bring the fun side out of him, but it was difficult, he was so driven.

Once they became a couple, Darryl rarely left Jan alone. He'd find out where she was having lunch, what time she was done in the emergency room; he knew her whereabouts at all times, and then he began driving her to work. When they finally discussed marriage, Darryl had the audacity to bring out his former girlfriend's ring, whom he'd politely dumped when he met Jan, telling her it was a perfect diamond, that she should consider herself lucky to have it. Of course, Jan refused to wear the thing, but Darryl just couldn't understand what the big deal was.

"One day I went to his apartment and he gave me a series of little notes," Jan reminisced. "There were ten of them. It must have taken him an hour to do these little notes and it was a scavenger hunt to ultimately open the refrigerator door and find this diamond ring in a cream puff."

Jan never thought Darryl was capable of being so tender. The ring he bought her was more stunning than anything she ever dreamed of, and she remembers the months preceding her wedding as being the happiest times of her life. Jan wasn't ambitious—she wasn't looking for a doctor and didn't want to be a doctor's wife— the lifestyle would be so demanding—yet here she had Darryl. And they were making all kinds of plans for their future together. They both wanted all the traditional things: the large upscale house, the yard filled with flowering plants, the kids, and perhaps a summer place on the water.

It's true that Darryl was terribly controlling, but then, Jan enabled that. She was Catholic, he was Lutheran, which made a huge difference somehow, and even before they walked down the aisle, Jan found out things had to be Darryl's way, or else. Since his father, Carlton, was a Lutheran minister, of course the wedding would be in a Lutheran church. Jan's mother and her requests were entirely ignored; it made no difference that she was the mother of the bride.

Darryl decided everything, right down to the style of Jan's wedding dress and veil. In essence, she became his puppet, although she never felt that way. Jan thought she understood Darryl because she could see how he had been brought up. He was used to a mother who sacrificed everything, and had a father who preached a fire and brimstone existence. Though Darryl would say he didn't want to repeat his parents' patterns, Jan realized Darryl could be extremely castigating and selfish. She knew he might be headed down his father's path of stubbornness, but she wouldn't let herself think it.

They couldn't afford much of a wedding—or a honeymoon, for that matter—so the two of them drove a couple hours, south to Cumberland Falls State Park in Kentucky, where things were rustic and isolated and they were stuck in a room with twin beds. It was the late sixties, the height of flower power and free love, but no one in the mountains seemed to care about that, which suited the newlyweds just fine.

As their marriage evolved, Jan realized Darryl was very much like his dad, which was problematic for her. She faulted Carlton for hiding behind the pulpit, always quoting gospel for answers, and now found Darryl to be hiding behind his medicine. Her husband didn't seem to be able to deal with real life, with close relationships. Everything for him had a pat response, a solution that seemed logical.

"The way he was raised, he went to church," Jan recalled. "He never did anything that wasn't becoming to a preacher and his family. He had to be careful about what he said. He cleaned the church, he was in Boy Scouts, but nobody ever took care of his soul."

As Jan grew closer to Darryl, she realized he resented being a preacher's son. He felt slighted, living under the strain of constant scrutiny by the congregation and the iron will of his father. As an adult, Darryl would complain about Carlton never being there for him. His only memory with his father was that of a single fishing trip.

"He would actually cry about the absence of his father," Jan confided. "That's how deeply wounded he was."

Yet Darryl was making the same mistakes. He was always at the hospital, never available to take a day off and relax. Finally Jan and Darryl sat down and had a talk. They promised each other they'd spend more time together, that when they had children, they would find ways to put the kids first.

In the early years of their marriage, Darryl made a strong effort to do things differently. He was still very involved in his career, but he'd take Jan out dancing every Saturday night. Darryl seemed to be an absolute dream back then. He was a tremendous connoisseur, and they ate out at the finest restaurants all over town. Jan kept a collection of matchbooks and menus as keepsakes, treasuring her time alone with her husband. Of course, that was during their first six years together, before they had kids.

And while Darryl was putting a wholehearted effort into building his career, Jan eventually talked him into buying their first house, a place he was hesitant to purchase, yet was quite happy to own. It was the early seventies, and the young doctor walked around with a twinkle in his eye, still very much in love with his wife. He loved to attend social functions so he could show Jan off to his colleagues—she had exquisite taste in clothes and carried herself well—and they dined on watercress and hearts of palm, and sipped out of demitasse at lavish receptions in places like the Banker's Club and Mecklenberg Gardens.

At home, Jan would host extravagant dinner parties for other doctors and their wives, and in the winters, when the Ohio weather got stormy, Darryl would find time to take her away to fantasy spots like the Bahamas and Las Vegas. Those were the residency years, when they were young and crazy about each other.

* * *

"When Debbie came, Darryl said over and over again that was the end of our relationship," Jan confessed. "He distanced himself from me and our child. He couldn't stand to be with us. To him that was the end of his needs being filled."

Just when Jan needed him most, Darryl became emotionally sterile. He had been excited during the pregnancy, but he wasn't present for the actual birth. Darryl had assisted on so many deliveries, Jan just couldn't believe it. When Deborah was born, she realized her husband required her full attention, that he didn't want to share, and he resented the child. Moreover, Deborah wasn't a boy, which is what he was hoping for, and although he never came out and said that, it became quite obvious years later, when John's birth took on a whole new meaning to him.

"I just kept denying that Darryl was avoiding me, and just thinking I'm so lucky to have this baby," Jan recalled. "He'd be gone all day and when he'd come home, he just wasn't involved with us, and I would keep thinking it would change."

Of course it didn't. Things got worse. In fact, when Becky was born, now there were two girls to contend with, both of whom demanded Jan's attention. Jan would do anything to please her husband, but for Darryl, no matter how many special dinners she planned, no matter what she tried in the bedroom, nothing was ever good enough.

As his income grew, Darryl resorted to material goods as a way to compensate. He would come home all excited about a new sports car or a fur coat for Jan, and that was supposed to make things better.

And for a long time, Jan admits, it did.

"I was addicted to Darryl," she reflected. "I was so grateful that he loved me, that he was willing to take care of me. But it was a funny kind of love. I found out that marriage was something that kept people together while they fell in and out of love."

But over the years, Jan understood she was paying a pretty high price for her lifestyle. With Darryl, she had everything she wanted—original signed artwork, a safe-deposit box full of diamond jewelry, fox-lined suits and coats, memberships to exclusive clubs—but she wasn't happy.

CHAPTER 25

*B*Y THE MID-1980S THE SUTORIUS FAMILY HAD CRYSTAL-lized. The kids were growing up and Darryl and Jan were already taking second-honeymoon-type vacations. There's a photo of the two of them at the Maison De Ville in New Orleans in 1985. They had the Audubon suite and were all dressed up for a big night out on the town. The excuse to be there was a conference for the American College of Chest Physicians, but Darryl's real goal was to go to all the fine restaurants, places like Brennans and Commander's Palace. He knew all the best places, and it was always Darryl's choice, but Jan liked it that way.

Though Darryl could be impossible to deal with, he provided Jan with a very good life. Jan and her husband attended such events as the Kentucky Derby and the Super Bowl, and were invited, on more than one occasion, to the White House. That was during Reagan's presidency, when America was plump and doctors were at the high end of the food chain.

It was during the Reagan era that the Sutorius clan had a number of time-shares they enjoyed regularly, one of them down in Cancún, the other in their favorite resort, Hilton Head. The family spent a lot of time hanging out in villas and cabanas, they stayed in super-contained villages with housekeeping and great dining, and took lessons in everything from fishing to horseback riding; and then, of course, there was always golf and tennis.

The family was active. John and his dad were avid fishermen, and the girls were athletic. They were all great swimmers, and their bodies showed it. In their photos, the kids look tan and strong, not an extra ounce of fat among them, just beaming faces with earthy smiles. They were the All-American family, and they looked like they were enjoying every minute of it.

Apart from the time-shares, there were family vacations to Disney World, to New York City, and, in fact, to most of the major cities around the country. Darryl and Jan took the kids to all the must-see places—the Broadway shows, the Empire State Building, the major museums, and, naturally, stores like Saks and FAO Schwarz—they did it all. Darryl was never the type to go second class, so when he traveled, even with the kids, he took limousines occasionally, and always stayed in good hotels. In those days, he could afford it; he could afford to have his family eat at private clubs and expensive restaurants.

There's a picture of Darryl with the kids, the girls all in matching dresses, standing in front of white airy drapes, brass chandeliers, and high ceilings. It's a backdrop that seems to fit them. The Sutoriuses were attractive. All the children were gorgeous, Deborah being the most outstanding. And the girls, in particular, were graceful, something they must have learned from their mother, since Darryl was always a bit clumsy, looking slightly disheveled whether he was in a sports jacket or a coat and tie. Jan, on the other hand, seemed to have the poise of a ballerina. Even when she was pregnant, she looked incredibly beautiful, her hair always up, her expression somewhat regal, and her smile just terrific.

CHAPTER | 26

"DAD WAS VERY PROUD OF OUR GERMAN HERITAGE," Deborah reminisced. "When I was little, he'd always tell me not to forget that we're German. That was one of Dad's favorite things."

Their family surname had once been Von Karlstein. Darryl wasn't quite sure when it had been modernized to the Latin, Sutorius, but he always reminded his kids that they were descendants of German nobility, that they had a heritage to be very proud of. He also drilled it into his kids' heads that they were Republicans; he wanted them to be conservative, to fit in with Cincinnati's high society.

Instead of moving to Indian Hill, which had always been his desire, Darryl settled for a house on Galecrest Drive, in a much less expensive part of town, but a place where Jan felt at home raising a family. As the years progressed, the Sutorius household became the most talked-about residence in the neighborhood. They had added a tennis court and swimming pool, and had even built an indoor habitat.

The habitat, of course, was a big attraction, having a rain and steam room with a whirlpool floor, and the Sutorius kids did a lot of entertaining, their friends bathing under the sun lamps in the sauna and soaking in the Jacuzzi.

The Sutorius family was the envy of the block, and besides having all the home frills, they were driving around in everything from BMWs to Jaguars. Each child, upon reaching driving age, was given a car, so eventually there were six cars in the driveway. Deborah tooled around in a 1982 red Mustang convertible. Just days after her seventeenth birthday, she wound up in a car wreck, but luckily she wasn't hurt. Then again, with Deborah, her parents had more important things to worry about.

Unfortunately, as Deborah approached college age, she was increasingly a problem. There was a growing strain between her and her parents—she was acting rebellious, smoking pot, dating a motorcycle guy—she was your basic teenage nightmare. Jan wouldn't allow Debbie's boyfriend in her house, and Darryl didn't approve of the young man, either. And that made Deborah all the more determined to stay with Ken.

The more Darryl made it clear to Deborah that he raised her to be a socialite, that he thoroughly disapproved of her riding around on a Harley, the more Deborah despised her father. Darryl described his poverty days, when he was a preacher's son, reminding her of the grind he went through to work his way through school and become a surgeon, and Deborah respected that, but she wasn't about to give up her bohemian existence with her boyfriend.

Deborah resented being prodded into a social status, and she didn't have designs on being rich, anyway. In fact, she secretly disliked the boys who existed off trust funds. She felt she had every right to choose her own men, and Ken was willing to support her, if necessary.

In a desperate attempt to get Deborah away from her boyfriend, Jan shipped her daughter off to Valparaiso, a Lutheran college that, to Deborah, offered little more than a view of cornfields. She couldn't wait to get out of there, but when she got back to Cincinnati, Deborah found herself kicked out of the house. It was Christmas break, and Jan was refusing to let her in the front door.

Jan was just furious that her daughter had made sneaky plans to transfer back to UC.

Caught between the two of them, Darryl decided to back Deborah's decision and help her find an apartment. She was only nineteen, after all, and too young to be entirely stable. Jan, meanwhile, became more and more irate about the situation. Ken was still in the picture, but she felt Darryl and Debbie were seeing far too much of each other, that Darryl was favoring Deborah over the other children.

As pressure from Jan mounted, Darryl agreed to spend less time and money on Debbie, but eventually he began to resent Jan for it. "They were having marriage problems," Deborah reflected, "but they didn't want to admit that, so they made me the problem."

By the time she was twenty, Deborah's relationship with her mother was nil, and her dad was under so much strain at home, he felt he had to leave the marriage. He rented an apartment in Olde Montgomery, a quaint complex right across from Bethesda North, but his stay lasted only a few short weeks. He just couldn't hack bachelor life.

When he decided to return home to Galecrest Drive, he and Jan agreed to let Deborah live her own life. They hired an expensive decorator, and started to completely redo their interior. They were giving themselves a second start.

CHAPTER | 27

*T*HE YOUNG WOMAN THEY HIRED WAS STILL A LITTLE WET behind the ears, but Lynn Cross had an instant rapport with Dr. and Mrs. Sutorius. A funky artist type with classic beauty and an elegant sense of style, Lynn was energetic and got along brilliantly with both of them, especially Jan. Darryl was concerned about the budget; though Lynn realized their house needed a lot of work, she assured him the costs would be kept down. Little did he realize that when the overall renovation concept was completed, he would sink $500,000 into the Galecrest place—money that would never show a return.

One of the things Darryl wanted was a three-story atrium with a game room overlooking their woods in the backyard. Then there was the marble entrance foyer, the big glorious breakfast solarium—there were limitless indulgences as they started to map out the blueprints.

"We became friends," Lynn confided, "because you really do move in when you're doing a project this size. Jan and I got so close, and with the kids, it was a constant zoo. She was running here and there, I mean, wow, what a life she had."

Since three of the children were still living at home, Jan had each of their bedrooms redone to their specifications, John choosing a sports theme, the girls going with a lot of pinks and pastels. She was the type of mom who lived for her kids, and she spoiled them terribly, without ever giving it a second thought.

Darryl's involvement with the interior decorating les-

116

sened as time when on—it took about a year and a half to complete the project—but he did have input on the master bedroom, which was done with the romantic notion that they could re-create one of their favorite hotel rooms in New Orleans. Lynn thought it looked a bit too much like a bordello when it was finished, but she figured it was Darryl's way of rekindling the marriage.

Occasionally she'd get a big grin out of the surgeon, but for the most part, he wasn't the type of man to pay Lynn compliments. Of course, Darryl wasn't the one orchestrating the job, Jan was, but Darryl liked to act as though he was always at the helm, and the decorator had to satisfy his whims.

"In terms of the design of the house," Lynn commented, "Darryl had to be pleased first. He was concerned with perfection."

Even though Lynn used the finest installers in town, Darryl would point out a slight variation in the wallpaper, perhaps a barely perceivable color mutation, and then he'd want the whole wall redone. He was definitely king of the castle when it came to home improvements.

By the time the project was finished, Lynn had helped them replace the carpets and most of the furniture, had suggested certain pieces of art, had gotten to know their tastes, and had become close enough to realize that Jan basically put herself last when it came to her husband, which didn't seem healthy.

In fact, Jan's dream kitchen was the final job to be done in the house. Even though she was a gourmet cook and spent a lot of time there, she was quite hesitant to go through with the project.

Suddenly money had become an issue.

"He wanted the house perfect, he wanted it stunning, he wanted it different, he wanted it practical," Lynn recalled, "and at some point I realized what a fortune it was going to be, but I was just working off ideas I got from him, and the place just kept evolving."

* * *

From Jan's point of view, the renovations only masked the same basic problems she was having with Darryl. He still had difficulty with intimacy. He would hide in the basement with his porno magazines, and it was insane, he just couldn't enjoy the new house. Instead, he'd blame Jan for wasting too much money.

When Jan chastised Darryl for having pornography in their Christian home, he responded by dragging her to shows across the river in Newport, where she was confronted with topless dancers, trashy lingerie, and red neon lights. Darryl thought it was funny; he was trying to show her what *real* porn was like, but Jan didn't find it amusing. In fact, she didn't think his behavior was normal, and she made an issue of it. Their many arguments led to Jan's decision to sleep on the couch in the family room.

By then, Darryl stayed upstairs watching porn movies, expecting Jan to come around and jump in bed with the video going, but she just couldn't have any part of that. When she tried, not only did she feel like a silly sex object, she thought Darryl was sick.

A turning point came when Darryl happened to break his arm playing tennis. Worried that he might not be able to perform surgery again, he became addicted to pain medication for a while and he seemed to go through a major personality change, becoming quiet and withdrawn, even with the kids.

Between problems in the bedroom and the troubles with money, Jan couldn't cope with him anymore and the two of them just stopped speaking. They lived under the same roof for a whole year without breathing a single word to each other.

By November 1991, Darryl came to Jan with a decision: He wanted a divorce. He said he just couldn't provide for her anymore, and explained that the changes in insurance coverage were really taking their toll on physicians, that he just wasn't making enough money to cover the expenses of the household.

At the same time, Darryl had gone out and bought himself a twenty-five-foot fishing boat. And not only did he dock it at the Four Seasons, the most exclusive marina in Cincinnati, he had also joined the Beckett Ridge Country Club and got heavily involved with golf and travel.

"He was spending money hand over fist," Jan said. "I mean, he went to Europe by himself, had a wonderful time, and it was not for family. All the money he was spending had nothing to do with his family."

CHAPTER 28

Dear Jan,

In January you sent me a letter through John asking me to return home. I didn't answer then because I was so hurt, angry, depressed, and felt I would not make the most thoughtful response that I could. I probably would not be responding now, had it not been for an "official notice" I found attached to my door, stating the Sheriff's Department had something to deliver to me. I assume this means you have taken some legal action and I wanted to respond to you before I receive that action so that cannot be looked upon as a motive for this letter.

Nothing could make me happier than to be with my family. I miss the children terribly, even though they call and come to visit periodically. It's really not the same as living with them, but I know they will also be off on lives of their own all too soon. That would leave the two of us together.

You remember that I left once before. You made an impassioned plea at that time and I thought perhaps all would be well, but that old pattern soon returned. You speak of communicating with each other but you have no idea how frustrating it was to talk to you about problems. You would either dismiss my concerns by saying that I could accomplish anything I really wanted to, argue that I did not have the proper facts, or, if no other recourse was available, turn and walk off, not saying anything for days to weeks unless it was to tell me to "just get out" which you did on three separate occasions early this year, two of which were done with the children around. That was the ultimate humiliation, to have you screaming at me about what a lazy, lousy provider I was, in front of the children.

I have tried my very best for 28 years to supply you with the best that I could afford. I would try to keep lists of things I knew you wanted and save up until I could purchase them for you. Think about the kitchens I put in for you, only to tear them out and revise them a few years later, the baby grand piano you wanted, the addition to our house, the swimming pool, the finished basement, and commercial kitchen most recently added.

When those items were obtained or projects completed, I expected some display of gratitude. What I usually got was a demand for the next project you had in mind. When the basement was finished and the new kitchen (the last one) completed, you had already checked on the feasibility of building a further addition over the garage with a sewing room for you, which would, of course, have eliminated Debbie's room. That was to your liking because you never wanted "that girl" in your house again and talked as though you had never had her.

I used to dream about coming home to my house and finding you waiting for me, having made arrangements for the kids to be elsewhere so that we could have a quiet intimate evening at home. That only happened twice in 28 years. I'll have to admit I couldn't believe what was happening when you surprised me with the "sensuous woman" routine, but that was an act never to be repeated.

Intimacy was something that you rarely had time for and never seemed to enjoy. I was always concerned I was to blame for that, and consoled myself with the fact that I had not had trouble pleasing women prior to our marriage. Whenever I would hope to have time to ourselves, there was always the threat that "the children will hear us" or "I have too much to do" which always meant something for the kids—school, soccer coaches, neighbors, babysitters, etc.

Darryl's letter went on for pages. He defended himself for having joined a tennis club, explaining it was something he did for the children, especially John, whom he hoped would also get into golf.

As he continued, he detailed how devastating it was to hear Jan complain about his lack of involvement with the children, detailing how angry he was that Jan called him "clumsy" in front of his medical colleagues when they visited the house, complaining that she never really entertained his colleagues enough, something that could have helped his referrals, if only Jan had cared.

Darryl moaned about bills, about Jan never getting a job, stating that he was sick of being ignored and being treated like a meal ticket at home, telling Jan that he was mortified to discover that "my only greeting when I would hit the door at night was a pewter dish filled with the latest bills to pay." He was tired of spending money on kids who didn't seem to appreciate it, and totally fed up with credit card bills that Jan pushed to their limit every single month "like clockwork."

He only wished he and Jan could have budgeted their time and money more wisely, that they had spent more time having fun with each other; he resented that Jan wanted to wait until the children were grown and out of the house. He thought they should have traveled together more, but explained that he no longer cared about that. In fact, he didn't have any more hope to be with Jan to enjoy grandchildren.

Now all he wanted to do was reassure her that he would not threaten the kids' security, that he would continue to pay the outrageous $18,000 a year in car insurance, along with everything else, and that he would continue to do his best to provide for them. He signed off by saying he felt totally uncared for, reminding her about their separate sleeping circumstances, repeating that all he was useful for was his money.

He hoped Jan would find what she was looking for in life. It seemed to him that the two of them were in constant competition, rather than in a marriage, and the only memory he had of her was seeing her rise from her "bed" in the family room, walking around the house in silence. He explained he wanted a relationship in which he would be needed and loved on a "more adult" level.

He thought he would find that.

To his friend Dick Brunsman, Darryl's marriage seemed to offer little or nothing. The guy had been hanging in there for the sake of his kids, but he was better off without Jan. For twenty-five years, Darryl appeared to be a whipped puppy, forever talking about his wife's demands. Darryl constantly complained about bills, acting like Jan had some strange hold over him. Dick would advise his buddy to put a limit on his wife's spending, but Darryl wasn't able to.

"It appeared to me to be a very typical situation," Dick reflected. "He was a brilliant surgeon, that was his

obsession, his medicine was his mistress. Eventually he
confided in me, and I began to realize he had a typical
doctor's marriage. He was interested in doctoring, and
she was interested in spending money. Then she became
more and more adept at spending money, and he became more and more disenchanted with what she was
doing."

CHAPTER | 29

"**I**F I WAS UP TO TAKING A DOSE OF POISON, I WOULD
talk to Darryl, but I spent the last year not talking to
him," Jan explained, "because he could just kill you.
He could just give you a tongue-lashing that you did
not deserve."

Darryl didn't look it. He looked like a big teddy
bear—but he could be incredibly cruel. If he felt
wronged, he would make his wife pay, and he knew just
the right buttons to push. He was good at using his
money as a way of wielding power and control, and he
caught Jan and his kids in that trap all the time. He was
always telling them, "If you do what I say, I'll give you
this," making it clear that if he didn't get his way, no
money would be changing hands.

"There was no security at all in his distribution of
money," Jan confided. "You didn't know what to expect.
You never knew if he was going to be taking it out from
under you, which he did from time to time, or what price
you were going to have to pay."

To Jan, it was a horrible existence. Even though ultimately she had all the creature comforts she could want,

she resented Darryl always placing a dollar value on her and her kids. There was an uneven distribution of money and there was favoritism, which caused problems. With John, the money was always more readily available. John was the one sent abroad as an exchange student, he was the one his father took skiing in Utah, and when he was given a brand-new car which he promptly totaled, Darryl went right out and bought him another one. With the girls, however, their father was never as generous. When Deborah crashed her car, she had to make do with a clunker. None of the girls attended private school, and Darryl gave them a hard time about spending money, annoyed that his daughters wasted cash on things like Clinique and Body Works.

Of course, the Sutorius girls were all fashion plates—it wasn't like they wore hand-me-downs or did without anything—but Jan was tired of hearing Darryl cry poverty all the time. He was always complaining that he didn't have enough money, and the big irony was that he'd take her to expensive restaurants and order hundred-dollar bottles of wine with dinner. Darryl would be having an extravagant night with his wife, but Jan would just cringe, thinking of all the friction he was causing with the kids over money. There was no rhyme or reason.

"He'd just go out and buy a Porsche, he never asked," Jan recalled, "and it wasn't a family car. Only Darryl could be in that car, and we had to use the van to go anywhere as a family. We never had any discussions about family needs and priorities."

For years Jan tried not to let Darryl's selfishness get to her. She was the best cook she knew how to be, she helped him build his private practice, she took care of the kids without the help of a nanny or a housekeeper. She basically raised four children by herself. Darryl was never there; he was always in surgery. But Jan was able to endure the responsibility as long as she didn't have to withstand his tirades.

"I thought I was doing really great," Jan boasted. "And it wasn't enough. It wasn't good enough. I mean, I don't think many people could have done as well as I did, but I got no acknowledgment."

Instead of praising her, Darryl resented Jan's care of the children and her involvement in the Green Hills school system. When John got to be high school age, Darryl pulled him out of Green Hills and placed him at Summit Country Day, the most prestigious private school in the city. Darryl just did it, without ever consulting Jan, and when she argued with him, he pounded his fist on the kitchen counter like a brute. He didn't want to discuss it.

And that was the problem. They could never be one big happy family with the way Darryl handled things. When Deborah was thrown out, there were no further discussions about her. It was like she was dead. Whenever Jan brought the subject up, considering a change of heart, she would get verbally abused for it. For years she'd gather her courage and try to reason with Darryl, especially when she needed to come to the defense of one of her children, but Darryl had a way of making her feel completely inadequate, of causing her to question her reason for existence.

"You can't talk to people like this," Jan would tell him. "You can't make people feel so bad about themselves."

But Darryl wouldn't listen. He'd just leave the room.

One day, Jan chided her husband for riding around on a $3,000 lawn mower, telling him how ridiculous he looked, suggesting that he should be out pushing a manual machine. She said he needed the exercise, even though she knew his ego wouldn't take such a blow. She was prepared for the consequences, because she absolutely couldn't stand the man anymore.

"He came up out of the basement and I really came unglued," Jan confessed. "I told him how embarrassed

I was by the way he looked, that he was so fat. I just really let him have it."

Not long after that, Darryl flew off to London with another woman—at least, that's what Jan suspected. She knew her husband had been taking other women out all along—just as friends, innocent dinner dates—but now he was pushing it.

Jan just couldn't make him happy; they couldn't even have a conversation about the daily news without arguing. Everything was always her fault and Jan's opinion was worthless. Meanwhile, she'd hear reports that he was having candlelight dinners with someone, and the London trip made her particularly leery, since he was supposedly there on business, yet he concealed all the information about his hotel and itinerary.

Their last formal dinner together had been in the Christmas season of 1991, and Jan had decorated the house with two Christmas trees, had invited doctors Fred and Ingrid Doud along with a few of Darryl's other esteemed colleagues for one of her five-course extravaganzas. She served everything from Waldorf salad to caramelized custard, had set the table up with place cards and fresh centerpieces, and had pulled off a wonderful evening. But as soon as the guests left, Darryl went into the kitchen to berate her.

"Don't you know that Dr. Harshman and Dr. Ferrar don't get along?" Darryl raged. "Why would you seat them together?"

"They don't? I didn't think that."

"Well, why would you seat them next to each other without asking me? Couldn't you see they were uncomfortable the whole evening?"

"I don't agree, Darryl, I don't think anybody was uncomfortable."

"Because you're too stupid to notice!"

"I don't think you have any reason to accuse me of this."

"You just don't *think*."

"If I made a mistake, honey, I'm sorry. But I think you're wrong."

So after all Jan's thought and preparation, that was how they ended the evening. Darryl never uttered a word of thanks.

Unfortunately, this kind of scene had happened so many times before, Jan was trained to expect it.

But after Darryl's secret trip to Europe, things were different. Jan wasn't speaking to him anymore, and by Christmas 1992 Darryl didn't appear at his own house for the family dinner. His kids waited until about noon and then opened their presents without him, choking down their turkey dinner without saying much of anything.

"And so you give up," Jan said, "you don't care, when someone doesn't bring any joy in your life. When someone only takes it all, you'd be better off without them. I didn't need him to tell me I was an awful mother. I didn't need people to tell me that. I already had my own insecurities."

Later that week, Darryl showed up to collect some of his clothes. He had found an apartment, a furnished place on a month-to-month rental, and he seemed somewhat relieved to rid himself of Jan. He arranged to pay the household bills through his office secretary, and he was acting thoroughly pleased with the new scenario.

"The sick part is, I would never have left him," Jan confessed. "I thought that if he could ever get it together and realize what he did to this family, then he could come back and say he was really sorry. I did love him. And I would have been glad to spend the rest of my life with him. I planned to. But after he left, I knew there was no chance."

In Darryl's absence, Jan had schooled herself through self-help books and she started gaining her own esteem back. She enrolled at Xavier University and was planning a career. Becky, John, and Chrissy were all for it, but Deborah, who had come back into the fold, desperately wanted her parents to reconcile; she didn't root for Jan's independence.

Of course, Darryl was shocked when Jan served him for a divorce. He had no intention of paying alimony, he made that clear. And because of his tenacity, their divorce proceedings became an all-out war. After two years and countless threats to go to court, the two of them finally settled.

"Darryl saw it as a black or white relationship; he looked at things as right or wrong," his attorney, Guy Hild, reflected. "When his wife, Jan, refused to speak to him, there wasn't a lot of compromise," Guy explained. "If you try to analyze his relationships with people, Darryl couldn't deal effectively. He couldn't deal effectively with his children. In medicine, he was well respected for his technical skills, but I assume that's why he gained the reputation of a tyrant."

CHAPTER | 30

IN THE YEARS OF HIS DIVORCE, DARRYL RAN TO THE safety net of his friends, Sue and Alan Browning, whom he had known since June 1990, when he performed open-heart surgery on Alan and saved his life. Alan Browning was a local celebrity, a shock jock back in the 1980s, and Darryl really liked the guy. He was a fan of his show, *Desperate and Dateless*, a local radio matchmaking spoof. The show did pair up couples, although it was really designed as entertainment, so people called in on Friday nights, delineating their weight, height, marital status, and occupation. It was a real hoot.

Alan's wife, Sue, a Farrah Fawcett look-alike, handled the jammed call-in lines and bolstered ratings by encouraging her husband to exploit local controversy. She produced the show, and together they created an audience of audio voyeurs, a vague precursor to listeners of Howard Stern.

In Sue's eyes, her husband was as big as Don Imus, and even if he really wasn't, Alan was enough of a radio personality to attract guests like Telly Savalas and Clint Eastwood over the years. He wasn't without his lineup of sex symbols.

But when Alan landed in Christ Hospital with a failed angioplasty, Sue immediately wanted him to retire. He had been on WKRC in Cincinnati for twenty years, had almost died because of the fast pace and aggravation, and now it was time to give it up and live the good life. They settled in a beautiful colonial-style house in Blue Ash, where their friendship with Darryl blossomed. The surgeon became extremely helpful in getting Alan through the healing process, and felt comfortable paying home visits to the Brownings. They were delighted to entertain Darryl; they quickly made him feel like family.

"He wanted to get real personal with us," Sue recalls, "and we never discussed it, but I wondered why this doctor was so intrigued with us being on the radio. Then suddenly he's getting divorced. If I had to bet my life on it, I think he hoped we had something in our files. Maybe he thought we had a listing of old broads that he could take out."

While Darryl was officially separated, he spent his holidays with the Brownings, mainly Thanksgiving and Christmas, and he couldn't have been a more generous and gracious guest, his hands always full, an expensive centerpiece having been sent before he even arrived. They would always scold him for spending too much, but that was Darryl. He only knew extravagance.

Darryl felt he could confide in Sue, and he told her about Jan turning the children against him, which made him intensely angry. He and Jan hated each other; they were at opposite ends of the universe. Sue saw it as the typical divorce scene, the mom teaching the kids to hate their father, the father trying to win the kids back with money. He confided to Sue that he had met someone when he was in London, that he had fallen in love with a woman at his medical conference. But apparently the woman wasn't interested and had insinuated that Darryl was too focused on his kids.

"He was complaining about money, about how his kids felt he had to give it to them," Sue remembers. "They were killing him financially, but you know, he gave them whatever they wanted."

With his newfound freedom, Darryl suddenly found God again and wanted the Brownings to accompany him to church Sunday mornings, but 11:00 A.M. was too early for them to be up and about. Because of their late-late evening air schedules, they had become night owls, and they lived on a different internal clock. But Darryl was welcome to drop by anytime, which he did, sometimes calling them from their driveway, where he would sit talking to Sue on his car phone until she fixed herself up enough to open the front door.

When they had first met in 1990, Alan talked about taking a trip to Hawaii after his recovery, and Darryl suggested that he and Jan go along. Back then, he was hopeful that his rocky times with Jan would end; he spoke of Jan with high praise, calling her an intelligent, beautiful woman who was a great mother and a wonderful wife. He seemed to think things would work out, that the four of them could have good times together.

Of course, by 1993 the only thing he wanted was a new mate, and he busied himself dating as many women as possible, but no one grabbed him. Since he loved to have a beautiful young woman on his arm, for fun, he would wine and dine Dick Brunsman's daughter, Laurie, who happened to be going through a divorce herself. A perky thirty-year-old with green eyes and an attractive face, Laurie worked with her dad selling insurance and investments to business professionals. She too lacked decent company. She needed someone she could trust as a gentleman.

"I'd heard Darryl's name over the years, and when he was getting divorced from his wife, he started hanging out with my dad a little bit more," Laurie explained. "They'd meet for drinks over at La Normandie, and my office used to be down the street."

When Laurie eventually ran into Darryl at the popular downtown pub, the two of them hit it off right away. He asked her to accompany him to a political fund-raiser that weekend, and they really had a blast. Darryl was a great dancer and an even better conversationalist, and it was a perfect setup for Laurie, because she just wasn't ready to be out dating for real. On occasion they would meet at Primavista or La Normandie, and most of the time they'd just be laughing and goofing around, although they did have heart-to-heart chats.

"I think he maybe looked at me as one of his kids," Laurie reflected. "I'm older than Deborah by almost ten years, and he would talk to me about her. He worried about her. He talked about all his kids, and was very proud of them."

Laurie would argue with Darryl, explaining that when she was in college, she had to earn her spending money. She wasn't sure if any of Darryl's kids were working, but from the picture he painted, it seemed like he was trying to shelter them, like he was denying them a sense of the real world.

"Look, I'm sure that you love your kids very much, and I'm sure that my dad loves me very much," Laurie finally told him, "but you two handle situations completely differently. You know, I feel I'm on my own two feet."

"Well, what would your dad do if you lost your job?" he asked.

"Of course, if I ever need my dad's help, absolutely, he'll help me," she admitted, "but the way you're handling things, your kids are never going to know when they're independent or not. They're always going to come running back to you because they don't know how to fix anything on their own."

"Well, my kids are smart and talented and—"

"Yeah, but, I mean, I don't have kids, but I just think you're too easy on them. You step in and solve all their problems and you're only perpetuating them running to you for help all the time."

"I know you're right."

"Your kids are never going to grow up if you don't let them, and you know, sooner or later people have to learn the value of a buck."

"I know."

"Or they'll be running to you when they're fifty years old."

Darryl didn't really want to argue, he saw her point, but when it came to his kids, if he didn't give them the money, he knew they'd turn to their mother. And then Jan would eventually make him look bad. It was a losing battle.

It hurt him that he wasn't on good speaking terms with any of his children. He told Laurie he was worried about John's emotional state because he had dropped out of Penn. And he was concerned about Deborah, who seemed to be doing nothing with her life—he didn't mention that she worked at Hooters. Then Becky was off in North Carolina—he had no hope of talking to her—and he wondered about getting through to Chrissy, who was still tied to her mother's apron strings.

"He would just try to prevent his kids from making mistakes," Laurie reflected. "Anything that would go wrong in their lives, he wanted to fix it."

CHAPTER | 31

"**W**HO WOULD WANT ME?" DARRYL PRODDED SUE, grabbing a moment of her time alone. It was a year since he'd been separated, and he was really down on himself.

"Oh, come on," she assured him, "you know you're a catch."

"But I'm big, I'm overweight. It just seems I turn everybody off."

"Well, you get too hot and heavy with a girl, Darryl, you just jump into things. You have to learn to take it slow."

"But what do I do to turn them off?"

"Darryl, I don't know. The only thing I can think of is that maybe you talk about your children too much."

"Yeah, maybe that's true."

"And people don't really like to hear that. They like you to talk about them. You need to be more attentive, as opposed to talking about your problems and your children and things like that."

Darryl wanted some pointers. He was having a hard time. He confided he just found out that a ballet teacher he was dating had only been using him to make her ex-boyfriend jealous. Darryl thought they were in love, he had lavished her with diamond earrings and expensive outfits, and then it turned out that she jumped back to her ex the first chance she got. He was crushed. At fifty-four, he thought he was just getting too old to stand a fighting chance with women. Sue Browning did her best to boost his ego, but she wasn't sure she was getting through to him.

Darryl had determined to make more sensible choices in dating, to find himself someone closer to his age, someone who wasn't a gold digger, so everyone was just astounded when he got himself involved with Lisa Johnson. She was only thirty-four, called herself a glorified secretary, and seemed to be looking for someone to take care of her. She was looking to quit her job.

Laurie Brunsman remembers talking to her dad about it—apparently Darryl was telling Dick about all of Lisa's problems—and they both wanted to see Darryl get himself out of that mess. Darryl had always given people the impression that he was very particular about what he did, that he was concerned with making good impressions, yet here he was involved in this odd relationship. Lisa was pretty, slightly overweight in a voluptuous kind of way, but she was quirky. Darryl told Sue that Lisa would make calls to him in the middle of the night. She'd follow him through his neighborhood.

Of course, none of this behavior manifested itself at first. Just weeks after they met, Darryl was telling people that they were very much in love. He and Lisa were all over each other and he was introducing her to his social circles. Alan Browning didn't approve of the young woman; he thought Darryl would be better off with some rich widow. But Darryl didn't think anyone like that really existed, and besides, he really didn't need the money. Still, there was a complication, because by then Deborah had come back into his life, and Darryl was starting to get anxious about her meeting Lisa. Deborah had just recently been coming over to the condo to take art lessons with him, and now Darryl was starting to get cold feet.

"You're going with the wrong people," Sue told him. "I don't want to hurt your feelings, but the people you've been going with want you for what you can give them. You've got to get with someone who has money and wants you for *you*."

"But Sue, what's so great about me?"

"Do we have to go through that again? You're an accomplished surgeon and a great person. How many times do I have to keep telling you over and over? We're not going to start with square one again."

But Darryl knew better. He couldn't get dates. He knew the types of pretty women he wanted just weren't attracted to him, and he'd tell Sue that, but she wouldn't hear it. She was sure there would be somebody at the hospital who'd just jump at the chance, but Darryl was having problems with nurses at the hospital, many of whom were scared of him. He never told Sue he'd been recently brought up in front of a hospital committee for behavioral problems. The committee had even required Darryl to get psychological counseling to help quiet his temper, an aberration he kept entirely to himself.

He tried to explain that most people didn't get along with him, and Sue's kind attitude helped him to change that feeling somewhat, but the fact still remained that he had a bad reputation. He was chief of Thoracic Surgery at Bethesda North, but his temper was his worst enemy; it undermined the respect he deserved for his surgical skills. While he was cool in a surgical crisis, outside the OR he deliberately sent nurses running for cover. And it wasn't only nurses, it was doctors, too. There was an incident when he exploded because an anesthesiologist walked in the OR sockless. It was a measure of the top surgeon's ego and arrogance.

He asked Sue if there was anyone she could set him up with, if she had a twin sister or something, but Sue couldn't be of any use in that department. "He didn't want anybody to live with him," Sue recalled, "but Lisa kept insisting that it would be nice, that the kids would be obedient. He understood all that, and he needed somebody."

After only a short time dating, Darryl agreed to let

Lisa and her kids move into his Blue Ash Condo. It was a place he had recently purchased, tucked away on Fallsington Court, just around the corner from the Brownings. It still lacked furniture, but that was fine with Lisa. She had her own stuff, and anyway, she liked the idea of getting involved in some interior decorating.

At least, Sue thought, this one was better than Darryl's last girlfriend. When Sue had met the ballet teacher, all she could notice was the girl's bad dye job, her black roots, which were too obvious against her blond hair, and her mascara, which was so thick it looked like false eyelashes.

Alan held the opinion that the ballet teacher looked like she belonged in a brothel; it was clear to him that Darryl was her Daddy Warbucks. But Darryl loved her appearance; he thought she was a knockout. The problem was that she was looking to have a child, and Darryl flat-out told her that he would never be interested in that. The relationship was going nowhere, and then there was always the ex-boyfriend lurking in the background.

However, Darryl was so attracted to Lisa he was willing to take a chance. He didn't care that she had two preteenagers, didn't care that people gossiped behind his back. And it didn't matter how many times friends tried to tell him it was a mistake. Darryl was crazy about the girl.

Before they moved in together, he had Deborah over to meet her, but the two of them seemed to barely tolerate each other. Just ten years apart, Deborah's beauty alone was enough to knock Lisa off her seat.

Lisa tried to like the girl, but in her view, Darryl's daughter was doing whatever she could to sabotage their relationship. It was an awkward situation.

CHAPTER | 32

"*I* KNEW LISA WAS A BAD DEAL FOR HIM," DARRYL'S friend Dick later confided. "She had these two kids, but he was saying they were getting along famously."

Dick Brunsman was trying to offer Darryl gentle advice. The two of them were preparing for one of their regular trips to Hilton Head with their golf group, having drinks at one of their favorite restaurants, a well-known steak house in Western Hills, Maury's Tiny Cove. They both frequented the place; it was a good meeting point and it had local character, being one of those old-time restaurants that served large portions and had bartenders who knew the regulars by name.

"Dick, I need to work out some problems with Lisa," Darryl blurted just as they were leaving. "Lisa and I have some things we need to talk over, and I want to bring her to Hilton Head."

"Huh?"

"Can I bring her?"

"I guess so," Dick said, his face turning red.

"I wouldn't ask if it wasn't serious."

"Are you thinking of getting married?"

"Yeah, I've been thinking about that."

"Well, I hope you're drawing up a prenuptial agreement."

"She doesn't want any of my money, Dick, that's not an issue."

"Yeah, right, Darryl."

*   *   *

137

For Dick, the trip to Hilton Head in the fall of 1994 was ruined. One minute, he and the guys were playing at Wexford, having a good old time, then all of a sudden they'd have to hurry back and leave the golf course because Lisa would be waiting at the condo with chicken wings. To add insult to injury, Darryl kept trying to get his buddy to give up the master bedroom with the Jacuzzi. He wanted his own private suite, but it was Dick's home, and there was no way.

It was supposed to be a *guy* thing, and Darryl was totally screwing it up.

"We were at one of the most beautiful golf courses in the world," Dick recalled, "and he would quit at halftime to hurry back because Lisa had asked him to meet her somewhere. And you know, then we'd find them cooing, and we'd be sitting there. We were just steamed."

It took a while for Darryl to figure things out, but the truth of it was, even though he wanted to marry her in the worst way, Lisa was refusing to sign the prenuptial. He had gotten down on his knees and given her an engagement ring, he had met her parents, and they had even shopped for a home together. The two of them had gone to a studio and gotten an official portrait taken— they were a real couple—but now Darryl was getting weary. All along, he suspected Lisa of having other male interests, which caused big blowups. And then there was the business of her children. Jonathan and Michelle were really getting on his nerves.

His real estate agent, Judy McCoy, a petite young blonde with terrific people skills, had been watching his relationship with Lisa unfold like a scene from a good soap opera. She had helped Darryl find the condo on Fallsington and had become friends with the surgeon. After he moved Lisa into his place and started feeling cramped, Judy was the one who helped Darryl find the house on Symmesridge. It was the dream house Darryl was planning to surprise Lisa with.

Judy never offered her opinion, but she gave Darryl a shoulder to cry on. All along he had been telling her about Lisa, and Judy was always enthusiastic and encouraging. But from what she could gather, his relationship with Lisa was doomed.

"They took a trip to Florida right after she moved in," Judy recalled. "He had taken Lisa and her kids to visit her mother. And there was this guy she used to go country dancing with; he was going to babysit the condo for them while they were gone. I think she had a cat, or some kind of animal. And Darryl didn't like the idea, but he was assured that there was nothing going on between Lisa and this guy."

By the time they returned from Florida, Lisa and Darryl had broken up.

Their relationship was volatile. When Darryl would accuse Lisa of cheating, Lisa would turn the tables on him. Immediately after the engagement, they had a tremendous fight because Darryl got a phone call from a female friend in Chicago, Lori Waiss. Darryl and Lori had been co-workers at Bethesda; she was one of his confidantes throughout his divorce, and they were friends, nothing more. Lori was just calling to update Darryl on her new life up north, just checking on the latest Bethesda gossip. Of course, Lisa didn't accept that. She became so infuriated, she clicked the phone off in the middle of his call, and Darryl stormed out of the condo.

He became so infuriated by Lisa's accusations and bizarre behavior, he decided to secretly reactivate his membership with Great Expectations dating service, fielding calls from his office for occasional dates. When the dating service accidentally called Darryl at the condo, Lisa told them they had made a mistake. She said it was impossible that Darryl was a member, explaining that the surgeon was happily engaged. Later that night, the two of them fought over it, and Lisa insisted that Darryl write a cancellation letter to the Great Expectations people.

But apparently Darryl never mailed it, and when Lisa got wind of another call from the service, she threw Darryl's ring back at him. Since she claimed she had no place to go, Darryl offered to let her stay in his home until they could iron things out. And, not knowing who to turn to, Darryl slept in his car for the first couple of nights.

Darryl now felt he made a big mistake. He was lonely and miserable and the dating service wasn't working for him; there were no good prospects there. He wanted to move back in with his beautiful, devoted Lisa, but he just needed time to think.

He wasn't sure.

For a few weeks, he stayed with his friends, Ted and Delle Jones, a couple with a gorgeous home in Indian Hill who thought the world of him. The Joneses had spent time with Darryl and Lisa, and were all in favor of the marriage. A top-notch jeweler, Delle had sold him the engagement ring and, having befriended Lisa, had even helped her shop for a wedding gown.

All along, Darryl was waiting on the financing for the Symmesridge home, and finally his mortgage came through.

The surgeon decided to surprise Lisa even before he closed on the house, certain that this would bring his fiancée to her senses. With a big smile and a dozen roses, Darryl appeared at the condo in the middle of the afternoon. He beckoned Lisa out to his Jaguar, but wouldn't tell her where they were headed.

When he walked her hand in hand to his new front door, decorated with a big red bow and a love note, of course Lisa was stunned. She couldn't believe Darryl had bought such an expensive house, and she marveled at every room in the place.

Lisa wanted to say yes, but she didn't. She just couldn't marry Darryl if a prenuptial was involved—she felt that wasn't what true love was all about.

The two of them drove back to Blue Ash in silence.

"He saw his friend Ted, just so happy with his wife in their hideaway in Indian Hill," Sue remembered, "and Darryl just wanted the same situation."

"I knew it was too good to be true," Darryl confessed to Sue, his face sullen.

"You know she didn't love you, Darryl," Sue said. "You'll just have to face the fact."

"Yeah."

"You'll see, there'll be somebody else, when you least expect it."

"Yeah."

While Darryl was waiting for the closing date on his new home, getting antsy with the Indian Hill living arrangements, he realized he'd have to ask Lisa to leave the condo on Fallsington. He had met someone through Great Expectations after all, someone closer to his age, and he needed his own place.

But Lisa was absolutely refusing to get out.

In desperation, Darryl agreed to give Lisa the money for a down payment on a new condo. Even though he had driven by her former boyfriend's place with Deborah and had been thoroughly humiliated, finding Lisa's car there, he felt a settlement with Lisa was necessary.

He later confided to Judy that of course he didn't like the idea, but he just wanted the girl out of his life. Lisa had a way of causing scenes, and he just didn't need that. Besides, she had already quit her job, and Darryl couldn't put Lisa and the kids out on the street.

CHAPTER 33

DATING SERVICES ARE A $300-MILLION-A-YEAR INDUSTRY in the United States, so one would think they would have a decent system to qualify their applicants. At least, Dr. Sutorius thought so when he signed himself up at Great Expectations, the second largest dating service in the country, with fifty-two centers nationwide and thirty thousand members.

He had watched the warm, cozy promotional video that promised a "change of pace" and a fun and easy way to find that special person. He had submitted to a lengthy interview process, during which he talked about his personal life and relationship failures. And as he sat patiently in their offices, located in the Bank One Towers on Montgomery Road, he was guaranteed he'd be able to select from a group of dignified female professionals.

Although he probably didn't believe their spiel about a seventy-five percent success rate—he really had no great expectations at all—Darryl liked the idea of meeting women through a screening process. He plunked his money down for a platinum membership, the most expensive level possible, and filled out all the paperwork.

On the member questionnaire, he listed himself as a divorced thoracic surgeon, six-four, weighing 260 pounds, Protestant, white, and very religious, with no wish to have any more children. His alcohol consumption was "occasional," his annual income he listed at $300,000, and he had a $20,000 credit limit on Master

Card and Visa, along with unlimited credit availability on American Express. He listed his savings and checking accounts, where he had well over $100,000. In response to the question "Are you dating anyone right now?" he checked the box marked "Yes."

Darryl liked the idea of being a member. With the consent system the service offered, at least he'd know that the person he'd be meeting had an initial interest in him. He wanted to find someone for a long-term relationship, someone who made him feel comfortable. He explained to the membership representative that he'd been meeting young, attractive women who "can't carry on a decent conversation."

About the person he was seeking: She had to be between thirty-five and forty-five, hold a four-year undergraduate degree, have a professional occupation as well as athletic and cultural interests, be a Christian, and of course, be very attractive. Darryl didn't care if the woman had been previously married or had kids; he just wanted someone who was "happy with life."

From January 1994 through March 1995, he made nine selections, of which four women responded yes, one of whom was Dante Britteon. The things she had been privy to were Darryl's photos, video, and member profile. And this is what she read:

"A former college athlete, football and track, I still enjoy physical activities but switched to tennis until a fractured wrist injury threatened my professional life and I took up golf. I've been playing two years (member at Beckett Ridge) but have only broken 100 on one occasion. Most of all I have fun playing and socializing."

Darryl went on to describe his interests in the arts— he was a supporter of the Art Museum and Contemporary Arts Center—and he mentioned the Bacchus Society, his love of food and wine, and said he had become "fairly proficient" at cooking since becoming a bachelor. He expressed an interest in traveling and said he planned to look up his roots in Europe someday.

Having practiced medicine in Cincinnati for twenty years, Darryl described the ten years he spent teaching medical students at the University of Cincinnati, explaining that economic pressure forced him out of a full-time academic practice, that what he did as a thoracic and vascular surgeon was to repair problems with the lungs, blood vessels, and heart.

He talked about his four wonderful children, ages eighteen to twenty-three, said he was politically conservative, and claimed that he enjoyed nightlife but also liked quiet nights at home, cuddling up next to somebody, just watching TV.

"What I want to find is a partner," Dante read. "I do not want to compete with that person but I want to share with her and enjoy life with her. I hope we can find activities we both enjoy but I have no problem with my partner having interests I cannot be included in. I want to find someone who knows how to have fun in life. I want to find someone who needs me and gains pleasure from me and appreciates my support."

There were a few photos of the man, two in a coat and tie, the other in casual attire. And Darryl didn't look too bad, not bad at all. His face was strong, if not handsome, his shoulders were broad and quite large, and underneath his shrewd smile there seemed to be a laid-back person.

Dante sent her profile his way.

In it, she reported that she was not dating, that she had owned a day-care service and an apartment building, that she had a four-year degree from UCLA. She was Catholic, five-two, 110 pounds, interested in everything from camping to ballet, and had been divorced for about two months.

She sounded comfortably well off, seemed stable in every way, and was looking for a versatile man, someone who was as happy roughing it as he would be going to the ballet. She did not list her year of birth, nor did she mention that she had any children, but she did note that her given name was Della.

She had signed up for an introductory membership, meaning she could pay in four installments of $323.50 apiece, and from July through November of 1994 Dante made seventeen selections, twelve of which responded yes.

Darryl looked at the video of the woman with light golden hair and hazel eyes, and was immediately swept away. She was beautiful; she looked like an angel. Sure, she was classy and businesslike in her expensive tailored jacket and heavy gold earrings, but she also had a way about her that seemed childlike; it was her pouty lips, her sparkling eyes. The surgeon was captivated.

In her member profile she wrote that she enjoyed movies, museums, theater, ballet, and dancing and dining out. "I haven't been camping since I was a child," she claimed, "but I would love to give it a try again."

She described herself as a very sensitive and gentle person, an intelligent woman who, in a relationship with the right person, could be very playful and extremely affectionate. "I'm very unpredictable," Dante wrote. "I'm fun and funny. I'm a definite hand-holder and hugger. Moral, loyal, cute, and adorable are a few more words that come to mind."

She was looking for an intelligent, sensitive man with high moral standards. She wanted someone who would be willing to compromise and meet her halfway. "At one time in my life I had seven pets," she wrote, so her man definitely had to be an animal lover.

She liked to go out, but she also needed someone who would be happy at home, just eating junk food and watching videos.

CHAPTER | 34

*B*Y THE TIME JUDY McCOY CAME UP WITH A REASONABLE offer on Darryl's condominium, he and Dante were already an item. The real estate agent called and said she wanted to stop by, she needed to go over the details in person, but when she got there, she felt awkward knocking on the door. The lights were dim and it looked like no one was home.

"I'm sorry, did I interrupt you?" she apologized. "If I interrupted you, I can come back another time."

"No, absolutely not." Darryl smiled. "Come right on in."

But Judy *was* interrupting.

"He answered the door, and he's got on boxer shorts and a T-shirt," she recalled. "And we're sitting at the table, negotiating the sale of the condo, and this little itty-bitty petite woman just comes walking in and sits down."

The Realtor realized she must have caught them fooling around, because for one thing Dante wasn't wearing a lot of clothes. All she had on was an oversized T-shirt, and her makeup was entirely smeared off.

Dante was very timid throughout the meeting, busy playing with Darryl's mobile phone, just pressing the buttons and saying, "Don't worry, I'm not going to call anybody." Judy couldn't understand why the woman was being so childish.

It was funny; as much as he and Judy had been in contact, Darryl never mentioned this Dante. Judy had no idea where she came from, but thought it possible she was visiting him from out of town. Dante seemed to have an odd accent.

Judy went back to her office and joked with her assistants about the scene she had walked in on. She thought Darryl's new girlfriend was a little weird, and then the next thing she knew, she happened to run into her at Kenwood Mall.

It was a few days later; they were both shopping at Lazarus, and Judy was waiting at a cash register when suddenly she spotted Dante in the same department. At first Judy had barely recognized her; she looked different with all the thick makeup and fluffed up hair. She was much more poised, hiding behind her Gucci sunglasses, and Judy walked over to say hello. When the elegant woman nonchalantly mentioned that she and Darryl were getting married, Judy was dumbfounded, absolutely caught off guard.

"She was this little girl that he had met," Deborah reflected. "She really didn't do anything, she just kind of lived off her ex-husbands."

When Deborah found out that Dante didn't cook, didn't clean, and didn't have a job, she couldn't fathom what the big attraction was. Then the day came when her father asked her and her boyfriend Bill to meet them for dinner, and Deborah bristled. It was just after Valentine's Day, and Deborah was praying her dad wasn't planning to do something stupid.

"I was hoping he was going to tell me he was maybe *thinking* about being engaged," Deborah remembered. "He couldn't have known her that long, because the last I thought, he was going back to Lisa."

Although Deborah was definitely not looking forward to the dinner, she pretended to be excited, then rushed off the phone into Bill's arms. Her boyfriend tried his best to get her to see the bright side of things, but all Deborah could feel was dread.

"Dante kind of stood back and looked at me," Deborah recalled, "and you know what it made me think of? One of those Hawaiian things that sit on your dashboard. That's what I thought of because she was so stiff, so proper, and her head was just bobbing up and down."

After the four of them exchanged a few pleasantries at the condo, they jumped in Darryl's new Lexus and headed over to the Olive Garden, one of Deb's favorite places for Italian. Deborah didn't say much along the ride. She felt emotionally overwrought, hoping against hope that her parents would get back together, that they would stop hating each other and just forgive and forget. She couldn't believe her dad was actually serious about this little woman.

As they sat waiting for their entrées, Deborah became rather sickened by her father's behavior. He seemed to just pant over Dante. She, on the other hand, acted cool, leaning away from him, barely accepting his arm around her. "It was like she had a rod stuck up her butt," Deborah confided. "She was so stuck up and all she did was talk about herself. Her eyes were cold, she was very cold and false. That was very apparent to me, sitting at this table."

No doubt Dante rubbed Deborah the wrong way, but after the problems she had with Lisa, Deborah was determined to like this woman, to give her a chance, no matter what. She knew she was going to have to accept Dante. there was no way she could publicly come out against the marriage.

By that time, she and her dad had become closer than ever; she didn't want to do anything to jeopardize that, and besides, if this was what he chose, she had to learn not to be so old-fashioned. Much as she didn't want to, she had to let go of her strict upbringing. The Bible verse on divorce, the one in Matthew that talked about man and wife becoming one flesh, that was now out the window. Her parents were never getting back together.

It was clear Dante had a very high opinion of herself,

bragging about her liberal arts degree from UCLA, hardly allowing Deborah and Bill to join the conversation, and Deborah quietly seethed. Dante seemed like a porcelain doll. She seemed to be practicing her poses, and it made everything feel even more tense.

"Well, did he tell you the good news?" she asked, blurting, "We're getting married next week."

Deborah almost choked on her bread stick. She had half of it in her mouth, and she just didn't know if she could swallow any more. A waiter came over and offered to bring fresh water, and the girl finally swallowed and managed to say congratulations. It was like Dante dropped a ton of bricks on the table. Debbie couldn't believe it was for real.

The daughter had been bracing herself for engagement news, but she never anticipated they'd be running off to tie the knot within *days*. For some reason, Deborah hadn't immediately noticed the big diamond ring on Dante's hand, and when she finally examined it, she didn't like the style. It was a diamond surrounded by rubies, not traditional at all.

"I don't remember much after that," she confessed, "because it hit me so hard."

All she wanted to do was get through that dinner and be by herself.

She had to process this. She was totally blown away.

CHAPTER | 35

WHEN PROPERLY DOSED, PRODUCTS LIKE CAVERJECT produce an erection that lasts for about an hour. It's an impotence treatment from Upjohn, and requires the use of needles for self-injection. It's a way of putting medicine inside the penis that allows blood to be trapped inside. The erection only takes about fifteen minutes to develop, and it's supposed to offer more natural results than a penile implant.

Darryl never wanted to explain all that to Dante, but when she caught him injecting himself on their honeymoon, she insisted he show her the process, and she spent time looking at the needles and the packaging, making Darryl thoroughly mortified.

He felt so bad about it, he was compelled to confide to Guy Hild that he was having trouble maintaining his sexual composure with his new wife. Darryl had gone in to see his lawyer about protecting his assets, and with this unexpected news Guy didn't know what to say. He felt humiliated for Darryl, and wondered why the surgeon had jumped into a marriage when his divorce papers were hardly dry.

Hild, a senior partner in the Cincinnati law firm of Katz, Teller, Brant & Hild, was the elected president of the American Academy of Matrimonial Lawyers, Ohio Chapter. He was, and is, the bar's top shelf, one of greater Cincinnati's true legal eagles. Involved in the area's biggest matrimonial endings, including those of Johnny Bench and Jose Rijo, Hild takes a businesslike approach to marriage negotiations. He looks at it like any other binding contract, and he knows how to help people get their ducks in line.

From his palatial estate on Grandin Road, where garlands of flowers spiral up red-brick walls, Hild's view of Darryl Sutorius could be nothing less than incredulous. Why a top-notch surgeon would spend a fortune redesigning a house in a moderate neighborhood, Hild never knew. He stood by Darryl as the surgeon bitterly fought for his property holdings in the first divorce, but now Hild was listening to Darryl with utter disbelief.

This was not the first office visit the surgeon made in 1995. Darryl had gone to see Hild just days before he wed Dante, foolishly insisting that a prenuptial was out of the question, that his bride-to-be wouldn't hear of it. With the kind of soft-spoken voice that can charm the skin off a snake, Hild tried coaxing some sense into his client. But Darryl was hell-bent on marrying her the old-fashioned way. There was no middle ground; he was in a race to the altar.

"He was probably socially inept," Hild admitted. "He was not the kind of person you'd meet on an airplane and have a soul-searching conversation with. You'd be lucky to get two grunts out of him. Darryl thought what a wife's role was, was to open him up and overcompensate for his lack of ability to be charming. What he wanted was a wife to take care of all the social engagements and arrange wonderful events, and enable him to come in at the last minute, as a surgeon, and everyone could applaud."

The only thing Guy knew to suggest, in lieu of a prenuptial, was a naked trust loophole, whereby Darryl's property would be owned by his own private corporation, and Guy handled the paperwork for that. Regarding Darryl's beneficiary designation under his corporate pension and profit-sharing plans—$1 million that Sutorius wanted to go to his children in the event of his death—that was a more delicate matter.

Guy advised that Darryl could not ask Dante to waive

her claim to that money until they were officially married, so there was a catch-22 involved. Dante could not waive the spousal rights until she was legally a spouse, so Darryl would have to get married before he could settle the problem. Guy suggested that Darryl have his business attorney, Mel Marmer, draw up the appropriate papers. The final result was a document allotting Dante a lump sum of $10,000 in exchange for her spousal consent to waive her rights to the pension money.

Just days after their return from Hilton Head, Darryl presented the papers to Dante. There were signatures needed from a witness and a notary public, but Dante wasn't signing so fast; she wanted to run it by some of her attorney friends. When Darryl started nudging her, Dante said she was having second thoughts. She wasn't too keen on signing anything.

In desperation, Darryl called Guy at home, wondering what he could do to persuade his new wife. The next day, Guy had Darryl come into his tower office, hoping to help the bumbling surgeon find a way out of his predicament. But ultimately Dante refused to sign, and legally there was nothing anyone could do about it. The marriage was off to a running start.

CHAPTER | 36

"AFTER THE BOMB WAS DROPPED, I WAS STILL DEAD SET on Mom and Dad getting back together," Deborah insisted. "I didn't like this woman, she seemed prissy, and I could tell she had tons of plastic surgery."

But it didn't matter what Deborah thought. They became husband and wife, and Deborah was given a tour of the new house on Symmesridge and became enlisted in helping them move out of the condo.

Deborah didn't care for the Symmesridge place. The basement was ugly, done in shades of yellow with a blue diamond pattern covering the floor; nothing matched. The bedrooms upstairs were dreary. Deborah thought it odd that Dante was mapping them out for her own use; but for Deborah it made the new marriage easier to accept, not having to think about them sleeping together.

Deborah had volunteered the use of her Toyota pickup truck. They wanted to move their most personal items themselves, and all along her dad was encouraging her to become buddy-buddy with Dante. So when moving day rolled around, Deborah spent the better part of the morning listening to Dante complain about her mother, telling the sad story of her childhood, that she got kicked out of the house when she was a kid, that she and her mother didn't get along. After a while, Deborah felt sorry for her. Really, she didn't want to like the woman, but Dante was pulling her in.

What she remembers most about that day was how squeamish Dante seemed about outdated foodstuffs; it was bizarre. As they were cleaning out the pantry, Dante was throwing everything out, even the spices, and Deborah thought it was nutty, so melodramatic.

At one point, Darryl reached in the garbage and salvaged a chunk of white chocolate she was tossing. It was perfectly good, yet Dante acted like he was crazy to consider eating it. In months to come, Dante would force Darryl to wash and wipe down every canned good before she'd consider touching the food and would give him a hard time about the expiration date on cold cuts and other packaged meats, insisting things be thrown away even before the stamped date.

Though she might have been quirky, she did seem independent, and Deborah was happy about that. Lisa had been so needy and clingy; that's what caused most of the problems for her dad. But Dante appeared to be self-reliant enough to handle a surgeon's schedule. She understood his job was number one with him, and she seemed to make a perfect bride. She could be an ice princess at times, but for Darryl, that was a preferable attitude.

"All he wanted out of her was for her to talk to him, to be good at conversation," Deborah reflected, "and he would take care of her, pay for anything she wanted, give her the world. He just wanted somebody to do things with and he wanted someone to love him. That's exactly what he said to me."

But the more she got to know Dante, the more Deborah started thinking gold digger. Once they moved into the house, Dante became snobby toward everyone and could hardly hide her phoniness. Upstairs in Dante's bedroom, Deborah noticed collagen syringes and all types of infomercial beauty products, weird hairpieces and potions that Dante obsessed about. It was like she was put together with glue.

Everything about the woman started to seem unreal. Between the creams, the bleaches, and fake nails, Deborah imagined her stepmother was pretty scary in real life. She'd hate to see her wake up in the morning. Not that it was a sin for Dante to spend so much time in her bathroom; it was just that she seemed pretty compulsive about her appearance.

"Is my hair okay?" she'd constantly ask. "Do you like this nail polish?"

It was just so annoying.

To look at Dante, one would think her a person whose whole life was devoted to charity, to be someone who would help beggars on the street. The clothes she wore were very innocent-looking, a lot of pleated dresses, things that were more befitting a little girl. She gave people the impression that she was fragile, and sometimes Deborah felt Dante would crack if she looked at her the wrong way. It was like walking on eggshells.

Everyone had to be so careful around her—so formal, polite, and genteel—and it irked Deborah to see how her father bought into his new wife's routine. Deborah wanted to say something to him, but of course she couldn't.

"She played the helpless role," Deborah confided. "She got guys to feel they were big strong men. She'd wear these long denim dresses with a big front, real girlish-looking, and she'd have this little baby voice, and my father would fall for it."

On moving day Darryl took a load over to the house and left Dante and Deborah alone, hoping they'd mesh. As it happened, they discovered one of Darryl's old trunks in a back closet, and right away Dante wanted to break into it.

At first Deborah didn't think it was right, but Dante convinced her, though it was hardly worth the trouble. All they found was a bunch of old medical stuff, some pictures of medical equipment, and a few outdated journals. But stuck in one of them was a love letter from Jan, written when they were newlyweds, and there was a joke Jan wrote about not having enough sex. Deborah thought it was cute.

"Well, okay, the lock's broken, so we'll just tell him," Deborah said as they moved out of the closet.

"No, here, I'll glue it back," Dante insisted, taking the wad of chewing gum from her mouth and pushing the lock back in place.

"But it's no big deal," Deborah protested. "He won't care if we tell him."

But Dante didn't want Darryl to know. She thought he'd be upset. The stepmom quickly changed subjects, distracting Deborah with talk about her wedding ring, pointing out how unusual the pattern in the gold was, telling her the full history of the stones set inside, acting like it was the Hope diamond.

By the time Darryl got back, the two of them were sitting on the couch yakking, and Dante was offering to take Deborah on a shopping spree. Darryl bragged that his wife was an excellent designer, that she had the right connections and excellent taste, and could help Deborah redecorate her place.

Dante thought she was offering a great service, but Deborah felt the offer was quite arrogant. Still, she figured it wasn't worth getting upset over. Dante was just an insignificant woman she would have to put up with; she could always outsmart her.

Eventually John went to visit his dad's new place, and some time later he and Deborah exchanged notes. John thought their stepmother was a joke. In his view, she was so empty-headed, a mannequin would have been more appealing.

CHAPTER 37

DARRYL WAS ONE OF THOSE PEOPLE WHO NEEDED TO watch his cholesterol; the nurses, well aware of the junk food he gobbled, used to kid him about who would do his heart surgery. He was the type who went on Nutri System and then turned around and would eat a big steak dinner.

By the summer of their first year together, Darryl had gained a noticeable amount of weight, partially because he did all the cooking, but mostly because Dante preferred fast foods and insisted on going to places like Wendy's and Taco Bell very late at night. During the week, these outings usually became a second dinner for

Darryl, because he would always grab something in the doctor's dining room before he went home.

Watching the newlyweds' lifestyle, Deborah thought Dante was subconsciously trying to give her dad a heart attack. He was gaining more weight each day. She finally felt compelled to mention it to her aunt Carlene, but there was really no remedy they could come up with. Darryl was so far gone on Dante.

By then Deborah had given up on liking the woman; between her germ phobia and beauty rituals, there were just too many quirks and too many strange incidents. Deborah remembers the time she listened to Dante page her dad because she wanted him to carry her up the stairs. Her back hurt, she said, and she needed him to drop everything and run to the house. She certainly got a lot of mileage out of that back, Deborah learned. But her father claimed he was happy, so Deborah let it go.

When it came to her stepmother, Deborah had learned to keep things to herself—it was much better that way. All along, Dante was giving her a hard time about her wedding plans, and the last thing the girl needed was more trouble. As it was, she was waitressing at a steak house, trying to save money to pay for bridal things, and her mom was offering to pitch in for the wedding because Jan didn't want Dante involved in it at all—there was a lot of friction. Of course, Jan didn't like Deborah hanging around with her dad and Dante to begin with—that always caused an argument.

"The way I saw it, Mom still loved Dad," she confided, "and whenever I would go anywhere with Dad, she would be mad at me. That's why I tried to stay out of my dad's personal life, because Mom would get very upset when I talked about it. It was hairy."

Jan was stunned and hurt when John came home with the news that Darryl would marry Dante, though she wouldn't admit it. Outwardly, she was still holding a grudge, still unable to forgive him, and was dealing with Darryl entirely through her kids. Of course, Deborah noticed that her mom never took her wedding ring off, which didn't make sense, but she never broached the subject.

"I had a much different reaction than I expected to have," Jan admitted. "I was very upset about it. Ultimately, I thought maybe we would get back together. Even though I knew I had progressed in a different direction, I thought maybe there was a chance he would've changed."

On March 2, 1995, the date of Darryl's second wedding, Jan officially put her home up for sale. She couldn't afford the expensive mortgage herself, and anyway it was just too much of a house. Dante ended up having legal rights to the place, being Darryl's new wife, so they were all present at the closing, where Jan met her replacement for the first time. To Jan, the thought of seeing Dante with Darryl was necessary, so she pulled herself together, threw on a suit, and went to the real estate office to get it over with.

"It was like one of those moments of inspiration," Jan said. "Like, I wouldn't miss this for the world. You know, if I'm not strong enough now, I never will be. I can do this. I arranged myself to be there with dignity. And I took a friend."

Of course, when Jan met Dante, she didn't expect the new wife to be so young and beautiful—she just wasn't prepared for that. She didn't make eye contact with Darryl during the meeting at all, so it was left to Dante to smile and make the small talk.

"She's nice," Jan's attorney later commented. "I really like her."

"Yeah, she's sweet," Jan said. "Very cute and attractive."

CHAPTER | 38

DANTE WAS FORCING HER TASTES ON DARRYL, ESPE-cially when it came to redecorating the house. She was driving him crazy with her ideas—and Darryl tried to give her everything she wanted, but he put his foot down when she suggested a purple kitchen. Dante insisted on doing everything herself, would only hire people for odd jobs, but Darryl had encouraged that; for the most part, he trusted her judgment.

When she asked Lyn Doll to come over to help her hang some mirrors and artwork, she ordered the decorator around like she was a servant. The funny thing was, the pieces of artwork Dante wanted hung were repro-ductions, just Monets and Renoirs in tacky frames. There were no original watercolors, no original works at all, except a pastel portrait of *her*.

"I went over to her house specifically to make sugges-tions about color combinations, and she questioned me on every penny," Lyn recounted. "She wanted an esti-mate for a very large gold-leaf type of frame, and then started talking about her wholesale connections."

It was obvious that Dante had no knack for design. The decorator was appalled to see such a hodgepodge job in such a beautiful home. None of the rooms looked coordinated, the furniture was poorly laid out, the paint colors and wallpapers didn't make the proper transitions. Lyn gave Dante some advice about centering the main pieces of furniture in the living room, but Dante refused to hear it, explaining her reasons for her peculiar couch and coffee table arrangement. Whatever Lyn came up with, Dante had a retort, and ultimately she asked Lyn to turn over her catalog of ready-made gold leaf frames, hoping to cut Doll's commission out completely.

Right before the holidays, when she stopped by the design shop to pick up some framed artwork, Dante scrutinized the bill minutely. She wanted separate pricing for the hooks and eyes, items that cost nickels and dimes. She had Darryl waiting out in the car, absolutely freezing, while she spent an eternity looking at the bill.

"She wanted him to put all of the pictures in the car; she was orchestrating the whole thing," Lyn noticed. "They were arguing back and forth about which ones to put on which seat. They were not happy campers."

Even though Dante had agreed to have the kitchen done in basic white, she went behind Darryl's back and found a suitable green. Dante was like that. She had to undermine Darryl's every decision, and then later make fun of his lack of style, his shortage of taste. Darryl's gourmet kitchen actually turned out fairly well; it was a room he was proud of, loaded with commercial cooking stoves and appliances. However, when Deborah complimented Dante on it, her stepmother took the opportunity to make a snide remark.

Dante didn't really like their house on Symmesridge; she had her heart set on a Victorian house over in the Calumet Farm subdivision and thought it was only a matter of time before she could talk Darryl into it. She had driven him by the cul-de-sac to show him her dream house, but her husband wasn't very impressed. More than once she insisted Beth drive her past the exceedingly large place, commenting on how much she loved the turrets and tall glass archways.

When Darryl refused to consider a move, Dante dragged him to the well-known Cincinnati "Homerama" show, where she henpecked him into all kinds of upgrades for their present abode. She nagged him about

the money he spent on his kids, and insisted he dole out
equal amounts to make their surroundings more
beautiful.

Of course, with Christmas around the corner, Deborah
was trying to keep the peace, so she wouldn't dare comment on Dante's lavish home expenditures. She had a
June wedding in the works, time was running out, and
she needed Dante and her dad to make some kind of
commitment. But while Jan was pressing for a date and
a location, Dante was holding Darryl up, asking him to
wait for her price lists on caterers and photographers.

Sometime during Christmas week, Dante listened in
on a phone call and discovered that Darryl and his
daughter were secretly making plans behind her back,
discussing the possibility of a reception at the Beckett
Ridge Country Club. She had already installed taping
and listening devices on her phones, and now she had
the ammunition to fight Deborah with. She had proof
that the girl was trying to cut her out of the wedding
altogether, and she used it to bully her. Suddenly Deborah's phone was ringing with hang-up calls, so she
started letting her answering machine handle it, which
was inadvertently taping parts of her conversations on
the automatic recording device.

"I hope you know you're not getting a *penny* for your
wedding," Dante hissed over the phone when Deborah
finally called back.

"You have no right to say that."

"You're just a waitress. You can't afford a big event.
How much money does your father give you a month?"

"Two hundred dollars," Deborah said, "for working
at his office."

"And you assume he's just going to keep handing you
over money for nothing?"

"I work in his office. I earn that money."

"I just hope you're planning to pay for your own reception," her stepmother howled, "because I've been

checking out prices and your father and I just can't pay for a royal wedding."

"You can't tell my dad what to do with his money because you sure don't do anything for it. You just sit around all day. Who do you think you are? You're nothing but a piece of shit!"

"And just what do you think you are?"

"Hey, bitch, I'm the one who's his daughter. All you are is one of his possessions, like a piece of furniture in the house."

"You don't call this house again if you can't talk to me in a civil tone."

"Just stay out of mine and my dad's life," Deborah shot back, "and just so you know, I'm not coming over for Christmas."

"Fine."

Dante slammed down the phone, and for Deborah, who had never cursed at an adult before, she couldn't believe how easily the words had flowed out. She was proud of herself, and so happy that she had the conversation on tape; she even let her boyfriend listen to it. Of course, she never dreamed she'd wind up giving that microcassette to her dad; but there came a day when she felt frightened enough she knew she had to.

Dante paged Darryl immediately after the telephone altercation, and as soon as the surgeon got home from the hospital, she wanted him to call Deborah in her presence. She demanded he tell his daughter that he would not be paying for the wedding. When he refused to make the call, it led to a knock-down, drag-out fight.

Dante threatened to kill him if he didn't obey. She told him she had a gun, and all at once there was something in her voice that scared him. It was like she was a different person. At first she ranted, then her tone changed to an incredible calm.

"I've done things before," she said, smiling, "and I've always gotten away with them."

"What are you talking about?"

Della Faye Hall
on her fifth
birthday.
*(Courtesy of
Olga Mello)*

Della Faye Hall
and Olga in rural
Kentucky.
*(Courtesy of
Olga Mello)*

Three sisters. From right to left: Della, Donna, and Cheryl. *(Courtesy of Cheryl Sullivan)*

Della hits puberty and feels ugly and left out. It's a traumatic time for her. *(Courtesy of Olga Mello)*

The house Della grew up in, in Norwood, a division of Cincinnati. *(Author's collection)*

Della Hall, standing on the far right. She dropped out of her exclusive private school. *(Courtesy of Olga Mello)*

Della's first wedding, to Joe Hoeffer, when she was nineteen. *(Courtesy of Olga Mello)*

The Mello clan. Top to bottom, left to right: Gene, Scott, Olga, Gene Sr., Carla, Nikki, and Cheryl. The family wouldn't allow Della to be in the shot. *(Courtesy of Olga Mello)*

Dante at a marina in California, on vacation with Jeff Freeman. *(Author's collection)*

Darryl and Janet Sutorius, in love in Las Vegas. *(Courtesy of Janet Sutorius)*

Dr. and Mrs. Darryl Sutorius on their wedding day. *(Author's collection)*

Darryl and
Dante on their
honeymoon in
Hilton Head.
*(Author's
collection)*

Dr. Darryl Sutorius
in his Great
Expectations
dating service
photo. *(Courtesy
of the Office of
Hamilton County
Prosecuting
Attorney)*

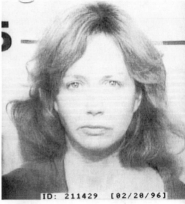

Dante Britteon in her Great Expectations dating service photo. (Courtesy of the Office of Hamilton County Prosecuting Attorney)

The mug shot of Della Dante Sutorius. (Courtesy of the Office of Hamilton County Prosecuting Attorney)

ID: 211429 [02/20/96]

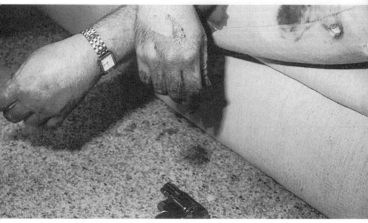

The bloody hands of Darryl Sutorius next to the .38-caliber revolver. (Courtesy of the Office of Hamilton County Prosecuting Attorney)

Lead prosecutor
Tom Longano on
the steps of the
Hamilton County
Courthouse.
(Terry Gaines)

Tom Longano celebrates victory with Jerry Kunkel
(center) and Steve Tolbert (left). *(Terry Gaines)*

"Well, I had to have someone's house burned down once."

"Why?"

"Because he cheated on me."

"Whose house? Where?"

"Just an old boyfriend. Nobody you would know."

CHAPTER 39

SINCE DELLA HAD BEEN SPENDING TIME WITH HER KID sister Carla lately, helping her redecorate her place, she decided to call her for a return favor. Della wasn't sure what she wanted, but first she needed Carla on her side. She certainly wasn't getting anywhere with Beth or Cheryl, and Nikki was just too young to understand.

She explained what a fruitcake Debbie was, how she was cursing and carrying on, and Carla tried to seem interested. It was obvious that the money for this wedding had become tantamount to the happiness in Della and Darryl's marriage.

From Carla's perspective, the whole thing was ludicrous. She and her young husband were just making ends meet, living in a trailer park south of Cincinnati in Florence, Kentucky, and Carla was already depressed about it; Della's redecorating hadn't helped. Now, as Carla listened to her sister's rage over the telephone, being eight months pregnant with her first child and consumed with the prospect of buying her own house, all she could think about was getting herself back home to Ohio. Here her sister was calling from the most exclusive part of town, complaining about money out of one side of her mouth while bragging about a $10,000 chandelier out of the other. It was so disgusting.

Carla had watched Della operate for years and knew her sister only came around with ulterior motives. When she couldn't get Cheryl's attention, she'd pretend Carla was her favorite. Della loved to play people against each other. She'd done it her whole life, and that's why Carla stopped accepting her fancy dinner invitations. Della could still fool Nikki with expensive restaurants and Indian Hill parties, but she couldn't fool her.

When the issue of a country club wedding was brought up, Carla agreed that it seemed extravagant. Della conjured up the formal and expensive places Deborah was considering, upscale locations like Kenwood Country Club, with its oriental rugs, tapestry curtains, and official coat of arms. But in reality, Beckett Ridge was none of that. It was a more down-home place, quite affordable and rather rustic, tucked away in a rural Ohio corner, overlooking farmland.

As Della continued to gripe, enraged that Deborah expected to be catered to, she had Carla believing that the girl was getting a $50,000 wedding, that Deborah was trying to order satellites, huge floral centerpieces, and a designer gown, that she was planning nothing shy of a *gala*.

To Carla, it seemed strange that Della was so controlling with Darryl's money. She knew her sister had gone into this marriage with nothing but a $200 car, that all she really owned when she met the surgeon was a ratty old Mustang. Her sister's attitude really amused her. Della had no right to question where her husband's hard-earned money was going, yet she absolutely believed his money was hers.

"I'm his wife," she insisted. "Legally, I have a right to everything he has."

All along, Carla suspected their newly revived "friendship" was nothing more than an act Della was putting on for Darryl. No one in the family had really talked to

Della for years, yet now that she had become the elegant "Dante," she was luring her sisters around, trying to coax them with gifts, praise, and attention.

But Carla wasn't about to be her lackey.

"Della was a difficult person to be close with," she confided. "She was just complaining all the time. She spent a lot of time cutting people down, and she would get close to me only when she wanted to."

CHAPTER 40

OVER THE YEARS, GUY HILD HAD HEARD SOME OUTRAgeous stories from doctors. When Darryl first came to him with weird details about Dante, the attorney listened with a highly trained ear. Guy was trying to understand the surgeon's position, but the doctor had no proof of Dante's wrongdoings; all he had were a bunch of allegations he was making based on Dante's threats. It took them about forty-five days to figure out who Della Dante Faye Hall was, and by then Guy had begun the process of the divorce. The attorney was trying to help Darryl through it, offering practiced advice, but it didn't seem to calm the surgeon down.

"Should I have somebody follow her?" Darryl finally asked.

"I don't care," Guy said. "If it will make you feel better, do what you want, but I don't need that information."

Darryl felt he really needed to analyze Dante, so he decided to break down and place a call to Olga Mello. Dante's mom had called the house on Christmas Day, and Darryl had jotted her number down from caller ID. She seemed pleasant enough Christmas morning, although the two of them only spoke a few words. Of course, Dante had made her out to be such a compulsive liar and a cheat, Darryl had no idea if she'd be trustworthy. But he had to give it a shot.

Olga, the type of woman who likes to help people, who believes in blessings from God, never really understood how her oldest child could turn out to be so cold. Della was one bad apple. Her six other kids were kindhearted and loving, but never Della. When Darryl called from out of the blue, telling Olga about Dante's threats to kill him, about his plans to get a divorce, her heart really went out to him. Della caused trouble for everyone.

"But I don't think she's capable of *that,* Doctor," Olga assured him. "I know she's really bad, but . . ."

"Well, she was just furious on Valentine's Day. She was expecting jewelry and flowers, you know."

"And what did you give her?"

"Six White Castle hamburgers."

The two of them had a big laugh.

"But Olga, do you know anything about her burning down a house?"

"Oh, Doctor! You know about that? I can't believe she told you. We've asked her about it for years, but she's always denied it."

"Well, she told me she did it. I guess she wanted to make sure I'd believe she'd hurt me."

"Oh, she's just scaring you," Olga promised. "The authorities talked to some of us, and I think they talked to her husband, Jim. But they never found any reason to arrest her for arson or anything."

"Did you say *Jim?*"

"Yeah, her first husband—no, wait, no. Jim was number two."

"But I thought her second husband was David."

"No, let's see, I think David was her fourth."

"Fourth? How many husbands did she have?"

"Oh, at least five, that I know of. And that's not counting the years she was out in California. God only knows what she did out there."

"Five?" Darryl's voice was rising. "She told me there were only two. What are their names, can you tell me? I'd like to write them down."

As Olga reeled off the list, naming Joe Hoeffer, Jim Beyer, Grant Bassett, David Britteon, and common-law husband Sid Davis,* Darryl was getting a sick feeling. The two of them continued to talk about his problems with Dante, mostly about the fact that she didn't want him paying for Deborah's wedding, and about her gripe that he hadn't bought Shawn a furnace.

"Getting Shawn a furnace is no problem," he told Olga. "I can take care of that."

"Doctor, you are just too generous. You don't understand; Della uses men. Shawn and her husband bought a house without a furnace, so it's their problem. If you cover for their mistakes, they're never going to learn."

"Can I ask you something, Mrs. Mello?"

"Sure."

"Did Dante go to UCLA?"

"Well, if she did, she went as a washwoman, because that girl never finished high school."

"She didn't?"

"No, Doctor. I spent all my money sending her to the best Catholic school in Western Hills, and she dropped out and never even bothered to get a job."

In Olga's opinion, her daughter didn't deserve any pity or handouts. Just because Della was threatening to do bad things didn't mean the doctor should be trying to pacify her. Darryl said Dante was intimidating him by promising to expose him to the IRS, and was also in the process of destroying his credit. Olga felt sorry for him, but was certain the doctor would find the means to outsmart her. She offered to help in any way she could.

"That's how she's gone through life," Olga confided, "on these acts of kindness from men who've fallen for her. Little do they know what a wolf in sheep's clothing she is. She's dirty, she's lazy, and she's always looking for easy money. That's right down her alley."

By the time Olga and Darryl hung up, the surgeon's head was spinning. He asked if it would be okay if he called back, and Olga encouraged him—under the condition that he never breathe a word about it to Della. Olga was frightened of her—the whole family was leery.

"You just don't know how wicked Della is." Olga's voice was ringing in his ears. "Be careful, because if she finds out you're talking to me, she's liable to do anything."

CHAPTER | 41

"WHERE ARE YOU CALLING ME FROM?" CHERYL asked. "Della doesn't know you're calling, does she?"

"No, I'm on my car phone," Darryl assured her.

"Well, where does the bill go? She'll check all the numbers, you know."

"No, she can't. This bill goes to my office."

"Oh, okay, good. I mean, Darryl, I'd love to help you, I know my mom told you to call, but if Della finds out, she could come burn my house down."

"What do you know about that?"

"Nothing, other than she denies it."

"Your mother said there was another boyfriend she tried to burn in his bed."

"Yeah, I heard that. I think that's true."

"Why didn't anybody ever tell me about all this?"

"You were already married to her, Darryl, and she's always denied everything. The only time she's ever been arrested is with Jeff."

Cheryl filled Darryl in on the aggravated menacing charge her sister had been convicted of back in 1990. Evidently she threatened one of her boyfriends with a gun because he refused to marry her. Darryl decided to call Jeff Freeman* and get as many details as possible, and when he identified himself as Dante's husband, all Jeff could say was, "I'm sorry."

Jeff explained that he initially brought Dante to court for terroristic threatening, that he really wanted her charged with attempted murder, but since the gun wasn't fired, it wasn't possible. Over the phone, Jeff confided that Dante had him so scared, he had gone to a police supply store and had bought himself a bulletproof vest. Back then, Dante was relentless, tormenting him at his brokerage firm, and even harassing his eighty-three-year-old mother. She claimed she was pregnant, but Jeff never believed her.

"It was like *Fatal Attraction*," Jeff confided. "With that type of person, you can't try to reach any kind of medium ground. You just have to be very forceful."

"When she pulled the gun on you," Darryl asked, "did you think she was going to use it?"

"Yeah. I have no doubt at all that she was gonna kill me."

"Well, I think my life could be in danger."

"You know, I would take her threats seriously. She looks sweet and innocent, but she's really crazy."

Jeff told the surgeon that he had every reason to be concerned. He gave Darryl the case number for her conviction in December 1990. The paperwork Darryl obtained from the courthouse showed that Dante Bassett had pled "no contest" to aggravated menacing. She had been fined $100, was sentenced to a year's probation, and was deemed "emotionally unstable."

Additionally, she was required to successfully complete the Crossroads program, which the court hoped would provide "some insight into why the torch of love is still being carried" by her, when it was clear that her ex-boyfriend had absolutely no desire to return her advances.

Throughout the proceedings, Dante was trying to gain sympathy, claiming to be pregnant. She was still hoping to establish the paternity of the child and wanted Jeff to have a blood test after the child was born. It was her first and only criminal conviction, and she walked away with a slap on the wrist.

CHAPTER 42

THAT AFTERNOON AT BETHESDA NORTH, DARRYL HAD trouble performing surgery. He had been so shaken up by the court documents, he had already run them by Guy Hild's office, claiming he was desperate to find a way out of his marriage. Guy suggested the possibility could exist that Dante was still married to someone else. Since there were so many hidden ex-husbands and boyfriends, the attorney was going to check into it.

In the hallway outside the OR, nurses and hospital staffers couldn't believe their eyes. Here was this demigod on the verge of tears. Dr. Sutorius, who had always been so careful about his reputation, who had never let people see his human side, was suddenly shaking with fear. Even though it was obvious that something was wrong, Darryl wouldn't open up about his personal life, not even to his favorite co-worker, Carla Smith.

"He just acted different," Smith recalled. "I don't know how to explain it. It was strange. He never mentioned that his wife had a gun, he never mentioned that he was scared at all, but he was just hanging around the hospital, like he had nothing better to do."

When Darryl confided his fears to Rob Coith, the cardiologist he shared a receptionist with in the Cardiology Center, his friend thought Darryl was paranoid and didn't really believe the surgeon's story. Darryl, a huge man, afraid of tiny Dante; it made no sense.

"Give me a break," Coith told him. "I mean, one swat from you and that little chipmunk goes flying across the room. That's crazy."

"You don't understand," Darryl said. "She's done it before. These threats are real."

Coith could see his colleague was honestly shaken. So much so, he went home and told his wife about Darryl—it was just so unbelievable to him that a prominent surgeon could have himself wrapped up with such an insane woman, that she had managed to convince him that he was in some kind of physical danger. Of course, Darryl never told Coith that he had located a gun in the house and had recently turned it over to police. He was too embarrassed to mention that.

"She had to be holding something over his head," Coith reflected. "There was something that she had on him, something that he held very dear that he didn't want exposed. That's the feeling that I got."

Darryl's strange behavior around his office lasted for about three weeks. In and around that period, he had been in personal therapy as well as marriage counseling with Dante, and he had started the official divorce proceedings, but kept wavering about signing the papers. Since he had taken the gun to the police on January 22, he was spending more and more time away from home.

Meanwhile, he finally told Deborah about the threats—Darryl had a scene with Deborah in his office one day—and he promised his daughter he'd find his way back to her, but asked her never to call the house or car phone again.

And it was then, for the first time, that Deborah realized the severity of the situation. She couldn't believe this was real. This kind of thing was only supposed to happen in horror films.

"I know God never gives you more than you can handle," he told his daughter, "but I've made some very bad decisions lately."

"I think Dante has some serious mental problems," she said. "Maybe she should go see a shrink."

"I agree, but I'm going to get rid of her, Debbie, so don't worry."

"Well, what are we going to do about my wedding? Should I just elope?"

"No, I'll help you with that. You can have it at Beckett Ridge or the Banker's Club, you two decide."

Darryl was sorry he couldn't be more involved with the planning. He had Dante on his trail constantly, he told his daughter. "She's got pretty much every minute of my time accounted for."

Unbeknownst to him, Olga had looked up Deborah's phone number and had been in contact with the girl, hoping to warn her about Della, and trying to keep tabs on the situation. Deborah was skeptical of Olga at first, but after she pinned her father down at his office, after she saw the fear written all over her dad's face, she decided to keep in closer contact with Dante's mom. Realizing that she might discover something, Deborah started checking in every few days, and Olga encouraged her.

Deborah just couldn't believe how nice the woman was—she was anything but the wicked witch Dante had made her out to be. From what Deborah could tell, Olga was just a hardworking woman who seemed to care, who had high moral standards. She wanted to help Deborah cope with Della, wanted her to explain to the other children that as soon as their dad got the divorce, life would go back to normal.

In the first week of February, Olga's phone rang early one night—it was Darryl calling to report that he had been talking to his lawyer, that Della was going to be served with papers sometime the following week. Olga had been in contact with him all along, and she was slowly learning about her daughter's evil deeds. For one thing, Della *had* reported the surgeon to the IRS, he had been asked to produce ten years of documents, something that Della later laughed about to Cheryl. Olga told the doctor it wasn't the first time Della had pulled that stunt.

Mrs. Mello was tired of her daughter's lies and troublemaking, and she explained to Darryl about her disowning Della years before, about what a bad mother Della had been to Shawn. She insisted that her daughter was an expert at deception, just number one in lies. She always played the victim, and over the years she used the abuse story to wrap men around her fingers. She'd have a man set up and carted off to jail, then would strip him of his every possession.

"Dr. Sutorius, all hell is going to break loose when she gets those papers."

"I know, Mrs. Mello, I've thought of that."

"And if you have anything of value in the house, get it out before she's served, because anything of value she will smash, she will destroy."

PART FOUR | The Little Girl

CHAPTER 43

WHEN SHE WAS YOUNG, DELLA WAS ATTACHED TO strange books. She loved *The Bad Seed*, checked it out from the library regularly, but Olga didn't bother to read what it was about. She never knew the protagonist was a twisted little girl, a natural-born killer who, among other things, drowned a schoolmate and burned a neighbor alive.

Olga had met Della's dad, Jim Hall, while he was stationed over in Liverpool. He was an American soldier, originally from Kentucky, and the two of them fell head over heels in love, leaving the ravages of war behind them. As soon as they got to America, they married and were settled in his hometown of Auxier. It was a backwoods place in the heart of Appalachia, not exactly what she had in mind, but Olga visited some distant family in Indian Hill, and she set her sights on relocating to Cincinnati as soon as possible.

As a young girl, Olga Brown had been through a lot of hell; during World War II, her house had been bombed. She and her siblings watched it blow up behind them and were forced to live in an air raid shelter. The kids lost everything but the clothes on their backs, and the war was still raging. It was the early 1940s and a highly traumatic time. Of course, Olga cried a lot, praying for wartime to be over; and for five years she was sent to North Wales, a place she hated but endured, at her parents' request.

"Some of the more miserable parts of it was when we'd get out of the air raid shelters," Olga recalled, "and we'd see the air raid wardens taking parts of bodies out of bombed houses. They had these great canvas bags, and you'd see arms or legs that went in a bag. We were little kids standing around watching this."

When the war was over, Olga was sent back to Liverpool, where she remembers dancing in the streets. She attended Catholic school and learned to properly starch pillowcases and bake breads and pies; she was reared to be a perfect homemaker, and she loved that kind of work. At home, she would practice ironing things like dustcloths, ribbons, and socks, whatever she could get her hands on.

Olga always thought the English school system was superior—there was no "tomfoolery" over there, and years later she was somewhat disappointed when her kids went to public school in Western Hills. She ended up paying for Catholic educations and thought they still had it too easy.

"I liked our schools much better. Your parents paid a lot of money to get you there," she said, "and you accomplished something. It was strictly business; there was no chitchatting in the hallways."

Before she left England, she went to business college and was typing seventy-five words a minute, which she thought was okay, though other girls were much faster. Still, she was good enough to get a job, having learned all the secretarial skills—shorthand, letter writing, and bookkeeping—and she worked in Gatwick Airport, where she met Jim, a good-looking young Air Force soldier.

By then it was 1949. She was sixteen, he was all of

twenty-one. After a year, the two of them made arrangements to move to the States, with the full blessing of her parents. Jim's family was poor, but they were loving people who welcomed Olga with open arms. The minute she got there, she was homesick, and she wanted to return to England in the worst way. After eighteen months in Auxier, she settled for a move to Cincinnati—the Queen City.

Olga quickly grew to like it; it was the early 1950s and all the modern conveniences were beginning to appear, which was a great help to her, since she was at home alone with two baby girls. Jim worked in a machine shop, earning $62 a week, good money back then, but then the Korean War broke out, and Olga started getting jumpy. She had a feeling Jim would get called back into service, that she would lose him. As it happened, Jim didn't get called to war, but disaster struck anyway. The young man died of cancer, leaving Olga with Della, age two, and Donna, who was still an infant.

Olga had developed into a beautiful young woman by that time, motherhood suited her, and her size-six figure was still intact. Within months of Jim's death, she was lucky enough to find Gene Mello, a man she met and married rather quickly, not caring what people thought. He loved her and she was crazy about him—that's all that mattered.

But little Della didn't take to Gene very well. She wanted her real dad, and throughout her childhood she kept a picture of Jim Hall in full uniform hanging prominently over her bed. This was her "daddy in heaven," she would tell her sisters, who had no idea what she was talking about.

As she got older, Della's memories of Jim seemed to grow more vivid. She would tell other kids all about him, insisting he was her only dad—the only one who ever loved her.

She hated her father, Gene, hated her mom, and she particularly hated their baby, Cheryl. No matter how many special favors her parents gave her, no matter how many new outfits and dolls, neither one of them stood a chance.

When Cheryl was still an infant, Della threatened to smother her; then as the Mello family grew, Della Faye Hall seemed more distressed. It was a shame because she was a beautiful child, the type teachers and neighbors would open their doors for, just to have a peek at what kind of new outfit she had on that day. Olga always made sure the girl was dressed like a living doll.

CHAPTER | 44

*H*ER SISTER DONNA HAS THE MOST VIVID MEMORY OF their childhood. She wasn't the least surprised when she heard Della was being charged with aggravated murder, and just before the 1996 trial, she confronted her sister in the Justice Center. She wanted to discuss their neighborhood bulldog, the one Della killed when they were little. Della claimed Donna was dreaming the whole thing up, looking for media attention, so Donna reminded her about their house on Wayland Avenue in Norwood, the place they lived before they moved to Western Hills, where the two of them played in the alley, in the days before kindergarten. She was hoping to spark Della's recollection.

"She was mean; she made me deathly afraid," Donna recalled. "She made me think that dog would tear my hands off."

According to Donna, the bulldog was a neighborhood

pet they played with when they were ages six and seven. He wound up killed and mutilated, and when Della brought her around the alleyway to see him, the poor creature was hidden between two deserted buildings. She says Della had a lot of fun torturing her with the gruesome sight.

"Do you like what I did to it?" she taunted. "Can you smell it?"

But Donna didn't understand. She was too young to comprehend what had happened. The dog just looked like a lumpy mass.

"We are really good sisters," Della told her, "so I saved the best part for you. You get to do the eyeballs."

But Donna threw the stick back at her.

As she watched in horror, Della poked at the dog's eye sockets.

The spectacle made her so sick, little Donna started gagging. She went to run to tell her mother, but Della caught up to her and threatened to do more harm if she opened her big mouth.

"Even before I was in kindergarten, she always let me know she could harm my mother in her sleep," Donna confided. "There was a time when she went and got the scissors, and snuck into my mother's room while she was taking a nap. She held the scissors close to my mother's neck, raising them up a little bit, and then stood there, posing like that."

At the time, Donna was only six, yet she recalls holding her breath, waiting to see what Della would do. According to Donna, Della was constantly plotting to kill their mom, and she was quite convincing about it, standing over their sleeping mother with the scissors raised and an evil smirk on her face.

When Donna tried to report the dog incident to Olga, her mom didn't want to be bothered with a bunch of kid stuff. She thought Donna was making up some kind of nonsense, and when she finally walked to the alleyway to see the dog, there was no such creature; there was only a dead squirrel covered with maggots, and Donna was scolded for playing in the filthy gutter. Donna later tried to convince her mother that Della did something really bad to this dog, but Olga had her hands full with two babies; she didn't want to hear it.

Throughout their childhood, Donna knew there was something wrong with her older sister. She feared her tremendously, but she never had any luck convincing others that Della was devilish. Della always managed to cover her tracks.

More than once, Donna watched her sister hold scissors over baby Cheryl's head, or sometimes Della would just threaten to twist the baby's neck. Still, these were early growing-up years, and Donna always forgave her.

For the most part, the two sisters did all the normal things, like playing Barbie dolls, and Suzie Homemaker, but then something would snap and Della would start scaring Donna again, pretending she was different people. Sometimes Della would use different names and voices, and she'd develop a strange look.

Back then, when they lived in the Norwood house, a big old Victorian place with a lot of nooks and crannies, the Mellos occupied the main level and rented out the upstairs floor for extra income. Olga was a stay-at-home mom, Gene worked as a housepainter, and they struggled to make ends meet. These were the days before Scott, Nikki, and Carla were born—the days before Della and Donna were shipped away from home.

According to Donna, at the tender age of seven Della became quite enthralled with the upstairs tenants, yet was claiming that the man living up there was a monster. In Donna's mind, the guy had fangs and sharp teeth, and was capable of biting little girls' legs off. That's what Della made her think.

Donna wanted to report the monster to their mom, but Della wouldn't allow it. Their mom would just get angry and punish them, she said. Then one night Donna climbed upstairs to rescue Della, and claims she found her sister with the scary man.

Donna professed, "I was pulling her arm, and the man pushed her back and grabbed me."

Donna says she remembers this "like it was yesterday," and says Della seemed to be enjoying the attention. She recollects the man shuffling the two of them out of the room.

"It was like her eyes kept changing, like Della was going blank," Donna remembers. "At first she wanted me to save her, but then she started fighting me, pulling away from me."

Donna believes these night visits continued for some time, but her memory is sketchy, she doesn't know the particulars, and there's no one to corroborate her story.

CHAPTER 45

"CALL ME SALLY," DELLA TOLD HER SISTER. THE words came from out of the blue as the two girls played with their dolls. "My name is Sally and I won't answer you unless you call me by my name."

"I don't want to play that game now," Donna argued.

"Della's not here now. I'm here. And my name is Sally."

"Okay, Sally."

"That's better. Now I want you to understand that you're going to have to pay for telling Mother about the monster."

"But I didn't, I didn't tell her."

* * *

Back in the fifties, when Della was growing up, Western Hills was a typical all-American suburb. It was segregated, very conservative, and considered itself special. There was a lot of local pride; the area was largely German, and there were plenty of mom-and-pop operations with names like Wassler Meats and Humbert's. Forget about Cincinnati and its chili; these west-siders were more into sausage, beef tenderloin, and pastrami.

By the time Della attended Our Lady of Lourdes Elementary School, the Mellos had become familiar faces in the neighborhood, living on a simple, tree-lined street. They had purchased a small brick house on Moonridge Drive, near the community swimming pool. Those were mostly quiet times; comparatively few police reports were being made back then, and there weren't nearly as many murders, although there was a terrible unsolved crime involving a whole family that had been slaughtered in their neighborhood. The Briccas had become rather infamous in Western Hills.

The victims happened to live just a stone's throw away from Della, and she liked to use their murders to taunt Donna. She liked to claim she did it; she had a lot of fun that way. She loved to hold things over her sister's head, especially when it came to making Donna keep secrets. Back when they were little, Della never wanted the monster story released. Donna was never supposed to tell anyone about that.

But Donna was too scared to talk about the monster anyway—she was afraid their mother was going to get angry—so she told Olga nothing about it. Olga now insists Donna's claims are bogus, that there was never a strange male tenant upstairs in Norwood, that Donna's memory is a mixture of dreaming and hallucinations. If her girls were being bothered at night, Olga is certain she would have known it.

Yet Donna recalls their tenant woman had a boyfriend who was sneaking in late at night, and she remembers being so frightened of the man that she would sleep with the covers over her head, afraid that the monster would appear to carry her off upstairs.

The more Della would disappear from their room, the more Donna wanted to tell their mom, but Della would threaten her, and at times things got physical between them. At least once Donna says Della tried to choke her to get her to shut up. When that didn't work, she resorted to the silent treatment.

"She didn't speak to me for three days," Donna recalled. "I followed her around, and she completely ignored me. She wouldn't play with me anymore; she wouldn't answer me when I talked to her."

Cheryl's recollection of the Mello household seems so different that it sounds as if the girls were brought up in two completely different worlds.

Cheryl has memories of camping trips and hula hoops, recalls the girls wearing matching starched outfits, and walking to church on Sundays. She remembers laughing with her siblings about their mother's strict rules.

She knows nothing about Della's threats with scissors, nothing about a dog with it eyes poked out, and she finds the story about the monster upstairs "absolutely crazy."

CHAPTER 46

"*I* WOULD DRESS THE THREE GIRLS EXACTLY ALIKE. They had the same little capes, the same little dresses," Olga said. "But, of course, when Della got older, she'd tell me I only did that to please myself."

In their childhood years, the Mello girls looked gorgeous; people would stop on the streets and stare. On holidays, they wore outfits trimmed with little pearls and had fancy purses with matching nylon gloves. Olga has them all captured on eight-millimeter film, her three beauty queens and her prodigal son, Gene. She and her husband took reels and reels of the kids—playing happily on swing sets, in backyard swimming pools, and at amusements parks. From outward appearances, their lives were full of Kodak moments, and Della appeared to be the star.

Perhaps that was because Della had been considered the prettiest of the lot. With her natural blond curls and her perfect dimples, she was an attention-grabber. But the girl's looks started changing after elementary school; Della's hair got darker, turning almost completely brown, and that was traumatic for her. She entered that awkward stage, and even though she was still pretty, Donna was getting more attention, as was Cheryl, which Della just couldn't handle.

"She would tell me she wanted to be an only child," Olga recalled, "and I would explain that children need each other."

But Della didn't understand. By the time she hit sixth grade, she was failing in school, so Olga moved her to Mother of Mercy Academy. She really couldn't afford it, but Della was the oldest; she needed to set the example for the others.

"She was getting all these extras in the academy," Olga complained, "but meanwhile, it didn't make any difference with Della. She was not putting in any effort. She was doing nothing. She just didn't care."

Even as a child, Della was greedy. She wanted all the attention, wanted to be treated like a princess, and wanted to get her way. When she didn't, she would protest with passive-aggressive behavior. For instance, at the dinner table she would mope and be slow and lazy about eating. Everybody around the table would be finished, but Della wanted to sit there for an extra hour, just picking at her food.

Olga always thought it was Della's way of getting out of doing the dishes, so it became a source of constant fights. No matter what chore Olga gave her, Della would always have a shortcut or a way out of it. As she got older, Della would taunt her mother about her work habits; she felt Olga was too strict about chores, that she acted like a drill sergeant at home. Olga was a work-horse, and Della would make it clear that she didn't agree with her values.

"I would never work like you," Della told her. "Nobody likes work. You can't tell me anybody likes work."

"I'm happy when I'm working," Olga insisted. "When I've accomplished something, that's when I feel good."

"That's just stupid."

"Just do the dishes. If you want to eat, you've got to work. That's just part of life."

"The water's too hot."

No matter how much Olga tried to light a fire under her, Della was not the type to get her hands dirty. She would much rather park herself in front of the television all day, which is what she managed to do with most of her time.

All her life, Della was preoccupied with TV characters; they were real people to her, people who were preferable to her own family. Della lived through the TV set and wanted to grow up to be just like the rich ladies she'd see on soap operas and sitcoms.

As a kid, Della wore Shirley Temple dresses and wanted to appear on the local kiddie show. As a young adult, she combed her hair like Farrah Fawcett and emulated TV bitches like Erica Kane. When she was in between marriages, she developed crushes on TV weathermen and news anchors. At some point she supposedly dated talk-show host Jerry Springer, a Cincinnati anchorman in those days. It was something she always bragged about.

She and Springer were reportedly seen together at a couple of Cincinnati hot spots, trendy places in Mt. Adams and Mt. Lookout, but officially Springer denies having known her. Jerry told local reporters that he barely recognized her name—he wasn't sure. But Della's connection with him was real enough, at least in her mind. She felt he was a part of her.

She talked about him incessantly, showed pictures of him to her subsequent boyfriends—most of her men heard about Springer—and she supposedly had one special snapshot of them together that she carted around. Hardly a day went by in which she didn't mention him.

She watched his broadcasts religiously, and when he made the jump to national TV, relatives would sometimes catch Della making bizarre comments to the television set.

"Oh, Jerry, that tie doesn't go with that jacket," she'd tell the TV. "You know better than to dress like that."

CHAPTER | 47

WHEN DELLA HIT PUBERTY, SHE HAD A FACE FULL OF zits. The whole family made fun of her, calling her "Pill" back then. "Her hair was just atrocious-looking," Cheryl recalled. "She was ugly, and there was a lot of name calling. She was being made fun of in high school."

Olga had a lot of problems with her because the girl didn't take care of herself. Della's hair was so stringy and unkept, Olga took an electric razor and shaved it all off. It was a decision she made the night she walked in on Della, who was supposedly taking a shower, only to find her daughter standing by the sink practicing makeup tricks.

"She was not bathing; she put the water on so I could hear the water running," Olga recalled. "I was screaming, calling her a filthy pig, because her back was just black, her bra was black, and I had to get a brush and scrub her down with Comet. That's how dirty she was."

Della's early teens were tough years. She had a recurring dream about falling, and then there were monsters, things like flying lions, and other weird dream-creatures she'd cry about. She was desperately trying to be accepted by the kids in her class, but none of the boys liked her. She never went to a prom, never went to any kind of dance, and as a result she took to the streets.

When she was just fifteen, she would coax Donna into leaving the house with her, and Cheryl remembers her two older sisters sneaking out quite frequently. They'd leave around midnight, and they got away with it for over two years. Cheryl shared a room with them and she would awaken to watch the two girls crawl out the tiny bedroom window. But Della would threaten her; Cheryl knew if she ever said anything, her sister would get even.

However, Della's midnight excursions did blow up in her face, because there came a time when police hauled her and her sister in for questioning. When they were escorted home in the early morning hours, Olga answered the door, absolutely horrified to discover Della and Donna were being accompanied by men in blue uniforms. She was shattered; she had no idea her children were capable of such bad behavior.

Back in those days, kids just didn't do that, and Olga became entirely fed up with the Hall girls. She decided she needed to do something drastic, and she shipped them off to distant relatives, certain that would straighten them out. Donna was sent to California, where she eventually became a permanent resident, with no desire to ever return to Ohio.

Della, on the other hand, hated living with her cousins in Maryland. She came running home within a year. But by then she had an even harder time winning Olga's approval. She was still a belligerent teenager who refused to work at school. Before Olga knew it, Della had gotten herself pregnant and was insistent about keeping the child.

Her boyfriend, Joe Hoeffer, became her first husband. Della was a beautiful young bride, yet she chose not to wear a wedding gown; she slipped on a short white dress and a headband, and her reception was just for family. They had some spiked punch and wedding cake at the Mello house, and that was it.

Della was nineteen, so was Joe, and predictably the marriage didn't last long. But it lasted long enough to bring Shawn into the world and to start a life together in an apartment on Queen City Avenue, in a run-down section of Western Hills.

Neighbors remember the Hoeffers as a happy couple, as young people with a zest for life, but that really wasn't the case. Behind closed doors, Della was miserable at home, and she made Joe's life pure hell. She didn't make the bed, she only cooked frozen TV dinners, and she hardly paid attention to Shawn. She was a rotten mother, by most accounts, and she loathed domestic life.

Part of the problem was that Della had been diagnosed with scoliosis, and as a newlywed, she had to undergo surgery and have a metal rod implanted in her spine. For months she wore a body cast, and even though she could walk and still had the full use of her hands, Della stayed in bed. At first Olga felt bad for her and would sometimes visit and handle the housework, but that got old after a while, especially since Olga had little Scott and Carla to take care of, who were both in elementary school.

Soon it became Cheryl's turn to help. Having rebelled against her mom's strict rules, she left home at age seventeen and moved in with her big sister, who had already filed for divorce and was going through a bitter custody battle. To carry her own weight, Cheryl worked at a burger joint, and whenever she could, she took care of Shawn. The household chores were designated as Cheryl's responsibility—Della just refused to have anything to do with that—which only caused fights and problems.

"She was a horrible mother with Shawn," Cheryl confided. "She would leave her alone in a place that was filthy. There was bird poop everywhere, bugs flying around, and crap would be everywhere. You couldn't walk in the kitchen, there were so many bags of her garbage."

In October 1972, a divorce petition was filed and an investigation was under way by the Hamilton County Court of Domestic Relations to determine who would receive custody of Shawn. Della and Joe had been married a little over two years, and their differences were irreconcilable.

"I remember my father banging on the door," Shawn reflected. "I remember Mom putting one of our kitchen chairs against the door and standing on it. She was screaming, and she threw a plate and it broke. I can remember standing there crying and looking at the plate."

At the time, Shawn was just two and a half; the kitchen scene was her first vivid memory. Of course, she wasn't sure what any of it meant until she got a little older. By the time she was four, the custody squabbles were in full swing, and Shawn was caught in the center.

To domestic relations investigators, Joe Hoeffer complained bitterly about child neglect, stating that while he was at work all day, his wife did not keep the child clean, that he had become aware that she left Shawn unattended. He felt Della did not understand the duties of a wife. He explained that in the time when Della had been in a cast, an eight-month period, he had taken

Shawn to their neighbor, Mrs. Bailey, for child care. Now he wanted custody of the child, with the provision that Mrs. Bailey's day care would be acceptable. He was going to try to arrange it.

Della, the plaintiff in the case, told the domestic relations official that her husband was coldhearted, that he didn't care about anything but himself. She said they would argue about important issues and Joe would just laugh at her; he would think it was funny. She complained that when he came home from work, Joe would not even say so much as hi.

When Della finally told him she was leaving—because the baby was biting her nails and becoming a nervous wreck—she had her sister Cheryl move in for support. Della wanted full custody of Shawn and a full disclosure of Joe's finances. She said she would not consider going on welfare, and even though Joe was struggling, living in an unfurnished apartment and working an entry-level job, she expected to receive full child support payments.

"She was the most piss-poor mother you'd ever seen in your life," Cheryl confided, "and she only wanted custody because Joe wanted her. It was a revenge thing. Della wanted to win. That's all it was."

CHAPTER | 48

W HEN THE DIVORCE WAS GRANTED IN 1973, THE ONLY assets the couple had were his 1970 Maverick and her 1964 Ford. Joe was ordered to pay $20 a week in child support and was permitted "reasonable" visitation with Shawn.

Three years later, Joe petitioned for a post-decree custody hearing, citing the "deplorable home situation"
Shawn lived in with Della. By then Joe was remarried,
and he and his wife were determined to save the poor
little girl. They felt it was absolutely necessary, because
from what they had seen, Shawn had no proper diet, no
decent clothing, was frequently ill, and was suffering
from a general lack of parental supervision.

Back then, little Shawn was living with her mother
and her stepfather, Jim Beyer, in a two-bedroom house
over on Gerold Drive. The six-year-old had her own
room, her own double bed, a furnished basement to play
in, and a homemade swing set and treehouse in the
backyard. Jim worked full-time with the Cincinnati
Sewer Department, Della was a full-time mom, and they
seemed to have a good marriage, having already been
wed for two years.

But even in the months prior to their wedding, Shawn
found herself being pulled between two sets of parents.
The child was increasingly torn between Della and Joe,
and in fact none of the parental figures were making it
easy on her. Della and Jim had one set of rules, and Joe
and Valerie had another. There had been problems with
visitation from the beginning, the Hoeffers often complaining about Shawn's general appearance, accusing
Della of abusing alcohol and drugs, of ignoring her
child's basic needs. Della denied this, insisting she only
had an "occasional drink." She felt the Beyers were
being completely unrealistic to want Shawn "dressed like
a princess all the time."

Della insisted that Shawn stay with her. She loved the
child, Shawn was happy in her home, and she was promising her daughter a play house and a piano, if only she
would stop whining so much. Della attacked Valerie for
being a "bad stepmother" who tried to interfere with
Shawn's prayer, actions, and general behavior. She believed that the Hoeffers were causing Shawn's emotional

problems, stating that Shawn would "talk back" to her stepdad whenever she returned from a visit.

Della complained that whenever she sent Shawn to the Hoeffers in new clothes, the items were always returned with stains. She further griped that Valerie was insisting on doing things like cutting Shawn's hair without Della's permission. Valerie countered that Della allowed one of her neighbors to "butcher" Shawn's hair.

Shawn told social workers that she loved all four parties involved; the child didn't complain about much of anything. She described herself as being well taken care of at her mom's home. When social workers asked about her meals, Shawn said that for breakfast she had a choice of cereal, pancakes, and sometimes eggs; for lunch she had sandwiches; for dinner she ate standing on a stool over the sink, because Della didn't want her to "make a mess." She admitted that it upset her to eat alone while her parents had their dinner in the bedroom, mentioning that at her dad's everyone ate together.

Regarding her grooming, Shawn talked about both her mother and her stepmother cutting her hair too much. She reported that her mother washed her hair every day in the shower, but said she was allowed to "use more water in the tub" at her dad's. She admitted that her mother sometimes sent her over to the Hoeffers in dirty clothes.

At the tender age of six, Shawn was subjected to adult problems, aware of the heated arguments between these four resentful adults. She spoke specifically of the fights between Jim and her mother which she overheard at night, and told caseworkers that she would "pull the covers over" and hold her ears shut so she couldn't hear them arguing about her.

"Valerie keeps lying and says my mom is a bad mom," she told one investigator. But later Shawn admitted that for punishment Della hit her, and sometimes slapped her in the face.

At that time, Della was twenty-six, and her husband,

Jim, also twenty-six, was earning $12,000 a year at the Sewer Department; the two of them seemed mature and settled enough to provide a stable home for Shawn. The Beyers were eventually deemed "adequate parents" by the psychiatrist who interviewed them for the Domestic Relations Court, but the battle over Shawn continued, and the Hoeffers petitioned the court again in July 1977.

In her desperate plea, Valerie wrote a letter to the judge trying to justify the reasons why Shawn should not live with her mother. In it, she pointed out that not all cases involved "battered" and "starved" children, insisting that Shawn would be "better off" in the Hoeffers' custody. She described Shawn as living "in constant fear" of her mother. She felt that justice hadn't been served, that by allowing Shawn to live with Della, the court was sentencing her to a troubled, unstable childhood.

Interestingly enough, Olga had testified against Della in the initial court proceedings, telling the court that her daughter was an unfit mom. Della wasn't surprised that Olga was supporting Joe and Valerie's suit against her, explaining to the court that her mother was "mean and cruel, just like Valerie."

For the record, Della stated that her mother was an impossible woman who ran her father "into the ground," and reported that when she was sixteen, she had run away and gone to the YMCA because her mother tried to take over her life. She told the judge that five out of seven of Olga's children had run away, and stated that her daughter, Shawn, was completely terrified of the woman.

Ultimately, the court ruled in Della's favor. After all, she was the girl's birth mother.

But before Shawn reached age nine, things had changed tremendously for Della. She had split from Jim Beyer and was living in a studio apartment, in a place that didn't allow children, and she had a new boyfriend,

Sid Davis,* who was rather wild and into the drug scene. With no income other than drug money, Della was practically destitute.

Along the way, she had decided to sign over custody of Shawn to Joe and Valerie—they could more readily afford to keep the girl. But an agreement was drawn up between the parties that allowed Shawn to return to Della—just as soon as her mom had enough money to provide her a place to sleep.

CHAPTER 49

DELLA REALLY CHANGED AFTER SHE STARTED CLASSES at the Barbizon School for Modeling. Shawn remembers how all of a sudden her mother became a sophisticated lady, focusing on makeup and clothes like never before. Shawn was only seeing her on visitations at that time. She was a ten-year-old kid. She felt funny about the way her mother dressed; it was too formal, and somewhat out of place. Della even tried to dress Shawn up to make the girl look older, which Shawn disliked. By the time Shawn was eleven, Della had her wearing satin pants outfits and was fixing her makeup.

Unfortunately, those makeup sessions were just for kicks, because whenever Shawn visited her mom's Queen City apartment complex, the girl was rarely taken out. Most nights, Della would leave her there unattended, and Shawn had to fix her own dinner and find a way to occupy herself. Della was spending all her time with Sid, but Shawn wasn't allowed to visit his place. Whenever Sid would drop by, she'd hear words like "coke" and "pot," but she thought they were talking about soda. It took years before Shawn figured out that her mom was into drugs.

Sid was sweet to Shawn—he called her Shawnster—and tooled her around in his Datsun sports car, always slipping her money for little goodies. On Saturdays he and Della would occasionally take Shawn to the zoo or the state fairgrounds. Shawn relished her time with them, especially because she thought things were getting so strict and unreasonable around the Hoeffer house. Valerie was grounding her all the time. Shawn was being scolded for not practicing her piano, being punished for refusing to wear corrective shoes. Shawn began to hate her stepmother and wished Della would take her back.

"I wanted to climb trees and play in the dirt," Shawn confided. "I was a tomboy, but for Valerie, that was no good. I remember her coming down on me really hard for stupid things like that."

When Shawn turned ten, Valerie and Joe had a son of their own, who suddenly seemed to Shawn to be their favorite. Shawn seemed to be the one who got punished all the time; she was their problem child, and her step-mom eventually decided that Shawn might have some kind of neurological problem. She and Joe decided to put the girl through a series of CAT scans and EEGs, hoping to find a medical remedy for her bad behavior.

"They did all kinds of testing on me," Shawn remembered, "and they found out that I was fine, that there was something wrong with my family. And when the doctors said that, Valerie just blew up. She turned red in the face. She couldn't believe she spent all this money to find out what was wrong with me, and here they are telling her she needs family counseling."

Shawn remembers many times when Valerie and her dad would fight and she would wind up being blamed. Apparently Joe didn't always agree with the way Valerie was handling Shawn, and it was causing a lot of grief at home. The upshot was, as Shawn tells it, she would get scolded for no reason.

"I was never allowed to watch TV," she recalled. "Valerie would yell at me all the time."

Shawn would hide in her room and listen to *General Hospital* on her transistor radio, often staying hidden there through dinner, eventually crying herself to sleep. Shawn loved her half-brother, Brian. But the way Valerie openly favored him, Shawn's natural sibling rivalry was exacerbated.

Unhappy with her situation, Shawn eventually spoke to a caseworker at school, and it was determined that she should be moved into foster care. A family conference was held, and although she was hesitant to leave her brother Brian, within months Shawn adjusted to her new family. Luckily, things worked out for her, and Shawn was officially adopted by the loving couple, moving with them to Indiana.

Della kept in touch with her every now and then, but it wasn't ever the same. Della was having quite a tumultuous relationship with Sid, and she just didn't have time for Shawn anymore.

PART FIVE | The Men

CHAPTER | 50

"**T**ODAY, SID DID BUNCHES OF ROTTEN STUFF," DELLA whispered to the tape recorder. She was taping one of their lovemaking sessions. She wanted to save it forever.

"No, I didn't," his voice answered.

"You called Paula twice in the last two weeks."

"Did not."

"Four times in the last two weeks."

"Did not."

"You told her you were gonna bring over some wine, gonna smoke dope and hang around."

"Did not."

"And had a nice long talk with Debbie, for hours and hours."

"Did not, you nasty mo-fo."

"And she told me exactly what a nasty mo-fo you was."

"I ain't no nasty mo-fo."

"So, we're having a nice time, his last night here," Della told the tape, as she giggled, started tickling him, suddenly breaking out in a child's voice, singing, "Oh, camptown races, sing this song, do-dah, do-dah."

"We're just a bunch of wild junkies, you and me," Sid

told her. "You can't do nothin' when you ain't got nothin', right, man?"

"And Sid knows about nothin'. Ain't got nothin'. Don't look like nothin'. Ain't goin' nowhere."

"But I got an awful good dick, don't I? I just sling that wild juice, man."

"Hits the walls, the ceiling. Juice everywhere."

"Juice city, you know, man?"

"Even juice in my ear once," she said, laughing. "Hey, watch it, tape recorder, he's gonna juice all over you now. He's getting his dick out."

"Okay. Tell me how nasty you are."

"Are you taking an interview? Is this a survey?"

"No, this ain't no survey. I just wanna know how nasty you really are."

"Sexwise? Well, let's see. I'm a pretty good fuck."

"Um-hmm."

"I can spank."

"Um-hmm. And you know, you got one of the tightest pussies I've ever had."

"I've heard that a million times."

"Hey, you still got that tape going?" he blurted.

"Yeah."

"Well, let me see it."

And the machine clicked off.

CHAPTER | 51

"Sid, you know the people. Go do it. Get her out of your life," friends would tell him.

"I can't live with her life on my conscience," Sid would insist. "She's just not worth it."

"Nobody believed the things I went through," Sid admitted. "Basically, it's like I was abused. You know, I was approached with three thousand cash in my hand to have her put her away."

Every time Della came around begging for a favor, Sid was always there for her. Just for spite, she would rat on him to his friends, then she'd come crawling back, claiming she never wanted to hurt him. It was an endless cycle.

Sid came from the bad side of Cincinnati, the kind of neighborhood where people were found dead in alleyways. Numerous times he had been approached to have Della knocked off; some of his drug friends were anxious to do it, but Sid never took the offers seriously.

Back then, in the late seventies, Sid was busy dating as many women as possible. He had a lot of luck picking them up in the discos. It was the pre-AIDS era, and most people considered one-night stands commonplace. Sid, a tall, muscular guy with long blond hair and chiseled features, had no trouble in that department. He was a swinging bachelor and he let women know that. With Della, there was always the understanding that he didn't love her. He refused to use that word, even when they were in bed.

Sid knew he intimidated women in nightclubs, so he would pick a target, zero in on the girl, and friends would always be amazed. He'd score every time. He could get, pretty much, anyone he wanted. Even though he was a railroad worker, when he dressed up at night he looked like a millionaire. In those days, he wore Brooks Brothers suits, drove Cadillacs and sports cars, and was very GQ. Women flocked to him. When Della first laid eyes on him, she fell so hard for the handsome young man, she became determined to leave her husband. She started an affair with Sid long before her marriage ended, lying to Sid about her marital status.

She was the needy type, she needed to be taken care of, so it was no surprise that Della hung around Sid relentlessly. Finally she started to move in with him. It started as a gradual thing, with her leaving bits and pieces of herself around his apartment. When Jim Beyer came pounding on the door one day, Sid found out the young lady was still married, but he didn't really care. He made it clear to her that he was just in it for the ride.

Della's divorce with Jim was finalized on September 20, 1979. Jim, the plaintiff, received the house on Gerold Drive; Della was divested of any right to it. In addition, Jim was deemed responsible for $750 of expenses toward Della's Mustang; $2,300 worth of lawyer's fees incurred for a previously aborted dissolution settlement; $126.51 to Master Card; and $432 to Deaconess Hospital for Della's cosmetic surgery. It was a quick and easy settlement, because Della didn't contest anything. She was pleased to have it over with, and loving every minute of her life with Sid.

Sid seemed rather happy to have such an attractive woman by his side. Della was quite an eye-catcher, especially in the dim lighting of a nightclub. But once they started living together, he noticed she was kind of like a genie in a bottle. She would drive him nuts with her makeup and beauty routines, but Sid tolerated it. Della really looked horrible when she woke up in the morning; she needed to put on all that glop before she could emerge and face the outside world.

When they first got serious, toward the summer of 1979, Sid was feeling really sorry for Della. He had taken her down to Disney World and he realized she was like a little kid; she needed to have her hand held all the time. She was the little chick that fell out of the nest; she needed a mommy and daddy. In their sex life, she liked to play "little girl" and wanted to be dominated and spanked. She wanted to role-play, acting like she was Sid's daughter, dressing up in little frilly outfits with garter belts underneath. She was creative in bed, even if she was ice-cold as a lover.

Before things turned sour between them, before Della's jealousy got out of control, on more than one occasion, Sid claims, she tried to have him killed. The first time, she had hired a couple of thugs to wait for Sid outside a nightclub called Lucy in the Sky. When one of the bouncers got wind of the trouble brewing in the parking lot, he escorted Sid out the back door. "I knew of two times where my life was in jeopardy," Sid confided. "Actually three, if you count the guys down at Lucy's."

In the beginning, Sid figured Della just didn't know what life was all about. He was an easygoing guy and never believed Della was out to kill him. He prided himself on not being violent, and whatever Della pulled, he just ignored it. Of course, deep down, he questioned her sincerity, especially when he considered the way she treated Shawn. The little girl was so bubbly, so deserving of attention, yet Della didn't seem to notice. Her attitude was that she didn't want anything to do with Shawn if it included Joe, period.

Della complained to Sid about a lack of family support. Sid himself was a twenty-five-year-old kid at the time; he was naive, and he believed her story. He just wanted to help. But even before they started living together, Della was accusing him of bedding every girl that walked by. To Sid, it was incredible. For the first time in his life he was being monogamous, but he had this nutty girlfriend who was totally paranoid. They got into many heated arguments about it, and then, days before she was scheduled to move in, she dropped by his place with a kerosene lamp and a plan for a romantic dinner. The poor guy thought she was trying to win him over; he didn't realize anything was wrong until he awoke in the middle of the night with his sheets on fire.

"We went to bed, and she climbs in with all her clothes on," Sid recounted. "She said she forgot she had her clothes on, which didn't make a whole lot of sense, but I was too drunk to really argue with her, so basically, we went to sleep. With the wine and smoking pot and things like that, she thought I passed out cold. And apparently she got up, turned the TV on, put an ashtray with a cigarette butt in my bed, put an empty whiskey bottle next to it, and then lit the kerosene lamp and slid it under the bedspread."

Sid literally woke up with his backside on fire. His bed was burning, the mattress was on fire, and Della was nowhere to be found. Sid's underwear was singed, he could smell flesh burning, but luckily he didn't suffer any severe injuries. His left cheek was just very red and sore for a while.

"If I would have been passed out and lying on the other side of the bed from where the fire started," he reflected, "I wouldn't have gotten out. I would have burned up in the place and they'd have come and dragged my corpse out of there. They would have done an autopsy and thought I got blitzed, fell asleep with a cigarette, and burned myself up."

Sid was so freaked out by the incident, he decided to try lighting the bed on fire himself, just to see how much time Della would have had to get away from the fire. When he relit the kerosene lamp and set it up under the already burned bedspread, it took seventeen minutes for the thing to catch fire. He realized that was just enough time for Della to go home, talk to her doorman and create an alibi, then climb safely into her own bed.

The next day, when Sid confronted her, Della just laughed.

"What the hell are you doing? Trying to kill me *in my bed*?"

"I have no idea what you're talking about," she said.

"You left last night and you put the kerosene lamp up against my bed. It would take a moron not to figure out what you were doing."

"Everything was fine when I left, Sid. I just couldn't sleep, so I decided to go home. You were passed out."

"Well, the corner of my mattress was burned. It's all black. I had to go out this morning and chuck the mattress and bedspread."

"Well, I had nothing to do with it. I'm sorry if you fell asleep."

"Like *hell*, you didn't."

CHAPTER 52

AFTER THE BURNING BED INCIDENT, SOMEHOW, DELLA weaseled her way back into Sid's life. They were on the phone fighting every other day, and she was playing the "poor pitiful me" act to the hilt. It didn't take long before Sid was sucked back in. He had no idea why he decided to let her move into his apartment.

"After all that had happened, after I knew what she tried to do," Sid said. "She reasoned out that I was some kind of pervert and tried to smoke me, but I gave her credit because the plan, the plot, was great. She had to be pretty devious. Her little head was just cooking away."

But things didn't seem to work out for the couple. Their living situation was unacceptable; Della was extraordinarily possessive. Sid thought they should remain a couple, but he asked her to find her own place. Della was just too nosy, too much of a problem around the apartment. Even after she moved out, the girl would come snooping around in the middle of the night. Sid would hear a noise at 2:00 or 3:00 in the morning, and he'd go downstairs and find the sliding door open, but no one would be down there. Sometimes he'd pull in from a disco around 4:00 A.M. and he'd spot Della's car in the parking lot.

He wasn't sure what exactly she was doing for money, but he'd see her hanging all over men at high-class places like the Precinct, where she'd be dirty dancing and carrying on. And somehow she moved herself into a ritzy apartment in Price Hill. Della had a sweeping view of the city, yet there was no way she was paying the money for it.

When Sid went up to Michigan with a buddy for a weekend fishing trip, he came home to find his apartment had been completely trashed. There was water throughout the place; two full aquariums had been dumped over, thousands of baby angel fish were dead, all his huge plants had been chopped down, the telephones were drowned in the bathtub, the TV was kicked in, all the barnwood shelves were torn down, all the photos were taken off the walls and destroyed, and the iron and toaster were stuffed in the toilet, plugged into an electrical outlet in the bathroom.

It wasn't the first time Sid's apartment had been tampered with. A few weeks earlier, his apartment had been broken into and some of his things had been destroyed. It happened while he was upstairs visiting a female friend and having pizza; when he got back, his plants had been knocked over, water had been spilled, his jackets were ripped up, and his pet, a parrot named Villain, had flown away.

He went up to see Della at Queens Tower to confront her, but he found her to be practically dying, she was so sick. Della was puking, completely dehydrated, and Sid wound up spending two days with her, nursing her back to health. At first he was only going to bring her to an emergency room, but the doctors were so concerned for Della, they loaded her with antibiotics and insisted she have someone look after her. Sid felt obligated.

"What am I going to do about the situation?" he asked his cousin as soon as he had the chance.

"Let me give you a piece of advice," the cousin said. "*Run*, don't walk. Just stay away from her. Get as far as you can."

But Sid didn't listen. Even though his cousin was a psychologist, even though he had been told the relationship was sick, Sid felt drawn to Della. He had a lot of compassion, he believed she'd been abused as a child, and wanted to save her. Even after his place was entirely destroyed the second time, he felt obliged to believe Della.

The dishes were broken, the terrarium had been contaminated, he lost everything he ever loved, but Della denied her involvement. It was the end of 1979, he was just turning twenty-six, and Sid found himself starting from scratch.

He got himself a roommate and an apartment in trendy Mt. Lookout, and for about six weeks he didn't hear from her. Then she showed up at his doorstep. She had no place to go, and Sid agreed to allow her to stay for a week, just until she got on her feet.

"This girl had a Teflon life," Sid reflected. "She could do things without any recourse. When she showed up at my new place, I started to get paranoid about her. I couldn't believe she was that smart. That she was able to do all these things without getting caught."

CHAPTER | 53

IT DIDN'T TAKE LONG FOR DELLA TO GET SID BACK UNDER her thumb. Not only couldn't he have girlfriends around, he couldn't have any friends, period. His roommate was away on business most of the time, so that left Della in charge.

"All of a sudden, the possessive crap started again," Sid confided. "I'd go to the grocery store and get accused of meeting somebody. I had to start using codes to call my mom. It was ridiculous. I couldn't even talk to my friends anymore, because she called people and threatened to come out and kill them. They were in fear of this lunatic."

Sid was losing friends, was completely fed up with Della. Then one afternoon while he was puttering around the basement, looking through her junk he stumbled on his old wallet. It was the proof he'd been waiting for, and as he dug through her boxes, he discovered many of the items that had been missing out of his old apartment.

"Get your shit and get out of here," he yelled as he came pounding up the stairs. "I want your fuckin' little ass out of this house."

"What's your problem, Sid?"

"Here! Here's the problem!"

He shoved the wallet in her face and backed her into a corner. Della started screaming and let herself out onto the back deck. The next thing Sid knew, she was yelling rape.

"You can stand there and yell all you want," Sid said, laughing. "I've got to go. I've got to get ready. I want you physically gone from here by the time I come back.'"

But while Sid was busy shaving, Della dialed the cops. She reported a rape and suddenly a team of officers entered Sid's home, questioning him about beating Della.

"Take a good look at this woman," Sid told them. "She's ninety-eight pounds soaking wet, and do you see anything wrong with her? Do you see a bruise on her?"

The officers were stumped. Della seemed fine, there was no indication of rape or foul play, and they sat down with the couple and made them promise not to fight. Sid told the cops to go down to his basement and check certain items that matched a police report on a theft he'd reported, but the cops didn't want to hear it. That wasn't their problem. They suggested that the couple keep cool; if not, they would file warrants for both their arrests.

Sid clammed up and decided to let Della stick around. He was still on disability back then—he had a major lawsuit pending against the railroad for a job-related injury and there was $185,000 at stake, so the last thing he needed was to jeopardize it with a bogus arrest report. He was coming close to trial and he was counting on that money. He had his case all lined up with a top attorney out of St. Louis. Unfortunately, what Sid didn't know was that Della had been in touch with the railroad company. She was promising to cooperate with their lawyers. Sid also thinks she set him up to be busted.

"We were going up to Mt. Adams to do some partying," Sid recalled. "We were driving up this very steep hill in the MGB, and all of a sudden the guy in front of me slams on his brakes, and the next thing I know, I have cops all around the car, pointing their guns at me."

The narcotics unit removed Sid and Della from the vehicle and found a half gram of cocaine under the driver's seat. They hauled Sid downtown, and while he was at police headquarters, Sid says Della took the narcotics unit on a little tour of his house, showing officers exactly where her drug-dealer friend kept his stash of pot and coke.

"They thought I was some big-time drug dealer," Sid confided. "They walked in and threw this bag in front of me, with all this coke and grinders and other stuff, and I was just wondering how the thing went down. I didn't really think she could have done that, not at the time."

From his jail cell, Sid landed himself one of Cincinnati's flashiest attorneys, Phil Pitzer, a city slicker who handled high-profile drug cases. Pitzer was hopeful that Sid would beat the rap, he got Sid released on bail. Della, meanwhile, said she needed to leave town—that a friend of hers had a sick mother she needed to attend to—and she packed her overnight bags. Sid was thrilled, glad to be rid of her for once—that is, until the phone rang just minutes after she backed out of the driveway. It was Lance Callas, his attorney in St. Louis, calling with bad news.

"Hey, Sid, what the hell's going on up there? Do you know your girlfriend's testifying against you tomorrow at noon?"

"What are you talking about?"

"I'm talking about Della Beyer. We go to court next Monday, and she's testifying against you in a deposition *tomorrow*."

"Oh, shit, you've got to be kidding me."

"Where's she at?"

"She just backed out of the driveway."

"Well, jump in the car and try to track her down. You've got to catch her."

"How the hell would I know where to find her?"

"Just do it, man. Otherwise she's gonna take the stand about this drug thing, and you not only will lose the case, you could lose your job, your seniority. You could wind up losing everything."

Sid called Della's mom, checked with her girlfriends, even went out to the airport. But it was all a waste of time.

CHAPTER 54

DURING HER DEPOSITION, DELLA TESTIFIED THAT SID was faking his injuries. She was asked by Lance Callas about Sid's drug arrest, about whether she had anything to do with it. Of course she vehemently denied prior knowledge.

In the end, Sid Davis took a settlement of $70,000 from the railroad. For the drug charges, he was sentenced to serve forty-five days in prison and was granted a week's stay of execution to get some of his affairs in order. Della had returned to Ohio and was planning a move to Florida. On the day Sid was turning himself in, she offered to drop him off at jail, then took off in her Mustang, ready to start a new life.

People thought Sid would kill her when he got out, but he just wasn't the vengeful type. As fortune would have it, Sid wound up a partner in a consulting business, and his headquarters became 1 Lytle Place, one of the high-end buildings in downtown Cincinnati, overlooking the river and the stadium. After taxes and legal fees, he had cleared $40,000 in cash from his settlement, he had invested the money wisely, and the next thing Sid knew, he was rubbing elbows with players from the Cincinnati

Bengals. It was 1981, the year the team went to the Super Bowl, so he was really flying high.

He and his business partner, Kevin, had gotten themselves a two-bedroom apartment in the Lytle Place tower, and they scheduled parties once a month, entertaining as many as three hundred people at a shot. There were still a lot of wild times. Sid had earned back everything he lost, and then some, so for Sid, life was good.

The Bengals had a big party as they were headed into the playoffs, and Wilson Whitland hosted the event, a black-tie affair at the Lytle Place pool. All the local media people were there—including Jerry Springer—and then there was Della, all dolled up and looking more youthful and stunning than ever.

Della was surrounded by men, and the minute she spotted Sid, she ordered one of her escorts to walk over and push Sid into the pool. Wilson Whitland, who watched Sid emerge soaking wet in his tux, promptly escorted Della and her cronies out of the party.

Two weeks later, Della popped up at Sid's Lytle Place apartment. Of all people, she was dating Sid's partner, Kevin. The two of them had heated arguments about it, Kevin insisting that it wasn't serious, that he was just sleeping with her, Sid adamant that he really didn't want the bitch hanging around.

"You think you're so smart?" Sid asked when he caught her alone for a minute. "Well, let me tell you something, Della. I can smell your stinky ass coming down the hallway, and you're not going to get away with this shit."

"I'm not Della anymore, I'm Dante."

"You're about as much Dante as the fairy queen," he sneered. "You're always Della to me, so what's your point? Just leave me alone. Just get out of my sight."

"You know, Sid, the police thought it was so funny when I took them around your house," she confided. "You should have seen their faces. They really got a kick out of it."

"You lying little bitch."

"I should have finished you off when I had the chance, you stupid bastard!"

"I don't remember exactly what happened," Sid admitted, "but the day she was yelling about the supposed rape, she picked up a kitchen knife and started walking toward me. She had a box of electric curlers sitting next to the sink in the kitchen, and I picked it up and promptly hit her with it and then took the knife away. That was when we were arguing, before she called the police."

CHAPTER | 55

DANTE HAD AFFAIRS AND FLEETING ASSOCIATIONS WITH countless men after Sid. There were all kinds of rumors floating around about her, one being that she was in love with Dr. Henry Heimlich, of the Heimlich maneuver fame, but as far as anyone knew she'd barely met him. Dante had quite a reputation; she was always on the prowl, spending time going on singles cruises and hanging around popular bars. For a while she even worked as a waitress at The Conservatory, a big singles meat market in Covington.

Dante always had to have a man, and once she made up her mind she wanted someone, she was like white on rice. Her only criterion: The guy had to be rich. She studied books about how to marry a millionaire. She practiced at standing erect, worked at maintaining eye contact, and pretended to project enthusiasm. Her best friend, Connie, once caught her standing in the mirror, studying her facial expressions. Dante was working at looking interested.

Dante spent time familiarizing herself with the most expensive designers. She'd go to Saks and try on clothes that cost over $500 apiece, memorizing the labels. She'd spend hours trying on expensive jewelry, go to showrooms and sit in luxury cars, and do anything to appear rich. With every man she met, she shared her discriminating tastes, and by and large they gave her the money and presents to support her purported lifestyle.

Olga found it revolting. Della would call every now and then, looking for a handout, and sometimes Olga would give in, but for the most part she was working hard at her own dry-cleaning business, and when Della was starving, she didn't want to bother with her. The girl never worked, yet she'd come around wearing designer clothes and expect Olga to dry-clean them for free. Olga let Della get away with that game for years, even though the dry-cleaning was sent out and cost her money.

It didn't take Dante long to get involved with Brian Powell,* a good-looking blond guy she met at The Conservatory just before Christmas 1981. They dated for a while and wound up living together. Their relationship lasted almost two years. At first Brian found his girlfriend's jealousy flattering, even amusing. Dante was so in love with him, so certain every woman walking down the street wanted him.

But she refused to do any work around the house, wouldn't even wash dishes, and after a while Brian decided they shouldn't live together anymore. He still wanted to be lovers, and Dante went along with that, but then Brian started dating other people, which didn't sit well with her at all. She was refusing to move out of his house, and finally he had to promise her rent-free living in one of his smaller homes just to pacify her. Brian was a successful contractor, building and selling houses for a living, and Dante knew he could afford it. Over the course of their relationship, her things wound up spread among three of his places—two of his homes and his storage facility.

By the time Dante moved herself back into an apartment downtown, Brian had become involved with a woman from Indiana; the two of them had started out as tennis partners. But one evening, as Brian was pulling out of the Westside Tennis Club, his new girlfriend realized they were being followed. She claimed it didn't bother her, but she must have gotten spooked, because she stopped calling him shortly thereafter.

"The same car's still behind us," she said, frightened. "It's the one with the dim headlights."

"I know who it is," Brian told her. "She's no one to worry about."

But as they had merged onto the expressway with the little green car following, going eighty miles an hour, Brian's new girlfriend was getting visibly upset. He was having trouble losing Dante.

When both cars wound up being pulled over by the cops, Brian said nothing as he was being written a ticket. He just wanted Dante to evaporate.

"Look, it's not gonna work out," he told Dante later. "It's just not working with us. It's over between me and you."

"Well, okay," she said. "We can just be friends."

"Yeah, we can be friends, as long as you don't get too involved."

Over the phone, Dante set up a plan for the two of them to meet at January's, a downtown nightspot. She wanted to see him and talk things out. Brian remembers it well. It was Friday the thirteenth, a hot August night, and he waited for two hours before Dante showed up. When she walked into the bar, she had a strange look on her face. She was the cat that swallowed the canary.

"You smell like smoke," Brian said. "Where you been?"

"Oh, I forgot where we were meeting. I thought we said the Conservatory, so I was over there looking for you."

"But you smell like a campfire or something."

"I guess it was really smoky over there."

After the two of them drank for a while, Dante talked Brian into spending the night with her; she had moved into her own apartment at 1 Lytle Place, and she was desperate for his company.

The next morning, Brian arrived back home to find his house gutted. The roof was burned off and everything he owned was gone.

When he called the fire marshals, they immediately determined it was an arson. The fire had been started up in his closet with charcoal fluid. Brian noticed that his tennis rackets were taken out of the garage and piled on top of his clothes. He couldn't imagine why someone would do that.

"The state fire marshal said it was definitely arson," Brian recounted. "He said it looked like a woman had done it, because the fire was started with clothes. If it was a man, usually they start it under a car, they burn something different."

Brian Powell's insurance company covered most of the damage, so he was trying to put the whole thing out of his mind. He was reluctant to think Dante had anything to do with it, even though one of the neighbors said he spotted a light green car, like hers, at the scene. Dante called Brian numerous times after the fire, offering her sympathy and help, but he really wasn't interested.

He was forced to move into one of his smaller houses, with no real furniture and a pile of burned items he was trying to salvage. His hands were covered in grit, virtually black, as he answered the phone to hear that Dante was feeling really sick, that she wanted to come over to see him.

"What are you doing?" she asked. "Can I help you do something?"

"Well, my back is killing me from bending over all day. I've been digging in the ashes, working on the list for the insurance company."

"I could bring you over some Bufferin. I have to go to the drugstore anyway, 'cause I'm coming down with something. I feel really horrible."

When Dante appeared with her care package, Brian thought it was odd. She never cared for him in this way before. She offered to nurse him, insisting that he take a break and rest for a while, and Brian considered a change of heart. Maybe he was wrong about her. She was being sweet, rubbing his head and bringing him some tablets with a big glass of water. They both took their pills and fell asleep; Brian went out like a light.

But he awoke the next morning and looked around in horror. What little he had left was gone. He had just bought a shaving kit and a few packs of underwear, and he'd had $500 in his wallet—all of it was missing. He still didn't want to believe that Dante could have burned his house down, but he called to question her.

"I was feeling better," she said, "and you were sound asleep, so I left."

"Well, I was robbed, Dante. Everything was stolen but the underwear I was wearing."

"I must have left the door open. I'm sorry. Someone must have come in after I left."

"If you think I believe that somebody else came into my house and stole my shaving gear and my underwear and reached under my mattress and got my wallet while I was sleeping on the bed, you're crazy."

"Well, that has to be what happened."

About a week after the robbery, Dante called to report that she was pregnant. She needed Brian to make a decision about marrying her, because she wanted to keep the baby.

"You're pregnant? Well, congratulations. Who's the lucky father?"

"You are, Brian. You know I haven't been with anyone but you."

"Well, I'm sorry. I know I haven't touched you since
your last period, 'cause I was afraid this was gonna happen, and I've been keeping track of it."

For what seemed like eternity, there was complete silence on the other end of the line.

"This is *your* baby, you fucking bastard. Why don't
you believe me? You know, I figured you would try to
walk away from this. I should've killed you when I had
the chance," she whispered, her voice deepening. "I had
a butcher knife at your throat and I just didn't have the
nerve to do it."

Dante slammed down the phone, but then dialed him
back a minute later.

"What're you doing tonight?" she asked.

"It's none of your business."

"I'm gonna have somebody come out and get you."

"Well, you know where I live. Come on over."

That evening, Brian locked all his windows and doors.
He took the phone off the hook, left the TV on, and
stayed out late. On the way home, about 3:00 in the
morning, he pulled his car over and slept in a parking
lot.

Dante called the next day, laughing about the game
he was playing with the phone and the TV. She thought
it was hysterical. For weeks she kept calling and threatening, until finally Brian was forced to play back one of
her conversations to her, telling her he'd been taping all
their talks. He claimed he had her caught on tape talking
about the knife she'd had to his throat.

And she disappeared from his life.

CHAPTER | 56

WHEN DELLA PACKED UP HER GREEN FALCON AND headed for California, she told her family she was tired of her mediocre existence in Ohio. It was time for a fresh start, and Donna had invited her out there. She hoped that she might get into acting. She wanted to be in front of the cameras; she needed the spotlight.

The minute she arrived in La Verne, a small town just outside Los Angeles, she was thoroughly annoyed by Donna's insistence that she find herself a job. They discussed it, and after much begging and pleading, Della agreed to apply for a position at a nearby convalescent hospital. However, when the next day rolled around, Della refused to get out of the car. She sat at the curb at the hospital, proclaiming she'd get sick working in a depressing place like that.

For months the two sisters quarreled. Donna was working sixteen-hour shifts, while Della sat around sipping soda all day. It was 1984, Donna was a single mom back then, struggling to feed two kids, and the last thing she needed was a freeloader. Every once in a while Della would announce that she had a job, but then she would always quit after a few days.

As this temporary work pattern continued, Della would live by leaning on men. If she wasn't taken out to dinner, she wouldn't eat. What little food she did consume, she kept in her car; she was never one to share. Donna was anxious to get rid of her and was grateful to hear her announce that she planned to move

221

in with Terry Armstrong, some "great guy" she met over at the Hollywood Bowl.

The same week Della was preparing to move, Donna realized there was a $100 bill missing from her purse, so she searched her sister's car, where she found a man's wallet, underwear, shorts, and a partial dental plate. Poring over the creepy items, Donna broke out in a sweat. For a moment she stood holding the man's wallet, trying to memorize the name and address.

The Oklahoma driver's license pictured a white Caucasian, last name Taylor. She crammed the stuff back into the glove compartment and rushed inside to help her sister pack.

CHAPTER 57

WITHIN A WEEK OF MEETING HER, TERRY HAD INVITED Dante to become his roommate. The two lived together for about eight months, during which time he became increasingly fearful of her sudden fits of jealousy. On more than one occasion, Dante threatened him with a knife. The first time, it happened because he made a comment about a female dance group that he saw on the TV show *Solid Gold*.

Terry had a job as a painter in the movie industry. He worked on stage sets and lived not too far away from work, in a singles apartment complex in North Hollywood, just off the Santa Monica Freeway. Before Dante came along, his life was going along just fine, and then suddenly she made him feel inept, like nothing he said or did was good enough. She made fun of his living quarters, berated his job, and insisted he move up the ranks and improve his life.

"She just wanted money," Terry later told authorities. "She took some jewelry that I bought her and sold it. She said she had one abortion with me and supposedly got pregnant again, yet she didn't want me to take her to the doctor."

Dante was incredibly domineering, and it got to the point that Terry decided to leave her in his apartment alone. He'd sneak his clothes out and stay with his brother just to get a night's peace. Dante was just so possessive and devious, she drove him to the point of madness. But Terry was a gentleman, so no matter how much she pressed him, he could never hit her or physically fight back.

As they got more involved, Dante determined to make his life utterly miserable. She refused to let him socialize with the other workers on the set. She couldn't tolerate other women, she referred to the men as "scumbags," and she'd tell Terry he was a "faggot" for hanging around such people. Dante wanted to monopolize all of Terry's time; she was only happy when the two of them would spend time alone.

It was okay for them to go out to dinner or down to the beach, but God help him if he tried to bring her around his work buddies. She had a real issue about associating with working-class people. On the rare occasions when he'd bring her over to the set of *Dynasty* or *Love Boat,* all she seemed to care about was meeting TV stars. In front of his co-workers, she tried to make Terry feel like a worthless pauper.

Things got so bad, Terry decided to temporarily move in with his friend Sue. He and Dante were still trying to smooth things over, but then an incident happened at Sue's house that caused their permanent split. Apparently, someone brought cans of paint thinner and paint stain over to Sue's place and proceeded to write graffiti and smear the place. The vandals covered everything

Sue had with paint, including her valuable oriental rugs; plugged up the sinks and turned on all the water and stole Sue's jewelry, which Terry later recovered with Donna's help. Sue made a full police report, but nothing ever came of it. She couldn't fully prove Dante was the perpetrator.

After the vandalism, Terry was actively trying to help Dante move out of town. He says he had already been approached by her with a knife enough times to be seriously afraid of her. Even though she was no longer living at his place—she was renting a room in a boardinghouse in Pasadena—and even though Dante claimed she was no longer interested in him, saying that she was thinking of turning gay, that she really preferred women—Terry used all his power to encourage Dante to go back east. He was even hinting that he would help pay for her train ticket.

In his view, it was no coincidence that Dante was still in the picture the day he was headed up the hill toward Sue's house and his brakes wouldn't work. Luckily he was able to stop the car without killing himself. He had to spend $400 to have a mechanic tell him that motor oil had been poured in the brake system.

CHAPTER 58

WHEN SHAWN GOT A CALL TO PLEASE COME GET HER mother at the airport in Chicago, the girl grabbed her boyfriend and drove up there. She hadn't seen Della in years, and she'd forgotten what she even looked like. As she stood waiting in the terminal, she spotted a petite woman whom she tried to follow around for a few minutes, but it wasn't her mom.

When Della came waltzing over, Shawn couldn't believe her eyes. Her mother was completely transformed, unrecognizable, and it wasn't until Della flicked Shawn's bangs that Shawn was convinced. Shawn was already eighteen, and Della appreciated seeing her. She thanked her profusely for the favor, explaining she was just so frantic when she left California she had no time to make arrangements.

In the years Della had been out there, she had kept in touch with Shawn. There were various postcards, including one from Mexico, there were a couple of birthday cards, even a Christmas box with Warner Brothers makeup and a teddy bear, and most recently a pearl necklace for Shawn's high school graduation. Aunt Donna was the one who sent the money to pay for Shawn's graduation dress; Della just couldn't afford it.

As they chatted throughout the lengthy drive home, Della catching up on family news, Shawn was surprised by how different her mother seemed. Her brown hair was dyed blond; her teeth were whitened; she looked young, especially in her face; and she had developed a new accent. As "Dante," she sounded and acted uppity.

It was the summer of 1988, and immediately upon her return, Dante was introduced to Grant David Bassett at a downtown Cincinnati bar called Benjamin's. She was there with her girlfriend, Judy Gottadero, a Joan Collins look-alike and a successful commercial real estate woman with whom Grant had done business. Grant was instantly intrigued by Dante. She had a lot of great stories about Hollywood and life in Los Angeles. Grant had lived out there for a while himself, and he could tell Dante was a real player.

He was thirty-nine, she was thirty-eight, and from the moment they met, he was sure they were perfect for each other.

On their second date, Grant took Dante to a dance club across the river in Covington, but the minute he excused himself to the rest room, she landed herself a fifty-year-old guy, the type who wore his shirt unbuttoned to show off his chest hair and gold chains. Grant never questioned her about it, although he later found out the man was someone Dante had been casually seeing.

The next day, when Grant took her to an event called "Toys for Adults," an expensive boat and car show, Dante made a point of mentioning how many phone calls she had been getting from other men, including the gentleman from the previous evening. She made it seem like her phone rang constantly, like she was so popular she was feeling harassed.

Grant didn't know how to react. He wondered if Dante wanted him to be jealous. As they became more serious, he started to accept Dante's name-dropping as a given. There was always some guy in a club who was after her, there was always some rich man offering her a vacation or an expensive gift, and then, of course, there was always Jerry Springer, whom Dante talked about obsessively.

"You should see his legs when he's in his underwear, they're so skinny," she'd say. "He does the funniest things when he's walking around half naked. He's such a prankster."

Grant never tried to extract any further details—he didn't care to know Jerry Springer's personal business—but Dante could never stop talking about the man. His name would pop up all the time.

"Jerry would do it this way," Dante would argue, insisting, "Jerry is the smartest man on the face of the earth."

Grant worked upstairs in the same office building that housed Benjamin's, so he was a regular there, and he'd run into Dante all the time. She would usually be hanging out with Judy, who had a knockout apartment in the same building. Complete with a fireplace and a wrap-around view, it was filled with fine art pieces and sophisticated furniture. To Grant, it appeared Dante traveled strictly in the fast lane. She was running with a crowd of pretty rich people.

But that hadn't always been the case. When Dante described her ex-husbands, for example, she described Joe and Jim as "nerds." Neither of them did anything right. They were both bad in bed, neither of them had any taste. She preferred to talk about her experiences at places like Hearst Castle, and she talked a lot about Hollywood. Apparently, she spent a lot of time riding around in Corvettes and fancy sports cars, making it sound like she blew a lot of money out in Los Angeles. She intimated that she had been so caught up in the high life that she wound up coming back to Cincinnati without a dime.

When late September rolled around, Dante started hinting that she needed money for a coat, and Grant took her shopping. Even though he had just come out of a fifteen-year marriage and had sworn he wouldn't support another woman, the new coat became Dante's signal that Grant was taking her on as his personal financial responsibility. And before he knew it, Grant was not only paying for Dante's meals, he was shopping for all her needs at the plaza stores downtown. Not that he minded. "She was very appreciative," Grant recalled, "very babylike, very little-girlish."

So Grant enjoyed doing things for her. Dante gave him that warm, fuzzy feeling and he was definitely falling in love. Back then, in the late 1980s, he had a great job working for an expanding communications company, and things were booming. His corporation was planning to relocate him to Dallas, and he explained to Dante that he was on the verge of a big promotion, slated to be the company's troubleshooter.

With this new job in sight, Grant felt like he was finally going to cash in on all his years of hard work.

CHAPTER 59

Hi, Princess:

Well, I got this far, and it was so foggy and cloudy, so I decided to stop at this place and go on tomorrow. It's kind of funny. We've never been so far apart from one another, but I feel closer to you than ever before, baby. I love you!

I had a great time talking on the phone. You'd think we were on a date or something. If you thought, for a minute, I could write a letter without getting smushy, believe me, I'll get better. It's my #1 priority. You're my #1 everything, Princess!

Your friend, Partner, &
Clothes consultant,
GB

Grant was writing a love note from the Braddock Motor Inn in LaVale, Maryland. He was headed out of town on a business trip. It was one of his last before he would relocate to Dallas, and he sent along a check for her, attached to a little shopping list:

Hamburger Helper
Hamburger
1 Brown Bottle "Rut Beer"
1 Clear Bottle "Clear Soda"
1 Bag "Crunchy" Cheese Curls
1 Box "Kudos"
1 Can "Biscetti O's" (Clean the lid first)
1 Carton of "Quick" (Look for the latest date)

1 Loaf of Wheat Bread (Whole wheat)
1 Pkg. Danish Ham (It doesn't have fat in it)

That was his Rx to her. At the bottom of the list, he instructed her to "take the rest of the money to the bank."

When Dante received it, she was busy with her own list of "things to do today." She wrote:

abortion? 2 kinds?
tubes tied?
same day?
cost (approx?)
how soon?
Women's Center on McMillan
3 wks in between $350
not more than 12 wks   D&C

Grant and Dante were married in Irving, Texas, on March 13, 1989. There was no honeymoon, not even a quick trip to Vegas, because Dante wasn't interested in any of that.

"The wedding night was at the justice of the peace, she just wanted to get married quickly," Grant recounted. "She was pregnant, allegedly pregnant."

Their marriage was rocky from the start—Dante was unsettled, being new to everything in Dallas, and she complained bitterly about being strapped at home with morning sickness. Grant tried to appease her, suggesting they go out socializing with his new co-workers, but she would have no part of that. On their wedding night, she told him to go in her bedroom and get ready—she had her own "princess room" from which she emerged in a black lace teddy. After she seduced him, she went back to her own bed to get some sleep. She was too uncomfortable to share a bed with him all night.

"She was constantly sick," he confided. "If it wasn't morning sickness, her head ached, her back ached, there was any number of things. I didn't know what drugs she was taking, but I know Xanax was being used."

CHAPTER | 60

*T*HEY LIVED WITH CLOTHES IN BOXES FROM JANUARY TO March, Dante still pulling off the "princess" thing, though Grant was thinking of demoting her. He couldn't get near her door without being screamed at; she didn't want him to even knock. They did a lot of shopping; that was how Dante liked to spend her time—buying and returning things. She was obsessed with the Galleria, with charging items on credit, keeping them at home for a while, then ultimately taking them back. She could never make a decision.

"I remember whenever she was getting ready," Grant said, "I was forever impatiently waiting." Dante would change outfits so many times, Grant felt like he was at a fashion show. He'd always tell her she looked great, but his praise was never good enough. Ten minutes later, she'd come out wearing something else.

"What the hell are we doing?" he would ask. "We've been screwing around for two hours while you figure out what you're gonna wear. What *is* it with you?"

"I'm trying to make myself look good for *you*, you jerk!"

At times Grant would get so frustrated he'd feel like slapping her, especially when he'd see her wiping off all her makeup with cotton balls, only to start the whole process over again. He'd go nuts, watching her repaint her face four or five times before an outing. She was in love with the mirror.

And when they finally got around to shopping, it was

always for the most expensive thing she could find. Their couch, for example, wound up costing $5,000. It was a replica of a large sofa pictured in the film *Out of Africa*, and Dante just had to have it. They had looked in every store in Dallas, Grant hoping to convince her to agree to something less costly, but she acted like she was Meryl Streep, like she belonged on this exorbitant piece. Whatever Grant pointed out was "cheap garbage."

With Dante, he quickly learned, everything had to be done her way, *or else*. He did all the cooking, all the cleaning, and she stood over him like a coach, giving him step-by-step instructions. He was taught how to open a can, how to sterilize the can opener, how to fry an egg. His lessons were endless.

"We have to wash the pan," Dante would say.

"But it just came out of the dishwasher."

"We have to wash it again."

"Okay."

"Now, when you crack the egg, be sure none of the egg white goes in. It has to be separated."

"What?"

"It has that white piece in there. It has to be taken out."

When Grant would try to get Dante to pitch in, she'd go into a rage about her mother burning her hands when she was young. She refused to get near the stove or wash anything, ranting about her mother scalding her under the hot water in their kitchen sink.

She'd lift up her hands to show him the scars, but there was nothing there. Grant was so tired of the story that after a while he just stayed out of the kitchen altogether, learning to live on fast food.

"Mrs. Mello, there are dishes in our sink since last Christmas," he complained to Olga, calling her long distance.

"I'm not a bit surprised."

"I'm sorry to bother you like this, but I just thought maybe you could talk to her."

"Grant, I don't know what to tell you. She would never listen to me. She makes me out to be the devil, you know. She tells everyone I'm no good."

"Well, she called the law on me, Mrs. Mello," Grant moaned, "she's out to get me."

"You have my sympathy. If you had talked to me before you married her, you wouldn't be in this jam you're in, 'cause I would've warned you."

"Della wouldn't let any of her boyfriends meet the family," Olga reflected. "She knew we had the goods on her, especially me. She knew she couldn't hook anybody with me around, because I'd give them some background. I'd tell them get out of there as fast as they could."

CHAPTER | 61

*E*ATING OUT MEANT GOING TO PLACES LIKE CHILI'S AND Tony Roma's. Grant was the meat-and-potatoes type, and Dante could tolerate those restaurants, even though they were only chains. Of course, whenever possible, she wanted Grant to spring for high-end places like Los Colinas Courtyard and Polo's Grille; she liked to people-watch.

At home, Grant spent his free time fixing up the garage and basement; he loved to fool with things from Home Depot; he was Mr. Fix-it and he would construct shelves and counters, though Dante never seemed to notice. She was always completely absorbed watching movies. She liked horror films and murder stories; she was into gore.

Grant didn't enjoy that genre, but he never asked her to rent something he wanted; in fact, he never gave her a hard time about spending his money, regardless of what it was for. Even though he wasn't exactly a millionaire, Dante made all her clothing purchases at shops like Saks Fifth Avenue and Bonwit Teller, and had her hair and nails done at the most exclusive salons in Dallas. Grant never kept score. He was a simple guy who liked to work hard and get ahead in business. When Dante announced she'd had a miscarriage, he believed her. She was crying in the bedroom, and he noticed a bloody hand print in the bathtub, but he couldn't get her to explain exactly what had happened.

"What's wrong, Dante? Why won't you tell me?"

"You really don't know, do you?"

"No, I don't."

For ten minutes, Dante sat shaking her head, tears streaming down her face.

"There's not going to be a baby."

Since they were already married, Grant just wanted to make the best of it. Even if it turned out she was lying about the pregnancy, it wouldn't have mattered much. He cared about her and wanted to share his life with her; there could always be another pregnancy.

But Dante was emotionally shaken, and Grant was getting on her nerves more and more. She'd made a mistake marrying him, he wasn't the man for her. Dante wanted someone more high-class, more intellectual, she made it clear, and one afternoon, as they were heading down the highway going sixty-five miles an hour, she picked up a loaded plastic bag from the backseat and started swinging at Grant's head.

"When are you going to learn how to talk?" she howled. "You're an idiot. You use phrases and you don't even know what they mean."

"You stupid little bitch," he yelped. "Don't fuck with me, or I'll pull this car over and throw you out."

As he grabbed the bag and threw it behind him, the car swerved a bit, but he was able to maintain his composure. He was ready to stop the car anyway, telling his wife he was going to leave her on the side of the road, but Dante quieted down.

"She was heading for my head, and I put my arm up and caught it good on my elbow," Grant recalled. "There was a glass Coke bottle in there, and it screwed up my elbow for a long time. She had a lot of leverage with that plastic bag."

After the highway incident, Grant started thinking maybe it was lucky that Dante had had a miscarriage. He was even considering a divorce, but then she became "cutesie" again, and she wanted to be with him. That Sunday, she bought a couple of plants, which she named Samson and Delilah, and she began treating them like children. Talking to them seemed to appease her.

Still, she was becoming an increasing problem, he couldn't picture her as a mother, and he seriously wondered about her as a wife. Her looks seemed to be all Dante was ever concerned about, and not long after the miscarriage announcement, when Dante decided she needed cosmetic surgery, she asked Grant if it would be okay for her to hock her engagement ring and use the money for a face-lift.

"We went and cashed in the ring," Grant admitted. "Not without some kicking and screaming, but we got the money and scheduled her operation for the same week. That got her off my back a little bit, which was good. We were getting ready to move to another place about two miles away because we'd driven the neighbors crazy with screaming matches. The police had been there a couple of times."

CHAPTER | 62

"**I**'VE GOT THIS LITTLE NAIL FILE MACHINE, WHAT ladies use for manicures," Grant confided. "I use it for airplane models, for attaching parts, and she comes down in her nightgown one day and asks me to go get it out of my tool box."

The next thing Grant knew, his wife had lifted her nightgown, produced an electric toothbrush, and started playing with it. She was going through the moves, acting like she was getting ready to climax, and she wanted him to get the file for her. She wanted to feel the vibration, she said.

"You and I have to get out more," he told her. "Why don't you get dressed and we'll go miniature golfing."

"Why? Am I too kinky for you?"

"Well, I don't know."

The nail file had a blunt end; it was a tool about six inches long, and she kept insisting he go get it. She didn't want to have intercourse with him anymore, she apologized. She just needed a toy.

"It's not that there's anything wrong with you," she whispered. "It's just me, you know, I'm just . . ."

And she made some kind of weird motion with her hands.

The morning of Dante's face-lift, Grant dropped her off at the doctor's office. He wrote out a $2,000 check to the medical receptionist and announced he was taking the day off from work.

"But why aren't you going back to work?" she wanted to know.

"Because we're moving in a week and packing has to be done."

"Well, my stuff's all packed, and you don't have that much left, really, so why don't you just go ahead in to work, and I'll call you at the office."

Grant got back in his car and raced to the house. From his wife's reaction, he knew something was fishy, so he started tearing through everything, the garbage, the drawers, the countertops, and he finally came across a pale yellow note that read, "Dear Harry, if I don't come back to the door, it's because I'm in the shower. Just come on in."

Grant kept the note and attached it to Olga's phone number. But that night, when he picked up his wife, she was covered in bandages; he certainly wasn't going to attempt a heart-to-heart talk. She was in pain, and Grant moved around her like she was the finest piece of crystal—everything had to be done with care and caution, so much so that when moving day came she asked Grant to put her in a hotel. She was too fragile to lift a box.

Their new place was only a one-bedroom apartment, so the couple was forced to share a bed, but she made Grant stay way over on his side, and he was so cramped he started sleeping out on the couch.

After a few weeks, she was recovering nicely, her stitch marks were getting better, when all of a sudden she broke the news that she'd been raped by her plastic surgeon. She said it had happened just a couple of days before her face-lift.

"I'm going to ask you something, Dante."

"Yeah."

"If this doctor raped you, then why did you have the plastic surgery?"

"Are you crazy? This guy's going to have a *scalpel* over my face in four days and he's already got half my money. What am I supposed to do?"

Grant started pacing back and forth. He would walk up to Dante and then put his finger over his mouth, thinking about what his next words should be.

"This thing has turned out to be such a mess," Dante told him, breaking down in tears.

"Look, I want you to get dressed," he insisted. "We're going to the police with this."

Dante quickly put on an outfit and they jumped into Grant's car. They were about five minutes from the police station when Dante came up with another way to handle the problem. She didn't want to get the police involved. She suggested they pull over for some coffee and think it through. By the time they were done talking, Dante had a plan to get the surgeon over to the apartment the following day.

Grant agreed. His wife should have the surgeon come by, while he waited at work for a two-ring signal. At that point, he just wanted to see what antics she was capable of. Dante had already told him that to get even with one ex-boyfriend she'd ripped out all his electrical appliances and flooded his place.

Grant figured that if the surgeon was really there when he arrived, the man would have some explaining to do. The worst that could happen was that he and the doctor would sit and have a talk. The next morning, he got the signal from Dante and rushed home, only to be told the surgeon had already left.

As it happened, the police knocked on their door to check things out, having followed Grant's speeding car. He explained to the officer that his wife had just been through surgery, that there was no real problem at the apartment. After that, the rape issue was completely dropped; it was like it never took place.

For the next few weeks, Dante didn't ask for much. She stayed in bed during the day and had Grant drive her around in the middle of the night, usually around 2:00 or 3:00 in the morning, when she couldn't sleep. She wanted to take him to see houses she was interested in buying, and they spent a lot of hours looking at tract housing developments, Dante jotting down subdivision names and Realtor numbers. Later that summer Grant told Dante he had a new business opportunity in Washington, D.C. His company was laying people off, and he felt it was the right move for him. As he watched her reaction, he could almost feel the room tighten, but she didn't argue about it. She liked D.C. and seemed open to the idea.

As usual, he fell asleep on the couch, but at 2:00 A.M. he suddenly awoke with Dante at his feet, her face half illuminated by light from the television, the rest of her in darkness.

"She stood there staring at me," he recalled. "It must have been for a minute or two, and she didn't say a word. She just turned and walked back into her room. But when I moved, my hand hit the floor, and it hits this newspaper."

When Grant picked the package up, he discovered a fourteen-inch butcher knife wrapped inside a newspaper he had purchased the day before. He got up and nervously started searching the house; he was sleepy, still groggy, but it occurred to him that Dante had been standing by the stereo after she left the couch area.

He investigated and found an eight-inch knife behind the stereo casters. He didn't know why, but he left it there and went back to sleep.

CHAPTER | 63

DANTE MOVED TO DALLAS THINKING SHE WAS GOING TO arrive on the set of South Fork; she didn't like living an everyday existence and she made fun of Grant, calling Cheryl back in Ohio to report that she couldn't force herself to sleep with him anymore. She said he looked like Woody Allen; he was just disgusting.

When they first met, she had made him feel like he was the brightest guy in the world. He could do no wrong. As long as he was doing her favors and lugging her stuff around, she made him feel like Superman. Grant missed that. In Dallas, there had been no hand-holding, no more compliments, and he started to feel alone.

What made matters complicated was the weird demands Dante had. For one thing, she was being really difficult about the furniture by putting masking tape directly on the wicker, and no matter how much Grant assured her he would personally supervise the help, promising he would cover the wicker in paper himself, his wife wasn't happy.

For Grant, the idea of going through a divorce again, of having to give away a portion of his $50,000-a-year income, was torture. Still, the reality was, when he'd tell Dante he loved her, she'd just shrug her shoulders. She never said it back. He wanted to patch things, but he didn't know how.

"She had steam rollers she wanted me to fix," Grant recalled, "and we got into this big goddamned argument, and I'm the one who made the phone call to 911, because I was frightened for me, and frightened for her. Little did I know that 911 was stalling me on the phone while the police were on their way."

Just before the cops arrived, Dante had gone wacko, tearing at her clothes and slamming herself into the wall. She took a two-liter bottle of Coke and poured it out in the middle of the kitchen floor, then headed for the knives.

But that's not what the police were told. Dante had run to the door in tears, explaining in her cute baby voice that her husband was beating her, that he had been tearing at her clothes and trying to rape her. She showed bruises on her arms, and Grant Bassett was immediately taken into custody by Texas officials.

"What did I do?" he demanded to know. "What rights do I have?"

"You know what you did," an officer allegedly told him.

"No, I do not! I have no idea what I did."

"Well, maybe you can explain the bruise on her."

"I didn't hit her," Grant insisted. "You ask her about yesterday. You ask about this morning, when she was tearing her clothes off and went absolutely crazy and started banging herself around."

The upshot was, Grant Bassett was arrested, Dante was pressing charges, and after he bailed himself out, he stayed at a friend's house for a week before his wife decided to drop the matter.

"Well, it looks like GB learned a lesson," she said in her tiny voice, smiling as she greeted him at the front door.

His adrenaline was still running, so Grant took the comment as food for thought. He didn't want to see any more cops.

"Sunday, August twentieth, 1989, I'm in St. Louis, I'm connecting from a flight from D.C. It was my fortieth birthday, and I made a phone call to the apartment,"

Grant recounted. "I made three or four phone calls during an hour-and-a-half layover, and there was no answer."

When he arrived at the Dallas-Fort Worth airport, there was no one there to meet him, and Grant waited almost two hours, continually calling Dante, hoping she was on her way. She knew he didn't have a nickel on him; they had spoken the day before and he mentioned that he was completely broke.

Finally he got in a cab and headed home, only to discover a note on the door saying, "For now, all you need to know is the keys to the apartment are under the plant. The instructions as to where you can find your car are inside."

Grant invited the cab driver into the apartment, where he scrambled through his pockets for loose change, but all the furniture was cleared out and the driver just didn't want to be bothered.

"You've got bigger problems, buddy," the guy said on his way out.

Grant read the note Dante left on the kitchen counter: "This is not going to work out. Your bank accounts have been emptied. You won't be broke forever, but, at least, I'm going to bankrupt you for now."

He called his boss and the two of them followed Dante's directions to his Chrysler. The car had been dumped at a U-Haul place twenty-two miles away. Grant had to go to his office to use the phones, where he called his mom to have her wire him $3,000. He picked up his cash at an IGA supermarket and was just beside himself.

Left only with his closet of clothes, he crammed most of that, along with his microwave oven, into his Chrysler New Yorker. He resigned from his Dallas job the same day and headed for Washington, D.C.

From the road, he called his new employers and asked them to speed up the paperwork—he needed to start right away. But he had to spend a couple of weeks in Cincinnati before they were ready for him.

Ironically, Dante found out where Grant was staying—she heard about him through the grapevine at Benjamin's—and she looked him up to ask for his help. She reported that the things she moved from storage had been damaged by bad weather, she was crying and wanted him to help her sort through it.

Dante was living with her brother Scott temporarily, and Grant agreed to meet her over at Scott's place on Labor Day. Together they drove over to U-Haul, where he was hoping he'd be able to repossess his $5,000 couch. On the way, he invited her to come live with him once he got settled in D.C.

Deep down, he was through with her, but there was something about Dante that made him feel the need to reconcile. She was so pathetic, such a little lost girl.

"It was just shambles," he confided. "The couch, all the stuff I had bought for her, the pictures of her father, her antique bedroom set, it was all just mildew. I was digging through the stuff, and basically, I helped her lay her clothes out to dry.

"I kind of savored it," he admitted. "I was in hog heaven."

CHAPTER | 64

WHEN SCOTT MELLO RECEIVED A CALL FROM HIS LONG-lost sister, he felt he couldn't deny her. Della led a hard life, and her days in Texas hadn't gone well. Scott was happily married and living in a three-bedroom house in Springdale, a sleepy Cincinnati suburb, so it was no problem for him to let her have a room. She had tried to go back to Grant—she had visited him in Maryland, where he was camping out on a cot in a studio apartment—but she had no desire to stay there. The two of them were officially separated, and Della was hoping to collect alimony, hoping that Grant's job would pan out.

But meanwhile, at Scott's, things were deteriorating quickly. Della didn't get along with her sister-in-law, Janet, and she could barely tolerate Scott's daughter. The first few weeks, she worked as a temp on and off, but then she just started hanging around the house. She never gave them a penny for bills, all her money went to designer clothes, and she monopolized the telephone and the bathroom; she was worse than having a teenage daughter. Janet worked hard at keeping her home shipshape, but Della didn't even keep her own room clean. When Della was out on a date, Janet would go in there to find clothes piled everywhere and a bed reeking with dirty sheets. It was creepy, and she felt funny about fumigating, but the smell was permeating the house.

"It was kind of an open-ended invitation to stay here," Janet admitted. "But after a while, I started to wonder, how long is this gonna last? Scott and I got into a huge argument about me doing all the work, about me not being a bully enough to tell her she's gotta carry her end of the load."

For Janet Mello, it was easier to do all the house-cleaning and keep her mouth shut. Having a confrontation with Della just wasn't worth it, because whenever her sister-in-law did a chore, it became a big production, just so aggravating. In all the weeks she stayed there, Della did the dishes exactly once, and she washed one dish at a time, pouring tons of soap and running extra water, standing at the sink for almost an hour.

The funny thing was, Della acted like Janet owed her, and she added insult to injury by trying to take over the house. Della had made a place for herself, she was the queen bee, but she excluded the Mellos. She had her own time for the bathroom, her own separate towels, her own separate food, and she was actually rude to anyone who got in her path.

The day of reckoning came when Donna pulled into town for a visit; she had driven across the country in her Datsun 280Z; Scott had invited her, hoping she might light a fire under Della. But instead, Donna received the cold shoulder from her sister. For two days, Della never spoke a word to her. She treated Donna like an invader. When Donna told Janet, "I just can't take this anymore," Janet pleaded with her to stay.

"Della just keeps her door shut all the time, like she hates me or something," Donna insisted, and after just forty-eight hours, Donna packed her bags and left, making Janet promise not to say anything to Scott until after she hit the road. She wrote her brother a thank-you letter, and when Scott got the lowdown from Janet, he was just furious about it.

As he entered Della's room to confront her, he walked in on a gallery of men: Della had all these pictures lined up against the wall, and she was staring at her ex-boyfriends, in some kind of weird daze. The two of them got into a yelling match, and when Della got up to collect her photographs, Scott pushed her up against the wall and told her to grab all her stuff and get out.

"She didn't call the cops until a day or two later," Janet recalled. "I was surprised when they came knocking at my door. They came and put handcuffs on Scott for domestic violence. They took him to jail, but he didn't hit her. I was watching."

Somehow, Della convinced authorities that her brother's push caused her an injury. Apparently, she had fallen lifting some of her things out of their basement, and she used the black and blue mark on her leg to bring charges against her brother. She actually dragged Scott to court, sitting in the downtown Cincinnati courtroom with no expression on her face, while the rest of the family begged and pleaded for her to listen to reason.

"You can't throw my son in jail for something that didn't happen," Olga pleaded. "Della, you just can't do this."

Just before the hearing, Della dropped the charges, but her sweetheart of a brother never talked to her again.

"She came over to Olga's at Christmas and knocked on the door," Janet recalled, "and no one would let her in."

CHAPTER | 65

INITIALLY, JEFF FREEMAN HAD GONE TO SINGLE VIEWS, a dating service in Cincinnati, just for kicks. He submitted a profile and a videotape, but he wound up being a member there for almost five years, looking at binders filled with women, reading their brief life histories. Occasionally he'd choose someone to date, but it had to be someone exceptional.

A top-notch stockbroker, Jeff had achieved great success in the business world, but he was at a loss when it came to finding a good woman. He'd never been married, had been engaged twice, but now he was well into his forties and felt the dating service was much better than chasing women in singles' bars.

The thing that attracted him to Dante was her cute way of expressing herself. On her tape, she was funny, very perky, and she struck him as someone from overseas; her accent wasn't from Ohio. She was soft-spoken, very sexy, and seemed perfect. He had an inexplicit hope that she could be "the one."

Right away Jeff realized how self-conscious the woman was; when he arrived fifteen minutes early, she was extremely flustered. It took Dante at least half an hour to pull herself together, and he noticed she used a lot of makeup, a lot of foundation, but that was okay.

As they sat at the Montgomery Inn, his favorite rib joint, they ran through all the typical first-date questions. She told him her mom was English, her dad, Cherokee; she talked about her daughter, Shawn, who lived in Louisville with her father, saying she visited whenever she was able to take off from work. For the moment, Dante had a job as a receptionist and a trendy apartment in Mt. Adams, but she talked about California a lot, acting like she planned to move back there. She certainly wasn't satisfied with her current status.

Jeff had the impression she was from upper society because she talked about certain local socialites, mentioning Jerry Springer quite a bit. As the evening progressed, she went into the history of her unhappy childhood, describing her supposedly abusive mother in graphic detail. Jeff thought it was odd. Most new dates didn't get that personal so quickly, but he listened. The bulk of the evening, he just asked her questions and let her do the talking.

For his part, Jeff talked about work at Smith Barney, that seemed to be his life—which made sense, because he was the epitome of conservative, with his double-breasted blazer and cropped blond hair. He had an apartment at The Bluffs, and before that, he owned a large Victorian house, something he had decided to sell because he was tired of handling the upkeep alone. He drove a German sports car, was well traveled, and gave the impression that he was rather comfortable financially.

On their second date, which they spent walking around a street fair called "A Taste of Cincinnati," Dante confided that she'd been living with a guy in Los Angeles with whom she'd fought a lot but tried desperately to love. They'd slept in separate beds, she claimed, but when she turned up pregnant, she tried to make things work. As Jeff listened, he felt sorry for her. He tried to be understanding. When she explained that somehow, she'd had a miscarriage because of all the fighting that went on, Jeff made no judgments.

He rather liked the idea that Dante wasn't too quick to get intimate; in fact, they went out on a number of dates with just a kiss good night. He was falling for her fast, and he suggested they take a vacation together. He wanted to get to know her, and he bought them round-trip tickets to California. At that point, Dante wasn't the only woman he was seeing, but he was considering becoming exclusive with her. The two of them saw eye to eye, Jeff thought. They both wanted the same things in life: the 2.1 kids, the house with the pretty fence, the complete all-American family.

Of course, there were certain strikes she had against her. She couldn't mingle well with his associates, and Dante kept a messy apartment. But those were surmountable little quirks. However, in California he discovered the two of them weren't really physically compatible; her bedroom techniques were lacking. Dante was only good when she was intoxicated, and that wasn't what Jeff was looking for. In the morning, whenever he would try to relax her, she had sweaty palms and wanted no part of him.

From the minute they had arrived in San Francisco, things had progressively gone downhill. Jeff had a driving trip planned—they were headed for Reno and then eventually down to Los Angeles—but he discovered Dante had no driver's insurance; in fact, she had an outdated driver's license. Regardless, she presumed he'd let her drive, which irked him.

Moreover, she was disappointing as a copilot: She couldn't read a map correctly and couldn't figure out the AAA book when they were looking for hotels. She failed miserably on all fronts. In Reno, when they checked into a gaudy red hotel, she made a big stink about the place, and they wound up moving over to Tahoe, with a view of the lake, which was fine except that Jeff didn't really appreciate her prima donna routine.

It bugged him that she could be so demanding, yet never once offer a financial contribution during the whole vacation. He didn't really expect her to pay for anything, but he wanted her to make an attempt, at least. They were out there for two weeks, and it seemed reasonable that she'd offer to buy a burger or an ice cream.

"She reminded me of a little kid," Jeff reflected. "It was like I was with a two-year-old. We'd see a Taco Bell and she'd start pointing, and it wasn't cute, coming from an adult. On one occasion, she was tugging at my pants, like a kid would tug at a dad's pants."

"Could we stop and get some candy? Could we, *pretty please*?" she'd squeal. "Look, look, there's a store! I want a soda! Let's stop, let's stop!"

CHAPTER | 66

DANTE WAS PERSNICKETY ABOUT RESTAURANTS, AND about things in general, he found out. One night he dared to check them into a Motel 6, and she wasn't a very good sport about it.

And there were other problems. The few days they had spent at a Napa Valley winery, she berated him for looking at the tour guide. "I explained to her I wasn't leering," Jeff said. "I told her the person means nothing to me, it was just someone I looked at, but she felt I was looking at the woman too hard, like I was kind of making a pass at her."

Another thing Jeff had problems with was Dante's behavior when she was drunk. They did a lot of sampling at the winery, and he noticed that she'd suddenly become obnoxious. They were staying at a nice place, Hotel St. Helena, yet she picked on it and made fun of Jeff's taste. She acted like she was the expert on California; having lived there, she knew of much classier resorts and restaurants than he ever suggested. Jeff got the impression she attended college in California, but he didn't remember UCLA being mentioned.

Once they returned to Ohio, Jeff wanted his space. Dante was telling him she loved him, but the feeling wasn't mutual. For one thing, Dante had quit her job. Jeff had advised her not to, but she insisted she could find something better. Instead, she started drinking a lot more, calling Jeff in the middle of the workday, somewhat intoxicated.

He was pulling away more and more, going up to Michigan for fishing trips with his buddies, going on business trips to the Northeast, and Dante was demanding to know his whereabouts, calling his machine and leaving endless messages. She was good at laying on the guilt trip, making him feel obligated to her, saying she'd lose interest in him if he didn't divulge his feelings.

"She was calling me at work and at home, telling me she stopped seeing everyone else," he recalled. "I told her I wasn't interested in her, from a marriage standpoint, and she tells me she's madly in love."

In August of 1990, Dante took a home pregnancy test. They had been back from the West Coast about a month, and she called him hysterically, reporting she was pregnant. Jeff was thinking she couldn't have even missed her period yet, he thought her claim invalid, but Dante's hysterics increased. She was threatening that if he didn't see her and spend time with her to figure things out, she was going to commit suicide.

"Who're you dating, these days, anyone I know?" she asked over the phone.

"Just a female friend, a platonic friend," Jeff said.

"Oh, you're such a liar. Don't tell me you're going out with someone and you don't sleep with them. I know you better than that."

"No, really, I'm just casually seeing one of my clients."

"That's a good one," she quipped.

Then Dante showed up at his door late one night. He'd seen her car out in the parking lot, but he was entertaining someone, and when Dante heard a female voice, she left before Jeff answered the door. She had dropped off a card that said, "Congratulations, Jeff, the 'Soon-to-be-Dad,'" and inside, she wrote that she loved him very much, and included a plastic green rattle and two diaper clips.

He was thoroughly horrified the next morning, when Dante called to report that she'd had an official blood test, with positive results. She threatened to go out and buy herself a derringer if he didn't agree to see her. She also threatened to call Jeff's mother, which was just the kind of inside publicity he didn't need, so he allowed her to come by his place, hoping to calm her down.

He wanted to defuse her threats without calling her bluff, so he took her to a cute Italian place that Saturday night, after which they went to see *Exorcist III*. Dante kept insisting that she needed him by her side, that she was sick, but she wanted to keep the baby.

That Monday night, she arrived with her dirty laundry in hand; she had wash to do, acting like she was ready to move in. Jeff offered her money to get an abortion, but she wouldn't accept it, so finally he agreed to help raise the chid, flat-out telling her that he was planning to marry someone else, an ex-girlfriend of his, Lynn.

Before Dante left, she stole Jeff's little black book,

and within days, Lynn got a threatening phone call. Meanwhile, Dante was agreeing to have the abortion, but she wanted Jeff to pay for a couple of procedures, one being sterilization.

"I advised her that she was crazy to be sterilized," Jeff confided. "But she said she never wanted to go through the same pain again, that she didn't feel stable enough to have another child."

She stopped by to see him on a Friday night, about 10:00 P.M., and Jeff gave her some canned goods and a check for $1,625. He knew that was more money than an abortion cost, but he just wanted her out of his life. He felt very uneasy around her.

A week later, Dante showed up at his door, unannounced, around 11:30 at night. She had a crazed look about her, but Jeff felt he had no choice but to let her in.

"What's up?" he asked as she walked in the living room.

"What are you talking about? You know what's up."

"No, I don't know. What're you doing here?"

"Who were you talking to when I knocked? I heard you on the phone."

"It doesn't concern you, Dante. Now, what do you want? Did you have the abortion?"

"You're still seeing Lynn, aren't you?"

"No, actually I'm not. But I wouldn't tell you if I was."

"I'm watching her because I don't trust her," Jeff recalled. "She tells me to sit down, and I'm looking at her handbag, she was standing right by the fireplace, and in a roundabout way she's telling me she's three months pregnant, she's mentioning the doctor, saying that it's a baby now."

Jeff told her he thought an abortion still made the most sense, but he would support whatever decision she made. This time her appearance was different; she tried to look very businesslike, had a more single-mindedness about her.

"She edges toward the chair that has her purse in it," he recounted, "and I see her turn slightly and reach her hand in the purse, so I jump from the sofa, and she's got a .22 revolver in her hand. I wrestled her and tried to bury the revolver in the couch."

Jeff forced the gun from her. He was able to keep her with him until police arrived, and a few weeks later he brought her to court on charges of terroristic threatening. After all the shuffle, Dante produced a lab report that showed she was, indeed, pregnant. She was sentenced to a year's probation and was required to pay a small fine. When all was said and done, she walked away virtually scot-free.

For months Jeff diligently checked the papers for birth announcements, he was looking for Dante's name, to no avail. He feared her so much that Jeff kept a file on her, with records of her threats, her phone messages, and his canceled checks to her.

But she never resurfaced.

CHAPTER 67

DANTE WAS A LIVE-IN GOVERNESS WHEN SHE MET DAVID Britteon. He was a tall, dark, and handsome type, very shy and charming, with a brilliant English accent; she met him in a bar, and for the first time in years she felt she was in love. She was just crazy about the guy and was determined to nab him.

David worked as a contract employee for Cincinnati

Bell Information Systems; he was in the United States on a temporary visa. He was thirty-two years old, in search of a good time, so it came as a complete shock when Dante announced she wanted to get married. They had only been dating a couple of months, and he was being forced to make a lifetime decision.

David's co-worker Amy Bules remembers that the first time she met Dante, the petite blonde was anything but warm. It was during a company Christmas party held on a riverboat, an event a select group had put together for themselves—something informal, so people could let their hair down.

"We were dancing and drinking and just being silly," Amy recalled, "and Dante was just sitting on the side. She wouldn't get up and dance, and I just felt this was not her type of thing."

As it turned out, Amy wound up leaving her scarf in Dante's car, and she had to make arrangements to go pick it up in Loveland, where Dante worked as a governess. When Amy got there, Dante was blunt with her. She refused to let Amy through the front door, and Amy got the distinct impression that Dante was jealous. She tried to tell her that she and David weren't dating, that they just got together at happy hour after work, and Dante nodded as though she understood. But Amy could see the look in her eyes. No matter what she said, Amy felt she was just digging a hole for herself, so Amy just took her scarf, got in her car, and pulled away.

By New Year's Day 1992, Dante and David were firmly an item, but from what David described, no one at his work thought much of the tiny woman. Amy in particular thought Dante was a poor choice. One minute David would tell her that Dante was a bitch, and the next he'd say she was kind of growing on him. He was wishy-washy about it, and Amy tried to help him break away by getting him a job in Kansas City, a four-month stint that would afford him time to think.

"That's when Dante started getting mad," Amy confided, " 'cause I'm calling over there, setting up these interviews, and David and I would talk for forty-five minutes. I know that must have just unnerved her.'

From that point forward, Dante started interfering in David's work life. She wanted to move in with him; she had the whole thing planned. She also had a lawsuit against her employers in Loveland in mind, and now Amy was ruining everything. To Amy, it seemed like Dante was determined to get David fired, calling him at work more than ten times a day.

Meanwhile, Dante was showing David her list of her employers' expectations, going over them with a fine-tooth comb. She wanted him to help her, hoping he would join her in a business venture. Dante hated her job, she told him, and wished she could start a day-care service on her own. Her Loveland employers expected her to do the laundry, collect the mail, stock the refrigerator, and learn to cook. On top of all that, they were trying to enforce a midnight *curfew*—it was just unbearable. She was forty-one years old and they were treating her like a child. She told David she'd been warned that these were difficult people to work for. Supposedly, she was the seventh nanny they'd hired.

"David, she's just using you," Amy blurted one day at work. "She just wants you until the next one comes along. You two don't have anything in common, and if the next guy has a little more money, she won't want anything to do with you."

"But the sex is good," he insisted, laughing.

"I know you're not that shallow, David, come on."

Amy reminded him that he had already made arrangements to take the position in Kansas City, and then all of a sudden Dante turned up pregnant. Amy thought it was a strange coincidence, especially since David now felt obligated to stay in Cincinnati. But she forced him to think rationally, to keep his job commitment, and to deal with Dante on an adult level. If the woman was faking it, time would tell. If she wasn't, David could always marry her at some point down the road.

"If you marry her, she's gonna take every penny you have," Amy warned. "She's not pregnant. She's just looking for someone to take care of her."

"Yeah."

"You already said you don't want any kids, right?"

"Yeah, but now Dante has a plan that if I marry her, she'll have an abortion."

"What?"

"If I don't marry her, she says she'll come after me for child support for the next eighteen years."

CHAPTER | 68

"**S**HE HAD THIS THING WORKED OUT ABOUT HOW A marriage should be organized," David reflected, "about why she had to have the joint checking account, that we were supposed to share everything, and there wasn't any arguing with it, really."

During a civil ceremony held in New Orleans, David and Dante became man and wife. It was February 14, 1992, and he had just started his Kansas City assignment two weeks earlier. That Monday, when he called Amy with the news about the wedding, his friend absolutely hit the ceiling.

"You dumb, stupid son of a bitch," she yelped over the phone. "I can't believe you did this."

"Well, she's going to have the abortion. That's the main thing."

"Abortion? Let me tell you, you better keep her

under control, because if she screws up this project, I can't help you."

Amy was disgusted. She couldn't believe David was so easy to manipulate. It wasn't that she was interested in him herself; a beautiful young woman with streaming long blond hair, she was quite happily engaged. But she felt sorry for David. As his liaison to America, she'd made an investment in the guy, and she didn't like to see him so obviously taken advantage of.

"Dave, in his own way, is a great guy," she confided, "but he's too trusting, and she played it to the hilt. She pretended like she got the abortion, she pretended she came back to Cincinnati and got it, but later she admitted to David that she never was pregnant in the first place."

"Dante didn't like me when we first met," David admitted. "She didn't think I had any money, and she slept with me just for fun. I never had any intentions of it going any further at all. I had this plan that I was going to make this woman fall in love with me, and then I was going to dump her, because she deserved it."

Dante was twelve years older than David, something he didn't find out until they signed their marriage license, when he noticed she was actually forty-four. Not that it mattered. Really, David married her as a way to assure himself of a green card.

Not that David hadn't been quite intrigued by her. Dante was a seductress, going out with many men at once. Even though he later realized it was a "stupid macho guy thing," he'd been pulled in by the competitive atmosphere. Dante made it seem like she was the biggest prize in Cincinnati, and he just wanted the conquest. When their weekend trip to New Orleans for Mardi Gras turned into a honeymoon, he had no idea what he was getting into.

"The ceremony wasn't any big deal to her," he recalled. "She didn't care about chocolates and roses and all that kind of stuff. She wanted her name on the piece of paper. It was a technical detail."

The two of them spent their honeymoon drinking all day, then sleeping all night. It was a pattern they continued through their days in Kansas City, when he was working for the Kansas City Gas and Electric Company and life was fun and simple. In the five months they lived there, she didn't give him much trouble at all—neither of them knew anyone, so they spent all their time together.

It was a perfect setup, as far as she was concerned, especially since David never complained about her lousy housekeeping. He knew it wasn't fair, but he could see that Dante was quite out of touch with reality, and he didn't waste his time arguing with her.

For a while, whatever Dante was doing seemed right, because under her tutelage, David was undergoing a metamorphosis. His hair, his clothes, the way he carried himself—he was much more sharp and fashion-conscious. By the time the two of them returned from Kansas City, David looked like a new person, and everyone commented about it.

For David, it was an okay existence—until his wife started spending unreasonable amounts of money. The first time, it was for a Ralph Lauren bed quilt. Then later, she bought herself a pedigreed dog. As the months flew by and their joint account dwindled, their arguments became more frequent. Not only was she throwing away all his savings, she was going nuts over his whereabouts, questioning him unnecessarily whenever he joined a buddy for a beer.

"Ultimately, she came out with this story that she knows all these people," David recounted, "and if I left her, she said she would do her absolute best to have me thrown out of the country.

"At the time, it kind of played on my mind a bit," he admitted. "I didn't want to risk that at all."

CHAPTER | 69

DAVID GOT USED TO A DIFFERENT LIFESTYLE. BEFORE Dante, he was out seven nights a week; now he was just going home after work and basically doing nothing. He thought the change was a step in the right direction; he was tired of the dating scene. Just before he got married, he invested in some trailer parks across the river in Kentucky; he liked the idea of putting down some roots.

As the months went by, Dante got more and more interested in the trailer tenants; David had an older couple living on one property, people who managed the place, and Dante would arrive and boss them around. She loved to play the role of being in charge. She liked overseeing his properties, demanding the rent and inserting her authority in people's lives. She was so mean, David would sometimes hear complaints about her, but for him that wasn't such a bad thing. *He* didn't want to be the one to throw people out of their homes. It was great to have Dante wearing the black hat.

Of course, her constant meddling ways were another matter altogether—that was something David could do without—but he had trouble keeping her at arm's length. She was always calling and checking on him. It had gotten so completely out of hand that he had become the laughingstock at his office. Whenever his phone rang, people took bets about Dante. Usually they were right. And if David happened to walk away from his desk, his phone would ring incessantly, sometimes twenty or thirty rings.

Then there were the calls that interfered on the golf course. This was before David carried a pager or cell phone, so Dante would get through to him by calling the golf course office, saying it was an emergency. Sometimes, when he'd finish a game, he'd find his wife sitting in the car waiting for him in the parking lot. It was crazy.

Whenever David's every move couldn't be accounted for, Dante would quiz him up and down. She spent hours dreaming up scenarios that he might have gotten himself into; then she would run her "hunches" by him. David was getting increasingly aggravated, she was making his life impossible, but by then he already had twelve months in with her and he figured he could serve another twelve. It wasn't such a great price to pay.

He tried to stay low-key. Other than for golf outings, he rarely went out alone. Most everywhere else, he had to take Dante with him. The couple wound up spending a lot of their weekends in Kentucky, where at least he could get some work done. In all fairness, she tried to be a help at his trailer parks, although often she'd start a project and just create more work for him. Like a child, she'd leave an unfinished mess for him to clean up. She was exasperating.

"Do you think I'm funny-looking?" she would ask.

"No, I don't think you're funny-looking," he'd assure her.

"Well, I'm not pretty," she'd say, "but sometimes, on my best days, I'm pretty. But do you think I'm funny-looking?"

This conversation went on over and over. David knew she wanted him to say she was beautiful, but he wouldn't lie to her about that.

"Do you love me?" she would ask.

"Yeah."

"But do you *really* love me?"

"Yeah, of course I do."

But actually David had grown to hate the sight of her. He was counting the days until he could leave. At times he'd feel bad, because he realized she was depending on his love. He had completely faked her out; all he was doing was using her.

Not that he hadn't considered the possibility of having a real marriage. In the beginning, at least, he'd thought things might work out between them. But Dante was forever laying on guilt trips and spending his hard-earned cash. No matter how "professional" he thought she was in bed, it never made up for her bad behavior. She would put on striptease shows, she would wear sexy lace garters, she understood a man's need for visual stimulation, but none of that was relevant to real life. He had done everything he could to be understanding, to try to care about her, but she was certifiably insane. She twisted all the good to bad. He couldn't have a simple conversation with her anymore; all his words were turned on him.

"Why don't you go to work, you fucking lazy bitch," he finally demanded.

"Because you won't help me go into business!"

"Okay, you want to be a nanny? *Fine.* I'll pay for you to get started. We'll put an ad in the paper tomorrow."

Of course, in order for her to do that, she felt they should be living in a better place. She insisted they move to one of the most expensive apartment houses in town, the Gramercy, and the minute he agreed to it, she went out shopping for all-new furniture.

She planned to watch six or seven kids, and David rented a two-bedroom townhouse, perfect for her day-care service. Before they moved in, Dante had been enthusiastic about it. Then again, she couldn't pull references from her previous employer because she now was suing the people up in Loveland. She had taken them to small-claims court over a car she felt they owed her. Still, she managed to sign up a few kids, and David hoped Dante could keep herself occupied enough to stop having headaches all the time.

But it sure didn't last long. Even though she seemed

pretty good with the kids—very detailed and organized, very childlike and fun-loving—she started to call the children monsters. She hated being stuck with them all day.

"She started off doing it," David recalled, "but then she always had these reasons why she couldn't. She said she didn't have experience. She said her IQ was too high. It was just pathetic, really."

Dante gave up on the day care, but, having been given access to David's checking account, she managed to slip $4,000 out—money she used as a down payment toward another face-lift.

"I can spend our money any way I want to," she insisted. "You can't tell me what to do."

"That was *my* money, not yours!"

"It was *ours*. And part of the reason I took it, David, is because this operation is just so important to me. Can't you understand that?"

"Well, what about the bloody day-care business?"

"You know, you took a whole lot of money and bought those expensive golf clubs, right?"

"That's right. I bought the most expensive golf clubs I could find."

"I hated that woman with a passion," he admitted. "I thought about killing her. I worked out how to do it. I thought about it a lot. I dreamed about killing her. You know, you go out, walking on a cliff edge, a romantic walk, and nobody would know."

CHAPTER | 70

NOT ONLY DID ALL HIS FRIENDS THINK SHE WAS CRAZY, they also thought Dante was stupid. The few people who actually met her couldn't believe what a dunce she was. Dante couldn't understand the simplest concepts, yet she'd try to hide her ineptitude by claiming she was *pretending* to be stupid. Just out of curiosity, David decided to test her on multiplication tables, but she couldn't calculate 2×8.

And Dante seemed to get angry all the time. She was severely prejudiced, having strong negative opinions about people of color, about people without money. Her elitism was so blatant she wouldn't even watch a movie if there was an "undesirable" element involved. She couldn't help it. She just wanted her world to be rich.

When she wasn't focused on money, Dante was paranoid, distrustful—mad at the universe—and she was obsessed with her mother. She would spend hours harping on her unhappy childhood, always retelling the story of her mom dunking her hands in boiling water.

"She talked about how her mother would make her sew until her fingers were bleeding," David recalled, "about how she got beatings all the time. She claimed her mother locked her in a cupboard under the stairs, that she got beat with a leather strap. I don't know if it's true or not, but I know she was always threatening to report her mother to the IRS. It was like she was at war with her mother, like she had some kind of competition going."

Dante always had something to prove, especially when it came to Olga. When David had taken her on a trip to Italy—a belated honeymoon vacation that he made possible by charging it on his Visa card—all Dante seemed to care about was bringing home Italian leather handbags and shoes so she could shove them in her mother's face. David didn't even try to understand it; instead, he decided to keep his distance from Olga and the rest of Dante's family.

Dante had no real relationship with any of her siblings at the time, anyway. In fact, after the European trip, she called Cheryl to report that she'd been in Paris, not Rome—just another one of those inexplicable lies she told.

To David, Dante made it sound like she was Cinderella, like she had been a girl running around in rags, while her siblings got the royal treatment. She told a story about her long-lost brother Gene getting a bike, when all she got for Christmas were a few pairs of panties. Of course, David thought most of the tales were trumped up, but some of Dante's childhood memories seemed real, and the few brief times he saw the Mellos, he witnessed the strained relationships Dante had with the family. But then, Dante had a bad habit of attacking the very people who took care of her, of lying and changing the facts, so David didn't know what to believe, and unfortunately, David knew about that firsthand.

More than once she threatened to report him to the IRS, but he reminded her that if she did, she'd be reporting herself, that the illegal nanny business was all *her* doing. Besides, David was totally straight in reporting his income as a landlord and computer programmer. He made good money and had every reason to be forthcoming with the U.S. government. He was proud of himself, even if Dante wasn't, and he hated the fact that she'd lie whenever she introduced him at parties, making him out to be some big-time consultant. She was such a little phony.

"She always pretended she knew about classical music and art and all this stuff, because she liked to mix with important people," he said. "But she really only knew tiny little bits, just enough to get by. She had all kinds of art books, but they were just for show."

Dante would bring home fancy books with impressive covers. They looked good on the coffee table, but apparently she hardly read anything at all, not even the newspaper. Her knowledge of current events was slim; she knew just what she'd glean from the nightly news on TV. Really, she was more interested in beauty treatments than anything else, and about crying over not being loved.

"You won't let them get me, will you?" she'd ask.

"Who?"

"I don't know. But don't let them come get me."

"All right."

"You'll look after me, won't you?"

"Yeah."

"And you love me? You won't let them get me?"

But David never knew what his crazy wife was talking about.

"There were certain things she'd repeat over and over again, and I never got any answers," he admitted. "I guess it didn't matter. It was insecurity, I suppose."

David had given up trying to figure the woman out. He had taken her to Europe, taken her to the Caribbean, he'd done everything to make his life with her bearable, but she couldn't leave well enough alone. He didn't recall the exact date regarding the first time she had him carted off to jail—but he remembered he certainly stopped arguing with her after that.

"We got in a big fight the first thing in the morning," he confided, "and she was thrashing around on the bed and kicking and everything. I didn't mean to hit her, but I got so livid."

"I spanked her," he admitted. "I don't know that I hurt her at all, but she freaked out about it, and she got up and smashed a vase with silk flowers on the floor. Then she called 911."

CHAPTER | 71

WHEN THE POLICE CAME POUNDING ON THE BRITTEONS' door, David actually asked them to take him away. Dante was screaming and yelling like a maniac, and he just wanted to get out of there. He didn't care if he wound up with a record. As it happened, she bailed him out the next day, dropping all charges. But it hit him, when she brought him home, that there was no use trying with her anymore. He would make it through the last few months of his marriage in order to get his green card, and be gone.

Of course, he couldn't trust Dante in the least—he'd known that all along. He certainly got bad vibes the day they first moved back to Cincinnati, when he helped her get her things out of storage.

"I guess, whenever she moved, she just threw her things in bags," he recounted. "This stuff was going back ten and fifteen years, but she never got around to throwing it all out."

As they sorted through her junk, David confirmed that Dante was lying about her ex-husbands, because the stories she told didn't match the dates on the things she'd saved. When he questioned her about her stories not fitting together, she just fumbled and acted confused, like she couldn't be bothered remembering the details of her past.

One minute she'd tell him she had only been married once—that was to Joe—and then the next she'd mention that she never lived with anyone without being married. Eventually she'd switch back and say she was never anyone's wife, that she only used people's names to change her identification cards, to change social security numbers so she could gain new lines of bank credit.

On certain occasions, when David would press for particulars, Dante let it be known that she'd had problems with men in her past. Sometimes she would talk about trying to kill somebody, mentioning the burning bed incident, for example.

"If you cheat on me, I'll kill you," she'd tell him, smiling. "I'll kill you, hubby. I don't care if I go to jail."

That's the way she said it when she was in a good mood. When she was angry, her threats to kill were more violent, more real. She'd repeat it hundreds of times, enough that when she came down the stairs pointing a .44 Magnum at him one evening, David took her quite seriously.

Luckily, he was able to grab the gun away from her, but that didn't stop her from trying to physically attack him. Often she would pick up blunt objects and threaten him, or she would lunge at him with her fists, even though she was too tiny to do any severe damage.

A few days after an attack, he'd sometimes remind her about it, but she would act like she'd blacked out, like she had no memory of hitting him. She'd seem to vaguely recall, but then she'd be surprised when David filled her in on the vivid details. "I don't know, David. I'm sorry," she'd say. "I just can't remember."

Obviously, Dante must have remembered something, because as their marriage continued to deteriorate, she became increasingly vindictive. When David was having lunch with his co-workers at his regular spot downtown, he noticed that suddenly Dante would be standing on the street corner, thinking she was hiding behind sunglasses. Her very presence was scaring his friends at work.

Dante was purposely disrupting the workplace on a daily basis, and everyone talked about it. Sometimes she'd call David's boss and curse, demanding her husband be given a raise. Other times she'd call making false accusations.

Amy Bules was still around, by then she was married and had just given birth. Still, she cared enough to listen to David and offer friendly advice. She warned him that he would lose his job if he didn't find a way to quiet her. When David confided about the gun threats, Amy begged him to get the guns out of the house. David needed them, he said; they were protection when he made his rounds in the Kentucky trailer parks. But, after thinking about it, he removed the bullets and kept them hidden in a separate room; that way, the most Dante could do was harass him.

By then Amy had grown truly afraid of the Dante situation. She had heard enough bad news from David to have reason to think the woman might be capable of murder. It was approaching the end of 1994, and David was talking about divorcing her, which Amy knew would create a big problem.

"I'm holding this six-week-old baby in my hands," Amy said, shuddering. "I had this little tiny baby and the phone rang, my answering machine picked up, and Dante just read my address off to me."

"Amy, I know where you live," the voice said, spelling out the street and number. Then the phone clicked.

CHAPTER | 72

"**S**HE HAD ALL THIS HATRED," DAVID REFLECTED. "She told me she hired some guy to burn a house down. Her boyfriend cheated on her, or she worked for him and he fired her. I thought it was a threat. That was one of the stories I really didn't believe at all."

People at work were telling David to write the stories down. There were so many, and they were so absolutely wild, everyone said he should write a book. Of course, he refused to believe most of it; Dante would sit down to dinner and tell him things like he was a priest offering confession. But from his own experience, he knew she made up stories without any reason whatsoever. She'd usually be talking just to hear herself talk, and most of the time David ignored her. He would lie on the couch watching TV and just let her ramble.

"When I left her," David confided, "we had gotten into a fight earlier because she threw my golf clubs out onto the street, and the two-year green-card period had ended, so I was planning to leave in another month anyway."

David announced he was through with the marriage, but he didn't drive off without Dante following him into the parking lot, banging on the car as he pulled away. She ran up the street after the car, and he had to admit, it was a great fight they had, their last blowout. He went to see his attorney that afternoon, and he came back and started packing up all his stuff. He dismantled his gun and packed it in separate suitcases, and he had those bags waiting in the foyer when Dante snuck upstairs. Her voice was strangely low.

"Are you really going to leave me?"

"Yes."

"Are you going, definitely? This is your last chance."

"Yeah, I'm leaving."

Dante ran downstairs and came back after a few minutes with something wrapped in a T-shirt.

"Where's the fucking bullets?" she howled.

She had both hands on the gun and she was pointing it at his chest. He just laughed, and she threw the thing down on the floor, but then she got the idea to hit him over the head with it, so she grabbed the gun and lunged.

"Look, if you're going to carry on with all this shit, I'm going to call the police," he yelled.

In a stern voice, he repeated that he was leaving, and he marched her downstairs so he could finish collecting his things. Within minutes the police were at his front door, and he could hear Dante telling them that her husband whacked her over the head with a gun, complaining about a bump on her skull. She was such a good actress, David thought she deserved an Oscar. This time David argued with police, trying to explain what was going on, insisting it was Dante who should be locked up. The cops hauled him off to jail without waiting to hear the whole story; it was his gun, he had a prior record, and that was that.

The next morning the judge issued a temporary protection order for Dante, so legally David wasn't allowed to enter their apartment. And because Dante refused to place his things outside, he had to make special arrangements for a police escort to retrieve his possessions. He already feared the worst, having commiserated with a cell-mate who told him he had been thrown in jail by his wife, only to find all his things burned up by the time he was permitted back in the home.

Ultimately, the disposition of David Britteon's belongings was moved out of the criminal courts and into civil litigation as part of the divorce proceedings. His lawyer was aware that while David was under restraining orders from the court, Dante had sold most of his possessions and had allegedly managed to store the rest in her U-Haul facility.

Evidently Dante thought she'd accomplished something, because she herself told David that she destroyed his clothes and his important paperwork.

"It was just like in *Psycho,* when he goes in the shower scene," she bragged. "You know, when he goes in there with a knife? Well, I freaked out, and I went into your clothes like that."

CHAPTER 73

ONE OF THE FIRST THINGS DANTE AND DARRYL DID TO-gether involved a Special Olympics event. Darryl was quite active in the organization, and Dante admired him for that. Secretly she cringed at the sight of people in wheelchairs, but she stood around and watched the race, signing herself up as a volunteer for future fund-raisers. The next day she called Cheryl to report how depressing it was to be around handicapped people. If the Special Olympics people called her, Dante said, she'd just have to come up with some excuse.

By Christmas Day 1994, Darryl and Dante were in that cozy stage of early romance. He was enamored with her kind-hearted ways; she loved to just listen to him, always taking his side and understanding his emotional needs. She made it clear that she never wanted to work, that she just wanted to be taken care of, if only she could find someone to pour her love out toward.

For her Christmas Day party, she decided to have a "lonely hearts" dinner, so she invited a few of her ex-boyfriends to her tiny apartment for a traditional turkey meal, encouraging Darryl to do the same. Darryl had no choice; he went along with the silly idea, even volunteering to cook for the event.

The day before, Darryl begged his friend Carla Smith to pop in at Dante's, but his pretty co-worker had no interest in posing as Darryl's love interest. For all his trying, Darryl was unable to round up any female friend to join him at Dante's for dinner, so on Christmas Dante wound up with six gentlemen callers all to herself. She was in her glory.

David decided to show up with a male buddy of his, figuring he'd have a free meal and, hopefully, reclaim some of his things. Their divorce was final and David was paying her $1,200 a month alimony, but Dante had managed to hold on to his green card, passport, and other documents. He needed the stuff back and was hoping to coax her into admitting that she was hiding everything, including his golf clubs, and possibly one of his guns.

"She had a way with men. She was an excellent flirt," David admitted. "She had some pretty dress on and she was prancing around, being cutesie and all. And I'm wondering, what are these other people thinking? I mean, the doctor isn't stupid."

While Dante entertained the guests, Darryl was stuck in the kitchen basting the turkey most of the time. Dante had no idea why her guests didn't bring any female friends, and acted like they had been asked to do so.

For a few brief moments, David went into Dante's kitchen to check Darryl out. The two of them chatted about national health care and the concept of price fixing, just medical shop talk. David watched every word he said because he could feel Dante pressing her ear in their direction. She had a knack for carrying on two conversations at once. She always listened from across a crowded room, especially when her name popped up. Even though David was thoroughly impressed with Darryl, he wanted to warn him. With Dante around, though, that wasn't really a good idea. He hoped the doctor knew what he was doing. It seemed like Darryl was overly infatuated with Dante. He wondered if she had turned over a new leaf. It was amazing that she hadn't caused Darryl any problems already.

Out in the living room, David had a private discussion with his ex-wife, at the end of which she handed him his passport and offered to let him buy back his golf clubs for $500. They arranged to meet at her storage facility the next afternoon, Dante promising to call first thing in the morning. She claimed she hadn't seen his green card, but David had proof the card had been mailed to her.

She promised to look for it, but didn't seem hopeful.

After they left, David's buddy said he thought the whole event was sick. He didn't understand what the big attraction was. He thought Dante just wasn't all that beautiful—she was scrawny, her hair was overbleached—the guy couldn't fathom why all these men were hanging around.

1-9-95
Darling Dante

You always look for mail when you get to your door, so I decided to be sure you had something to read. Another "mushy" note? Probably, but nevertheless, I suppose I can put my thoughts down more specifically on paper than by spoken word.

You asked me tonight what I think about you and I tried to respond. Obviously, anyone with reasonable eyesight would think you are one of the most beautiful creatures God ever created, and I must agree. Your beauty, however, goes far beyond the contours of your face and figure. You are a compassionate, caring human being, who I believe can love someone completely and give yourself to them totally, once you have decided to do so.

You're funny at times, playful at times, brooding at times, selfish at times, generous at times, intellectual at times, earthy at times (I like that), always tasteful, always lovable, always adorable. You have shared things with me I suspect you have not shared with most other of your admirers, I take great pride in that and hope this means you have some feelings for me, similar to those I have for you.

Is it silly and sophomoric at this point in our relationship to say I love you? Again, probably, but I had a feeling the first night I met you that I have never lost. Probably impossible to put into words, I only know that you have become the very central person in my life. I want so much to please you, I want so much to gain your respect and hopefully someday, your love. Don't fool me like you did your friend you moved to Texas with, I'd rather never have you than think you loved me and have you leave. If we stay together, I never want a separation as long as we live.

I want a lifetime partner to share things with and enjoy life with. We seem to have many common interests, which is good. I also have interests which bore you to tears (sports primarily as far as I can tell). Our tastes are different in food, art, music, architecture, but we both admire quality and I'm sure, could come to happy compromises when differences of opinion occur.

When arguments occur, know always that love is there and nothing is worth breaking that bond. I will always try to be considerate. Sometimes I can be a real blockhead but if I cause you discomfort or pain it will never be intentional. Let me know what I've done and I'll try to improve and keep you happy. I want so much to see you have a wonderful life with everything you could wish for. I don't know what the future holds for me, but I'll do my best for us, I promise.

To say those things to someone when you have yet to share a physical relationship probably sounds old-fashioned, I'd have to plead guilty to that. The other point this makes is that being close to you and tied to you emotionally is more important than the physical.

You've asked me would I love you if you gained weight, etc. I am extremely proud to be in the company of someone like you who is so beautiful from a physical standpoint. There is no question that your beauty was the first thing to catch my eye. What will keep me close to you and loving you forever is not physical beauty. It will be a commitment from you that you love me.

If that ever comes, the only thing that will separate us will be death, and that will only be temporary as I would hope to spend eternity with you as well. Forgive me if I have overstepped the bounds of our relationship at this point.

Love, Darryl

CHAPTER | 74

THE FIRST PERSON TO CALL THE POLICE WAS OLGA Mello. That kicked off their investigation on February 19, 1996, the day Darryl Sutorius was found dead in his basement. She had called to find out if her daughter was being held in custody, and Detective Bob Wessler gave her a call back, reaching her in Old Town, Florida, just after 6:00 P.M. Minutes before, Olga had received a call from her daughter Nikki and was aware that her daughter was all over the Cincinnati evening news.

Mrs. Mello gave Detective Wessler a quick rundown of Della's husbands, referring to the list she had written out for Darryl. There had been so many, and there was the common law husband, Sid Davis, so Olga just wasn't sure she could keep track of them all. She was ranting about Della having sent Sid Davis to jail for marijuana possession. The detective tried to get her to slow down, but Olga was worked into a lather, calling Della "such a bully," and offering the phone numbers of Joe Hoeffer and Grant Bassett.

"Della thought Bassett had a lot of money 'cause he used to bring gifts over," Olga told the detective. "She was thrilled to death she got a rich man."

"Her real name is Della?" Detective Wessler asked, somewhat surprised.

"Della. Della Faye Hall," Olga said. "She thought that sounded like a little black girl's name or something, and she made up Dante because it sounds rich. Is she still being held?"

"Yes."

"Because my other children are afraid that she might come out and do something to them. They're all in fear of their lives right now. Is she getting out tonight?" Olga asked in a panic.

"I don't know."

"I hope and pray she doesn't. I mean . . ."

"Okay. Anybody else that she threatened, shot, burned out that you know of?"

"She threatened my life. I have that on tape recorder. She said if she ever found out she had a half-brother or half-sister, and I didn't tell her about it, she definitely would kill me."

"Oh, okay."

"But she's good at threatening people's lives, and then we all think her bark is bigger than her bite. Everybody is afraid of her, but we didn't think she would go this far."

Before Olga hung up, she had supplied the detective with as many phone numbers as she could find, had filled him in on how she tried to help Dr. Sutorius, and mentioned Darryl was planning to divorce Della.

The next morning, Grant Bassett was brought into the Hamilton County Sheriff's Office to talk with Detective Dennis Goebel. He described Dante and was very graphic in detailing her weird habits.

"Has she ever threatened you?" Goebel asked.

"To quote her, she said, 'Don't fuck with me, or I'll kill you. That's not a problem. It's not beyond me. It doesn't bother me one bit, especially when it comes to a weirdo like you.'"

Bassett described the two occasions when Dante was contemplating killing him: the time when he found the two knives, and the time he called 911 because she was going crazy and seemed capable of beating him to death with a household object.

Bassett talked about the unfair justice system, about

how he had been sent to jail for no reason. He gave Goebel the whole story—the way she traded in her wedding ring for a face-lift—but said he didn't really care to repeat it for a grand jury. Bassett wasn't happy about testifying and asked not to be called. He still feared Dante and was visibly shaken up.

While Goebel was busy with husband number three, Detective Hinrichs was questioning Dick Brunsman in an adjoining office. He was listening to Darryl's buddy talk about meeting the surgeon for dinner for the last time. They sat at Chester's Roadhouse and Darryl discussed Dante's previous criminal activities; she had a record involving something about threatening a guy with a gun. Brunsman told Hinrichs about Darryl breaking into Dante's bedroom, finding a .22-caliber pistol, and turning it in to police. Before Brunsman left, he informed Hinrichs that Darryl's profit-sharing and pension plan was worth over a million dollars. In the absence of a will or a beneficiary designation, Brunsman said, that dollar amount would go to Dante.

"He was afraid she was gonna kill him," Dick asserted, "so afraid that he canceled a trip he already planned."

On February 21, Detective Patrick Dilbert made a couple of calls to Darryl's faraway female friends. Lori Waiss, Darryl's ex-co-worker who had moved to Chicago, gave a statement that detailed Darryl's problems with Dante. According to Lori, Darryl didn't like his wife's idiosyncrasies and didn't think their marriage was going to last. Darryl had poured his heart out to Lori just three weeks prior, apologizing for not returning her calls sooner. He said he couldn't make phone calls from home because of Dante's accusations, and promised to keep in touch. She was shocked at the news that Darryl might have killed himself, and wanted information on the funeral arrangements. It was a particularly sad phone conversation; Lori was in tears when they hung up.

When Alanna Conrad was contacted, she, too, had spoken to Darryl about three weeks earlier. She couldn't remember the exact date, but she recalled his tone was unusual, that he sounded extremely anxious. Darryl wanted to know if she had been contacted by anyone in Cincinnati because her name was missing out of his Rolodex. He was sorry for bothering her and sounded depressed and fearful.

"He mentioned he thought she would kill him?" the detective asked.

"Yes," Alanna said, "and I'll tell you why this comes into such a big play with me, is, unfortunately, five years ago my sister was murdered."

"Okay."

"So I think he felt like he could talk to me about this stuff. It was a terrible situation."

At the time, Alanna suggested that Darryl give up his practice and consider moving to Palm Springs. She would help him start his practice all over again. Of course, Darryl appreciated her support, but he had four children in Ohio that he wanted to stay close to.

Later that afternoon, two detectives appeared at the Cardiovascular Laboratory at Bethesda North Hospital. They were there to interview Carla Smith, someone known to have been friends with Darryl for eight years.

At first Carla was hesitant to talk; she had no real information about the death. But she described Darryl's first divorce, from Janet, telling detectives how he was annoyed because it was costing him a fortune. She tried to remember the beginning of the relationship between Darryl and Dante, but couldn't. Carla admitted having a peripheral awareness of their domestic disputes and said that while the two of them were reading vascular studies one afternoon, she noticed scratch marks on Darryl's face.

It was in early 1996, Carla told police, that she realized Darryl was no longer wearing his wedding ring. At some point in January he confided that he was going to have to give Dante $3,000 a month in spousal support. He told Carla it was a small price to pay for his life.

When Goebel left Bethesda North, the detective headed over to see Jeff Freeman to discuss the aggravated menacing conviction against Dante. Freeman described the actual offense at length, insisting that he never trusted Dante and suspected that she still carried around deadly weapons in her purse. He elaborated on the phone call he had received from Darryl Sutorius just a few weeks before his death, and also mentioned he had recently received two phone messages from Dante.

She was calling to thank him for not giving any comments to news commentators, and also to report she had something important she wanted to tell him. Freeman had not called her back.

Lisa Johnson came next. She was called into the Symmes Township Station and seemed frightened and extremely upset. Lisa was interviewed by Dilbert and Wessler, and described her engagement to Darryl and their difficult breakup. She mentioned a phone call she made to the Fountainbleau Hotel in Miami when she first realized the surgeon was intimate with Dante. Originally Lisa was supposed to go on that trip; it was for a medical conference Sutorius was participating in. Lisa explained that Darryl had encouraged her to call him, but when she did, Dante answered the phone.

That day, Lisa reported, she and Dante had a spat over the phone. Then a few weeks later Dante started harassing her. Lisa told police that Dante would call and play one or two notes on the piano, then just hang up. Eventually Dante called and mentioned she knew the color of Lisa's car and the names of her kids. She threatened to contact the children while Lisa was at work, and Lisa was nervous enough to let the receptionist hear the threats on the speaker phone. Apparently Lisa had made an official complaint to Blue Ash police, and she handed Detective Dilbert the telephone harassment report.

When David Britteon was being interviewed by Detectives Hinrichs and Goebel he described his ex-wife "brandishing a gun." Britteon contended that Dante thought it was loaded when she held it up and pointed it at him. Before he left the marriage, he explained to authorities, Dante had stolen a .22-caliber pistol from him. He told Goebel she was currently in contempt of court for failing to return his belongings.

"Have you seen that weapon since you left?" Goebel asked.

"Not until just now," Britteon said.

"Okay. And the weapon we just showed you, that's the weapon that was yours?"

"Yeah."

"How do you identify it as being yours?"

"It was a Browning that I had. And more specifically, I had an unusual mounting for the telescopic sight on it."

"So you know it was yours?"

"Yeah."

"Have you had any conversation with her since you left?"

"Yeah, she called me yesterday afternoon, that would be the twentieth."

"And what was that conversation?"

"She told me that her husband died. She sounded really upset, hysterical. She said that she didn't want to talk about it. She wanted me to talk about my trip to England. She basically wanted to talk about other things."

"That would have been Tuesday, the twentieth? Yesterday?"

"Yeah."

"And have you had any conversation with her today?"

"Yeah, she called today asking if I told the news-people about her threatening to kill me after the divorce. She talked about a cocaine charge or something. She wanted to know if I remembered a little box that she had from a long time ago that had cocaine in it, and I didn't remember anything about it.

"And then I asked her, I asked her if . . ." he continued. "I don't know how I put it, but I guess I asked her if she killed him, and she said, 'Well, I might run a bad temper, but I wasn't that bad. I wouldn't do that.' I forget how the conversation went exactly."

"During the course of your marriage, did she ever threaten to kill you?"

"Verbally, I guess, many times, yeah. Just how serious she ever was, I don't know."

"Did you take the gun incident as a threat, as serious?"

"Oh, yeah. I believe that if the gun had been loaded, she might have shot me with it."

CHAPTER 75

As Della sat at home clipping newspaper stories about Mrs. Iran Alavi, the eighty-two-year-old woman slain in her neighborhood earlier that week, police investigators were listening to hair-raising stories from two of her former lovers.

Sid Davis started off talking about his apartment that Della had completely destroyed, but Detective Hinrichs wanted to hear about the burning bed—Olga had made numerous references to it.

As Sid described the kerosene lamp Della once brought over for "atmosphere," the detective listened in disbelief. Sid recounted waking up with his mattress in flames, certain he would have died if he had been taking any kind of other drug at the time.

"Well, did you receive any injuries?" Hinrichs finally asked.

"No, just a red cheek."

"Okay, and did you question her about these incidents? Like when she tried to burn you in the bed, and when your apartment was broken into?"

"Yeah."

"And she basically admitted to doing them?"

"Yeah."

"Is that correct?" the detective wanted to be sure.

"Yes. She wouldn't come directly and say 'I got you this time,' but she would make it known that, yes, she did do it."

Sid told Hinrichs about the time Della pulled out a butcher knife, and described her testimony that ruined his lawsuit against the railroad, asserting the cocaine found in his car wasn't really his, that she had planted it there. The last contact he had with her was through her brother Scott, who had called asking him to testify on his behalf when Della was falsely trying to take him to court. But Sid had refused to do that; he felt he couldn't chance any face-to-face contact with her.

If the Sutorius case came to trial, Sid hoped he wouldn't be called as a witness.

That same day, when Brian Powell talked to Sergeant Tom Boeing, describing Dante as insanely jealous, he took no time to zero in on the night she showed up smelling like "campfire smoke." She had kept him pre-occupied downtown that evening, and the next morning he returned home to find his house torched.

"Was the fire determined to be an arson?" the sergeant asked.

"Yes, it was. It was an arson," Powell told him. "The state fire marshal said it looked like a woman done it, because if it was a man, they usually start it under the car, or they burn something different than clothes. Plus the insurance company said it was arson. It was actually sheets hung over the windows, so people wouldn't discover the fire."

"So I want to understand you right. You tell her one evening you want to break off the relationship. She talks you into meeting for one last time."

"Right."

"And she shows up a couple hours late," Boeing repeated.

"Right."

"Smelling like . . ."

"Smoke."

On February 25, two days before Della was arrested for aggravated homicide, Detective Dennis Goebel got hold of Donna Hall out in California. He conducted a taped interview during which Donna quoted Della as having said, "Anybody can die." Donna out-and-out accused her sister of being a killer, claiming Della had slain numerous men.

"She really scared me because she was laughing like when you see people in the movies when they totally lose control," Hall told the detective. "She had fallen to the floor she was laughing so hard. All I remember is something about a fat man, and he was so fat, and she just kept stabbing him. I don't know if she said stabbing, I think she said sticking. And she was doing this thing with her hands and showing me."

"Okay, and then what did she tell you about this?" the detective asked, trying to get Donna to focus on the facts.

"That's where she was telling me, 'Anybody can die,'

and it was like, 'Ask me, I've done it three times, almost four.'"

"She told you she killed someone, and she could do something to you?"

"Something like that. Or my kids. It seems to me it was a threat about my kids."

Donna described her sister as being "incapable of love," talking about a time when Della tried to strangle one of her sons. Apparently Donna had received a call at work from her eleven-year-old boy, wanting her to come home because Aunt Della was trying to "do something" to him. When Donna arrived, she couldn't get the straight story out of her son, but the boy was clearly frightened. Not long after that, Della moved in with Terry Armstrong.

"If she's jealous," Donna reported, "like she told me, she can't take rejection very well."

"Hm. Hmmm."

"You know, what is bugging me, I'm trying to figure out what it is about the fourth one, why the fourth one got away. It's nagging at me."

"The fourth husband?" Goebel asked.

"No, the fourth one she tried to kill."

"What's that?"

"I know when she left L.A. all of a sudden, she ended up in, I think it was Laguna Beach. At the time, I thought she was the weirdest thing going. I didn't know there was something wrong. I guess I had just blocked out the murders she told me about."

"Well, she seems to have messed with a lot of people's lives," the detective said, trying to wrap up the conversation.

For the most part, Goebel just listened. Based on Donna's accusations, he made a notation to check with LAPD. Still, it seemed evident that Donna was exaggerating about her sister. There were no names connected with these supposed murder victims, no dates, no specific details at all, and in fact, when a search was done, Della had no criminal record in California.

Before Goebel ended the interview, he gave Donna his desk number, asking her to call him if she had any further information. He was politely trying to hang up the phone, when Donna blurted that she had a husband who had been murdered. His name was Mitchell McDowell, and his killer had never been found.

Donna tried to imply that Della might have been involved.

On March 21, 1996, Detective Cutch of the San Bernardino Police Department was contacted by Bill Smith, a detective with the LAPD. Cutch confirmed that Della was never a suspect in the murder of Donna Hall's ex-husband.

As the victims came forward, Sergeant Tom Boeing, who had supervised the investigations of more than five hundred deaths in his career, realized he had never seen anything quite like this. Still, as the head of the Sutorius death investigation, he was concerned with only one thing: what the coroner's report would show. On February 19, 1996, Della Dante Sutorius had given them a six-and-a-half-hour statement, but had left them with the same unanswered questions.

"The officers kind of had to talk their way into the house," Boeing recounted, "and then at her first opportunity she runs down and miraculously finds this body that's been in the basement, and that concerned me. When you take a look at the physical evidence, the blood splatter evidence, where the gun was found . . . all these things didn't fit a suicide."

CHAPTER | 76

ONE OF THE FIRST THINGS TOM LONGANO DID WAS hang pictures of Della on the back of his office door. With the case turning into a media circus, he needed to stay focused, and seeing her innocent posture whenever he hung up his coat made him all the more determined to win. Of course, the case was entirely circumstantial, one of the most unusual murder cases Longano ever tried in his twenty-three years as a prosecutor.

"I'll be honest with you, I probably feel that she has multiple personalities," the prosecutor reflected. "She is probably convinced that she was abused as a child. But when we talked to her relatives or anyone that knew her early on, they say that's just not the way it happened."

For tactical reasons, R. Scott Croswell decided against filing a plea of not guilty by reason of insanity. Had he done so, Della would have been examined by psychiatrists and psychologists, and those reports would have been turned over to prosecutors. Generally speaking, those kinds of findings only work well for the state.

With a witness list that reached over 150 people, Hamilton County Prosecuting Attorney Joseph T. Deters needed his best men on the job. He assigned two of his top criminal prosecutors, Jerry Kunkel and Steve Tolbert, to work under Longano, and the three of them worked out a strategy, trying to keep it simple. They divided up the witnesses and worked day and night, each one being told stories that curled their fingernails.

Brian Powell, for instance, told Longano a tale about finding another man's wallet among Della's storage. Powell actually spoke to the guy, only to discover that Della met him in Daytona Beach, had followed him to his motel room, and while he was in the shower, jumped into her car with all his earthly belongings. The man was legally blind without his glasses and had to fumble to dial O for an operator, making an emergency call to his mother.

It was one of the many Della side stories that seemed to grow day by day.

"There's a tendency in cases like this to want to bring in everything," Longano explained. "You end up really clouding up the issues and muddying up the waters. We had a choice: We could bring in every bad act she ever committed and try her on her reputation along with the facts of the case, or we could try it the way we did."

Prosecutors decided they didn't need to paint Della as the most evil person in the world; they thought the jury might have problems with that. They actually threw Della's prior bad acts out the window and didn't put any boyfriends or husbands on the stand, other than David Britteon. Longano thought it might backfire if they started dishing dirt, and his cocounsels concurred.

"See, Della didn't have good sense," Tolbert reflected. "I mean, Della could have played this thing out for a very long time. She had it made. She married a guy who earned a decent income with a good long-term financial outlook. The ironic thing is, she tells people he's overbearing and disgusting and she wants nothing to do with him, yet he leaves the house for ten minutes and she's on him like Sherlock Holmes."

Anxiously anticipated were the arrivals of Olga Mello and Donna Hall. The two women had tickets confirmed on Delta for May 29, 1996. That afternoon, they would be met in the lobby of the Omni Hotel in order to discuss what kind of questions they could expect on the witness stand. By the time the date rolled around, Della's trial was well under way, opening statements having begun on May 20, just three months after the surgeon's death.

In the courtroom, prosecutors found that Scott Croswell had a whole new set of tactics. There were more than a few observers who thought he went overboard. Perhaps. But most everything he pulled was admissible in court.

CHAPTER 77

"*E*VEN THOUGH THE JURY IS NOT SUPPOSED TO RELY ON sympathy when they deliver verdicts, you still want to make the victim into a living, breathing person that has friends and family," prosecutor Kunkel confided. "So here we are, confronted with the Sutorius family, and none of them, other than Deborah, had any communications with their father in months."

In his opening statement, Longano gave the jury the short version of what the case was about. He read the indictment, explaining Count I, aggravated murder, which meant Della Dante Sutorius acted with prior calculation in causing her husband's death; and Count II, drug possession, for the small amount of cocaine found in Della's belongings, a Schedule II controlled substance.

He described Darryl Sutorius as a successful fifty-five-year-old vascular surgeon, earning in excess of $300,000 a year, who was a perfectionist, a tough guy to work with, but a well-respected man who worked hard to provide for his wife and his children.

Then he talked about Della, a forty-five-year-old woman who was virtually broke when she married Darryl, her fifth husband. She met the doctor through a dating service and after they decided to wed, Darryl attempted to draw up a prenuptial agreement, but Della refused to sign. He mentioned the doctor's retirement and profit-sharing assets, which, when he married Della, amounted to a million dollars, and explained that Darryl had drafted an agreement that detailed the exact amount of money in the plan, asking Della to waive her spousal rights to said money in exchange for a $10,000 payment. But Della balked at the contract.

Tom Longano moved on to March 1995, when Della and Darryl moved into their house on Symmesridge, which the jury had inspected the day before trial began. The prosecutor claimed that their honeymoon was over the minute the couple took possession of the place, Della inhabiting her own private bedroom upstairs.

Longano pointed to the patterns that characterized the Sutorius marriage for the next eleven months: Della was outrageously jealous, snooping through his mail at the office and his things at home; meanwhile, Darryl was cut off from his children, his co-workers, and his friends.

As Longano spoke, he was good at giving nonverbal cues. He had a Superman cool about him, something many women would find sexy, and his thick head of hair, sleek dark suits, and piercing steel eyes didn't hurt any. With a perfectly calm tone, he described the fierce arguments that started to develop over Darryl's expenditures for his daughter's wedding. Della was presented as a conniving, deceptive shrew, the antithesis of the lady the jury saw before them, a wisp of a woman sitting there with her hands clasped over her delicate Laura Ashley skirt.

When Longano moved to the time frame of November

and December 1995, he told jurors that the doctor had expressed fear to his daughter, that he had been physically abused, scratched, by his wife. In January 1996, Darryl sought the services of a psychiatrist, Dr. Louis Spitz, at which time Darryl confided, in Della's presence, that because of his first divorce, he had once considered suicide. The two went on to see a marriage counselor, Miriam Warschauer, after which Darryl called to privately express his concerns for his own safety, describing his fear of his wife.

"Della cut those sessions off," the prosecutor's voice boomed, "because Miriam formed the same opinion about her that Dr. Spitz did. Della was exhibiting all this anger towards the doctor."

Longano presented events as the atmosphere became progressively worse in the Sutorius household. The surgeon eventually went to his attorney, Guy Hild, asking for advice. He was very concerned about keeping his house, but made the decision to draw up legal divorce paperwork. On January 24, Darryl turned a .22-caliber pistol in to police. He told Corporal Huber that his wife was threatening him, and at that time a temporary restraining order was filed to prevent Della from making any physical attacks.

The divorce papers were supposed to be signed on Monday, February 19, 1996, the day Dr. Darryl Sutorius was found dead. As Longano described Della's well-plotted plan to carry out a murder, citing the forensic evidence that would back up his theory, the jury hung on to his every word. He promised to present evidence of motive, of purpose, telling jurors that Della married not for love, but for money. And, had the death of Darryl Sutorius been deemed a suicide, she stood to gain close to a million dollars.

Scott Croswell's opening statement only lasted about ten minutes. He raised the issue of reasonable doubt, referring to Darryl as being "suicidal," an "alcoholic," "impotent," and "depressed." The type of lawyer who would pull out all the stops to make his point, Croswell had once brought an ax into a courtroom, swinging it in front of jurors in the high-profile murder case of Jack Hennessee, who had killed and mutilated his wife. Croswell got him off by proving it was self-defense.

Now, for the jury in the Sutorius trial, he played the country bumpkin to the hilt. His Ohio drawl was at its peak, and his mannerisms were friendly, yet self-assured. He was brilliant at making himself out to be the underdog.

"This is my opportunity to tell you what I believe the evidence will show," Croswell said, getting up close to the jury, "and I have to be absolutely candid with you. I am not sure what the evidence will show."

Croswell was complaining that since almost none of the witnesses would agree to be interviewed by him, he was at a tremendous disadvantage in defending Della. The defense attorney had no idea what the expert witnesses for the state were about to testify.

"My client tells me that she is innocent," Croswell crooned, "that she knows absolutely nothing about the death of her husband.

"You have heard the prosecution discuss suicide for the last couple of days," he continued. "I have to tell you that *I don't know* if it's a suicide. I'm not suggesting to you that I can prove that it is. I'm suggesting to you that the prosecution can't prove that it isn't."

CHAPTER 78

WHEN DAVID BRITTEON STOOD BEFORE THE COURT-
room and spelled his name for prosecutor Steve Tolbert,
one could have heard a pin drop.

He was tall, about six-one, with thick dark hair and a
perfect smile, and Della couldn't take her eyes off him,
though David hardly looked her way. Tolbert's soft-spoken manner seemed to help the witness get over his
nervousness, and David identified Della, who was sitting
behind the defense table in a floral print outfit.

He testified that her assets had totaled no more than
$1,500 when he married her, that when their divorce was
finalized in January 1995, he was ordered to continue
paying Della $1,200 a month spousal support. His ali-
mony payments stopped, however, when she married
Darryl in March of that year.

David examined State's Exhibit Number 1, a .22-cali-
ber revolver, telling the story of Della trying to hit him
over the head with a gun. When 911 was called and he
lost entrance to his apartment, he explained to jurors,
Della stole his .22 Browning. Since that time, he had
been unsuccessful in getting it back.

Tolbert asked him about the conversation he had with
Della on February 21, 1996, and David described her as
sounding distressed. She had called to say her husband
had died, and then called back the following day, asking
him not to talk to reporters. Before he ended direct
examination, Tolbert established the fact that Croswell
and his team had never contacted David.

*   *   *

Carla Magaveny was the next witness, Della's sister, an attractive dark-haired woman 15 years her junior, and she told the court that in 1994, Della's money was running out. Apparently Della had no skills, was complaining about her bad back, and was "a bit worried."

"She didn't know where her money was going to come from," she testified, looking thoroughly disgusted with her sister.

Carla talked about the men Della was dating at the time, claiming that she didn't love any of them, that it was only after Darryl bought her a Lexus that Della agreed to marry him. Responding to Tolbert's well-crafted questions and his mild manner, Carla described Della's lifestyle with the doctor, noting that Della had never lived in such luxury before. Suddenly, she told jurors, Della had expensive antiques, a bunch of fur coats, and vacations to exotic places.

"Do you recall a comment she made about what her financial situation would be if something happened to Dr. Sutorius," Tolbert prodded, "what would happen if he would leave the planet?"

"She came out with, she'd be worth a million dollars if he wasn't here. And I thought, you know, of course it was a joke. And then I said, 'Does the man have a million-dollar policy?' and she said, 'Well, I'd have to split it with his kids.' "

"Did Della ever make a comment to you about the status of your personal life or your marital life?"

"Well, she didn't come right out and say it, but definitely, you know, I had married a working man and that was beneath her."

Later, on cross-examination, Croswell tried to undermine Carla's testimony, mocking her memory and trying to diminish the million-dollar comment.

"Would it surprise you to find out that there isn't a million-dollar life insurance policy that she is beneficiary of?" he wanted to know.

"I would find that odd."

"Find it odd. I tell you what you do for me. If you find a million-dollar life insurance policy that she is a beneficiary of, bring it to us, will you?"

Later that day, Melvin Marmer, Darryl's attorney for estate planning, took the stand, telling the court that he met with Darryl just ten days before the doctor remarried. They had a meeting to discuss how they could comply with Ohio law while still protecting his retirement benefits, since Della wouldn't sign a prenuptial. They came up with an alternative plan, and Marmer produced the pertinent document. It was a letter directing Della to waive her rights to his retirement funds.

"Let me rephrase it, then." Longano clarified. "If Della Sutorius got married to Darryl and did not sign that waiver, if he were to die, she would take the proceeds of the retirement plan?"

"Yes," Marmer confirmed.

When it was Croswell's turn, the defense attorney brought up the fact that Della only had an eighth-grade education, that she wasn't well versed in the law of pension and profit-sharing plans. He had Marmer admit that in fact the Sutorius children were the beneficiaries of the plan, though Marmer was quick to point out that, upon the doctor's death, a new law would allow the surviving spouse to receive all benefits, regardless of the named beneficiaries.

For the court, Marmer went on to describe the doctor's life insurance policies: a $1 million policy payable to the children; a $600,000 policy payable to his first wife, Janet; and a $200,000 policy with no named beneficiary, meaning it would go to his current spouse. Marmer testified that there was actually only $650,000 in the pension plan at the time of Sutorius's death. Thus Della stood to receive a total of $850,000.

"That could mean in addition to playing for a murder case, we are also playing for $850,000?" Croswell cajoled. "In other words, if she is found not guilty, not only do we celebrate that she's found not guilty, but we also get the eight hundred fifty thousand and the children don't get it. Is that correct?"

Hypothetically, of course, that was correct. But just before the trial began, Della had already entered into a deal with the Sutorius children to settle for $229,000, forfeiting all her rights to any other additional property of Darryl's, regardless of the trial's outcome. When it came out in court that she needed to take a settlement because she was indigent and couldn't pay for legal costs, Croswell wanted to know why the Sutorius children would have agreed to give her that amount. Why would they settle with her?

"I can only presume that you, Mr. Marmer, recognized, as did the Sutoriuses, the possibility that Dr. Sutorius could have taken his own life," the defense attorney said. "Why else would you pay $230,000 if you didn't believe that was a possibility?"

CHAPTER 79

*B*ECAUSE OF HIS BLISTERING CROSS-EXAMINATIONS, THE prevailing opinion in the corridors of the courthouse was that R. Scott Croswell had raised just enough doubt about the state's case to enable jurors to vote not guilty. With Della sitting quietly in her ladylike designer clothes, and her attorney doing everything possible to undermine and discredit the doctor, the groundwork was being laid for an acquittal.

For the first few days of trial, Judge Richard Neihaus and the members of the jury heard about money and vanity, about Della's need for control. But that wasn't enough to make them believe that she shot her husband while he was asleep on his couch, that she had been clever and calculating enough to concoct a fake suicide. She was the prim and proper doctor's wife, and Croswell took every opportunity to elicit sympathy for her, to make it seem like she was living with a suicidal maniac.

However, as the trial continued, Court TV carrying the Sutorius case live, *Inside Edition* was poking around, looking for ex-husbands and family members to interview. Local media coverage was fierce, painting Della as a "small woman with a big past."

"The defense believes that the decedent in this case had dealt with issues of suicide and had contemplated taking his own life," Croswell told an already-fueled media throng, but no one in the press seemed to believe him. As drips and drabs of horror stories came in from Grant Bassett and David Britteon, it became evident that she wasn't such a sweet person. Della liked to devour men, taking whatever she could get—using blackmail and harassment to get her way.

The jury was admonished not to listen to any news accounts but nonetheless Croswell had his work cut out for him. He knew jurors would soon hear about the threats Della made, and about her menacing behavior. Still, all he needed to do was convince *one person* that the evidence wasn't conclusive. Since everything was circumstantial, he felt confident prosecutors had no real proof. And no matter how much they might trash her reputation, that wouldn't lead to a murder conviction.

"Don't cut her a break because you feel sorry for her," Croswell had told jurors. "We don't want breaks here. But don't punish her because you don't like her. . . . And I doubt very seriously, when this case is over, you'll like her."

Deborah Sutorius took the stand dressed in a beige linen suit. She leaned respectfully toward the jury, refusing to allow cameras to photograph her for Court TV, and spoke softly into the microphone. The day she testified was her twenty-sixth birthday; she considered it a gift to finally tell the truth about Dante, to have someone listen without thinking she was exaggerating. She told the jury she was currently attending Xavier University, earning a graduate degree in biology and secondary education, with plans of becoming a biology teacher. She seemed the epitome of the all-American beauty. Somebody did something right in raising her; she held herself well.

She talked about working for her dad, doing filing and cleaning out the waiting rooms in his office, explaining that he had paid her $200 a month to help her work her way through college. She talked about meeting her dad's fiancée—the woman whose real name was Della—and described their first dinner at the Olive Garden, where she learned her dad and Della were about to be married.

A tall, slender young bombshell with a beautifully stunning face, Deborah was the only person designated to testify on behalf of the family. She spoke with a confident, somewhat lofty tone, mentioning that Della seemed kind of cold to her, but nonetheless she agreed to help her and her dad move into their new house on Symmesridge. When asked, she confided that Della moved into an upstairs bedroom, but that really hadn't fazed her at the time. She wasn't thinking about the dynamics of their relationship because she was too focused on her dad. From the moment Della entered the picture, Deborah was never allowed to have any "alone time" with him.

"My father was who I talked to about everything," she said, quickly wiping away tears.

"Take your time, Deborah, don't worry about it," Tolbert said in a calm, fatherly tone.

"She always had to be there and it was very frustrating to me, because *my* personal business is none of hers."

Deborah told Tolbert about her announcement to become engaged, and she described how happy her dad was, how he patted her on the back, elated by the news. She didn't want an elaborate wedding, she testified, but it didn't really matter what she asked for, because Della immediately piped up and told her she was just a waitress, that she couldn't afford any kind of big wedding. Shortly after that, Della started listening in on her phone conversations with Darryl, and Deborah described several calls and hang-ups. A couple of days before Christmas, Deborah got tired of Della's threats, so she called and cursed her out. Deborah said it was the principle of the thing. She didn't want Della bossing her dad around.

Tolbert handed her a transcription of an answering machine tape, which she identified as the words her father spoke in the last days of his life. The exhibit was entered into evidence—under an exception of the hearsay rule, the tape was allowed in—and the entire courtroom listened to Darryl's voice:

"Don't *call* Dante, don't *speak* to Dante," his weeping voice pleaded. "Deborah, I don't know if I'll ever be able to talk to you again. *Please,* Deborah, you just don't understand. . . . I don't know if I'll live through this."

CHAPTER 80

IN THE ABSENCE OF FINGERPRINTS ON THE GUN, IN THE absence of any eyewitnesses, the first few days of prosecution testimony didn't seem very damaging. The turning point came, however, the day Miriam Warschauer took the stand.

The clinical social worker offered an explanation for

the phone calls that came in from Darryl following their January 11 session: He was frightened, he seemed very scared. He described a fight with his wife in which she became completely out of control.

"He said that she made threats to ruin his career," Warschauer testified, "about spreading lies about the IRS and about his hygiene, that she would tell lies to doctors he associated with, and he'd be ruined."

"Did he express fear for his life?" Kunkel asked, his eyes wide, his brow furrowed.

"Yes. He said he was very fearful that she would kill him."

"Did you give him any advice?"

"I suggested that he see a lawyer as soon as possible in order to protect himself."

By the time Warschauer was finished testifying, describing Darryl finding the gun behind Della's bolted door, his panicked phone calls, and the information Darryl had from Della's mother, including the fact that Della had supposedly hired someone to burn down a house, members of the jury seemed to see things in a different light. When Warschauer testified that Darryl's greatest fear was that Della would kill him in his sleep, the jury was paying close attention. It was difficult to imagine the little woman in the pink dress capable of such a thing, but the social worker classified her as a truly dangerous character, as being one of the most dangerous patients she had encountered in over twenty years.

When Croswell began his cross-examination, he appeared to be holding back a smile. He seemed to be questioning Warschauer's professionalism, making her out to be a nitpicker. She wasn't a medical doctor with patients, he pointed out, she was merely a counselor, a social worker paid to console people and "hold their hand," he suggested.

"Do you believe that there are those in America," he smiled, "experts that know more about suicide than you?"

"Probably."

"And of course, of your own personal knowledge, you don't know whether Dr. Sutorius took his own life or not, do you?"

"With the information I was given and that I observed, I'd say he was not suicidal."

The marriage counselor somehow managed to turn Croswell's cross-examination around, pointing out that Darryl Sutorius was making plans for the future, stating that suicidal people usually don't do that. Even though her response was stricken from the record, the jury heard it, and they were left to interpret its significance.

Darryl's sister, Carlene Shultz, also testified to Darryl's healthy frame of mind. She claimed that when her brother came to visit on Super Bowl weekend, he looked better than she had seen him in a long time. According to Carlene, Darryl was wearing new clothes, was very upbeat, and seemed excited about Debbie's wedding. They had a wonderful evening, and in between football quarters Darryl was even talking about the new rose garden he was going to plant.

The jury learned that shortly after Super Bowl weekend, Della entered the PNC Bank on Montgomery Road. Records indicated that she went on February 7, to close out two CDs, each valued at about $1,000. The bank branch manager testified that Della seemed upset, that she said she and her husband were having marital problems and she didn't want him to get "her money." At the time, the manager mentioned that Della's checking account was overdrawn, and she replied, "that fat son-of-a-bitch was supposed to deposit five hundred dollars." Once Longano had elicited Della's nasty comment from the young manager, no matter what Croswell did to try to stump the young man, Della's statement couldn't be undone.

When Marian McCausland, a Target World employee, later took the stand to tell jurors that Della Sutorius was a "motivated customer," the murder plot started to really unfold. Della spent a good half hour testing weapons, gaining pretty extensive knowledge of what they had available in double-action revolvers. Before she selected a snubnose Smith and Wesson revolver, a used gun that came with two holsters, the Target World employee suggested a stun gun instead, thinking it might be a better idea. But Della wasn't the least interested.

Della "dry-fired" the handgun, double-checking the trigger, and then put $100 down, filled out papers to satisfy the Brady Bill, and was scheduled to pick up the gun ten days later, February 17, at which point she would receive a free hour of range time, as well as a credit toward a lesson.

She grabbed the yellow receipt from the counter and casually mentioned that she didn't want to be contacted at home, explaining that her husband didn't like the concept of guns in the house.

The clerk noticed that the date on Della's renewed driver's license happened to be the very day she was in there ordering the gun, but according to her testimony that wasn't uncommon. The Target World employee didn't question Della about it.

CHAPTER 81

"**D**ID SHE INDICATE TO YOU WHETHER OR NOT SHE HAD fired a handgun before?" Longano asked Rob Robertson, the Target World handgun instructor. The courtroom was packed and it was the last testimony before they broke for lunch that day. Robertson had just finished describing the preliminary shooting instructions he gave Della on February 17, 1996, having told Mrs. Sutorius about safety, sight alignment, and basic firearms marksmanship.

"For Ms. Sutorius," Robertson explained, "we moved on to the weapon she had purchased prior, the Smith and Wesson .38 Special."

"How did she do with the model you described?" Longano asked, looking over at Della, who quickly moved her gaze downward, away from his piercing glance.

"I would describe it as extremely well, especially for someone who hadn't fired a weapon before."

"And what kind of targets were you shooting at?"

"The standard police qualification silhouette target. It has a black silhouette outlining with scoring rings on it."

"And how was she doing in terms of hitting the target with the .38?"

"In my opinion, she was doing outstanding."

Robertson identified the gun Della used in the lesson as the same gun held before him in court, the one found at the Sutorius death scene.

After lunch, in the afternoon session of a busy court

day, Dr. Louis Spitz took the stand, describing the initial meeting he had with Dr. and Mrs. Sutorius as being very disturbing. Back in January of that year, he learned that Della was nosy, that she went through the doctor's private papers and had hidden things, among them a letter from Mel Marmer detailing Darryl's financial status. He also discovered that Darryl had considered suicide during the breakup of his first marriage, a point that Scott Croswell wouldn't stop mentioning. He harped on the fact that the doctor was irrational when it came to problems with women.

No matter how vehemently Dr. Spitz denied the notion of Darryl Sutorius being truly suicidal, Croswell tried to make Dr. Spitz's diagnosis of his patient seem fairly sketchy. He threw around statistics about white male doctors being more susceptible to suicide, but Spitz scoffed at these claims.

Time and again, Croswell returned to Darryl's suicidal thoughts of the past, asking Spitz to detail the triggering factors for Darryl's earlier claim that his kids might be better off without him. Dr. Spitz was quick to point out that Darryl only *thought* about suicide, that he hadn't ever *attempted* it.

"Did you look at Darryl and say, 'Doctor, I would like to explore specifically why you considered suicide in 1991'?"

"I felt that I had enough of the answer of things going on in 1991," Spitz explained, "that I could proceed with treating him in 1996."

"You never asked the question, did you?" Croswell pointed out. "Now that he's dead, a lot of other things are important that you couldn't predict, aren't they?"

"That's true."

"And that's the very reason you decided you would swing in here and make this six-page report, addendum to your treatment notes, because you figured you better get it covered, because there were a lot of things that were becoming important now that hadn't been important before. *True?*"

Answering Croswell's questions with a tone of icy disdain, Dr. Spitz looked disgusted by the attorney's attempt to make Darryl out to be a man who was miserable and psychologically depressed. Still, there was no denying the fact that Darryl was taking Effexor, an antidepressant; that he was treating himself with penile injections for impotence; that he was upset about his rocky relationship with his children; that he was mortified by his wife's threats to expose his physical and financial problems to his medical colleagues.

Croswell brought out all of Darryl's supposed reasons for considering suicide, even mentioning Della's threats to expose Darryl for having bowel problems, for soiling his pants. In spite of his gritty details, Croswell seemed to gain back some ground. When Dr. Spitz left the stand, it wasn't so clear that Darryl Sutorius had any kind of forward-looking view at the time of his death.

With all the problems Darryl faced—a messy divorce, public humiliation, financial ruin, the sleazy dating scene, utter loneliness, legal fees—suicide started to look like a viable long-term fix.

CHAPTER | 82

*H*E TALKED ABOUT SUICIDE. HE TALKED ABOUT A PERson taking a gun and placing it in an awkward position where he shoots himself so it appears to be an accident. Without coming right out and saying it, R. Scott Croswell did everything he could to imply that Darryl had shot himself and had set it up to look like a homicide, thus allowing his children to collect on his life insurance policies.

He talked about Darryl's daughter Deborah, "the little wildcat," and tried to blame her for the problems Darryl suffered with Della. Deborah was the one causing all the fighting, the verbally abusive one who wanted her dad to pay for a wedding he couldn't afford. According to Croswell, her demanding ways put her dad in a tough spot, making him feel like the living he was earning simply wasn't good enough.

Victoria Nicole Mello walked into the courtroom with a pleasant smile and not the slightest care in the world about testifying. Nikki was tall, with a stylishly cropped head of dark hair, and her little pearl necklace and white lace collar made her seem the epitome of proper. She was one of the best-dressed in the parade of witnesses, and she looked straight at Della as she identified her half-sister, staring at the woman in the light brown suit behind the defense table as though she were the devil herself.

"Could you tell the ladies and gentlemen of the jury the substance of the conversation you had with Della on Saturday, the seventeenth of February, 1996?" Tolbert asked.

"Saturday she called and asked me what my plans were for the weekend," Nikki said politely. "She told me she was going to Blockbuster to get a movie. She wanted to meet me to go to Mardi Gras in Mt. Adams, if she felt up to it."

"Did you, in fact, see Della on Saturday night?"

"No, I did not."

"Did you hear from Della on Sunday?"

"Yes, she called and woke me up. It was around noon, and she asked me to go to a movie with her. I said I was sleeping, that I would talk to her later."

According to Nikki's testimony, Della called her back

later that afternoon, practically begging to take her to a movie. She even offered to pay for the tickets, which was unusual. Even though Nikki refused, Della kept calling, reaching her again at 9:00 that night. She claimed she had been paging Darryl, but couldn't seem to locate him. She also mentioned that she and Darryl had a big talk Saturday night, that Darryl wanted to work things out, but she wanted a divorce. Della insisted to Nikki that her marriage just wasn't salvageable.

Among the more colorful witnesses to appear before Judge Neihaus and the ladies and gentlemen of the jury were two savvy waitresses from a Bob Evans Restaurant. They seemed as close to Darryl as anybody, having served him breakfast every day for over a year. Neither one of them backed down when Scott Croswell tried to belittle their perceptions. Both of them thought the world of Dr. Sutorius, and neither noticed anything strange about him—no body odor, no bloodshot eyes, no reddened skin, or any of the telltale signs of drinking.

When Dr. Joe Todd, a thoracic surgeon who worked closely with Sutorius for thirty years, later testified, he, too, assured the court that he "never noticed any uncleanliness" in Darryl. Dr. Todd insisted that Darryl had a very good medical practice, that he was an excellent surgeon. But when Croswell cross-examined him, the attorney continued citing Darryl's poor state of affairs as a given, attempting to turn the doctor's poor hygiene and lagging medical practice into a recipe for suicide.

"Over the entire time that you have known him," Croswell asked, "did he complain about money?"

"Yes, Darryl was preoccupied with money problems," Dr. Todd was forced to admit. "That's the reason he and I were never partners."

"Would you tell us about it?"

"Well, from my standards, I thought he was financially irresponsible."

"He apparently told everybody he was broke," Croswell asserted. "He was always pressed for money, wasn't he?"

"I don't think it would make any difference what his income would be," Dr. Todd said frankly. "Whether it was minimum wage or two million dollars a year, I think there would be the same preoccupation with money."

"Never enough money to satisfy him?"

"I think Darryl would probably spend at the level of whatever was available."

As Croswell pushed the subject, he got Dr. Todd to confirm that Darryl would panic whenever he had a "light week" at work. That was just Darryl's way, to feel he was out of business if he wasn't performing back-to-back surgery at all times. The press later had a field day with this—emphasizing Dr. Todd's refusal to go into medical practice with Sutorius because of his financial instability. They clipped excerpts from Dr. Todd's testimony that made Sutorius seem greedy. The media blew everything out of proportion, including Dr. Todd's comments about Darryl's mood swings, about the fact that Darryl didn't have many friends at the hospital.

Todd's words had been twisted by the media to the point that they didn't resemble anything he really felt about his friend and colleague. Dr. Todd had come out of semiretirement to take over Darryl's practice after his death; he was the one who sat with Darryl for an hour on Saturday the seventeenth, the last day of Darryl's life, listening to his friend talk about the prospect of another divorce, yet he was made to look like Darryl's enemy.

Croswell apologized for putting Dr. Todd in a difficult position, hoping that he hadn't offended him in any fashion—but obviously he knew he had. In front of God and everyone else, Croswell had forced Dr. Todd to talk about his friend's *hemorrhoids*.

CHAPTER | 83

*T*HERE WAS TREMENDOUS COURTHOUSE FLAK INVOLVING the revelations of Robin Zygmont. She was an admitted drug addict and felon, and it was a wonder that the prosecution bothered to call her at all. She wanted to testify that Della had confessed to the murder while they were jailmates together. The state was taking a chance—but it was a bad move.

Robin explained her compassion for Della stemmed from her familiarity with Dr. Sutorius from her days as a lab technician at Bethesda North. When they later became friends, when Robin thought Della needed a shoulder to cry on, she visited Della at the Justice Center. According to Robin, she found the two of them had a lot in common: They both had married into money; they both had difficult husbands to contend with.

But during the course of questioning by Tom Longano, Robin seemed too foggy to be credible. She couldn't remember dates, she blanked out on key questions. It was clear that she was a mess, perhaps even high on drugs. She said that Della confided that she shot Darryl twice, watching him die, and testified that Della pre-planned the suicide defense, that she admitted the suicide was a cover-up. But her statement was a package wrapped too neatly, and it came as no surprise when Croswell started to tear it to shreds. Not only was she a criminal, the attorney pointed out, Robin Zygmont was a liar and a snitch. It seemed that Croswell had her on the stand forever, chomping away at her in bits and pieces. And as she desperately tried to defend herself, everything Robin said started to make the state's case seem somewhat distorted.

"You're a drug addict, did you say? A drug-addicted person?" Croswell asked.

"I believe I said that," she told him, her voice weak, her knees visibly shaking.

"Have you ever been in treatment for drug addiction?"

"Yes."

"And did you learn about the profile of a drug-addicted person? Did they talk to you about that in your counseling?"

"Yes."

"Do they talk to you about how *manipulative* a drug addict can become?"

"Yes."

Everyone could see the road Croswell was traveling. Before he even got warmed up, he had Robin admitting that she had lied and cheated, had done just about everything and anything to satisfy her own purposes. He was cruel with her, mocking the pretty young woman for being a loser, pointing out that she'd already been divorced three times. When Robin said that she had only been divorced twice, Croswell was happy to offer himself up as the bearer of bad news, handing her a copy of Gregory Zygmont's suit for divorce as she sat helpless in the witness chair.

With Robin, the defense attorney saw his chance to poke a hole in the state's case. He did everything short of crucifying her, spending hours combing her criminal records, mentioning her aliases, quizzing her on her sketchy "friendship" with Della, which he claimed was a figment of her imagination, something she pulled from media accounts, in hopes that her testimony would gain her leniency with the law for her most current drug-related charges.

* * *

"You didn't get the interest in cracking the Sutorius case until you were sitting in jail charged with drug abuse," the attorney mocked. "That's when you got your interest in the Sutorius case, isn't it?"

"No."

"I see." Croswell smiled, pausing as though thinking about it. "So you're out on the loose. You know all about this. You're carrying the confession. You have the keys to the vault. But you don't tell anybody, even though you're here today as a good citizen? That's what you want us to believe?"

Up until that point, prosecutors had been braced for Croswell's attack, even if it was rougher than they might have anticipated. But when Croswell suddenly produced letters Robin had written to Della in jail, letters that hadn't been previously entered into discovery, Tom Longano hit the roof. He objected, citing the rule on reciprocal discovery, but was overruled. He and his team sat steaming as they watched Croswell gloat, reading the letters verbatim in open court.

It turned out that Robin's letters were written in late April 1996, weeks *after* she claimed to have received a confession from Della about the murder. In them, Robin was praising Della for being such a strong woman, for having the strength to tolerate all the bad press in the wake of Darryl's suicide. Croswell wanted to know why Robin would write so many supportive notes to a confessed killer, and of course Robin had no answer.

Furthermore, by referencing local papers, Croswell was able to make clear correlations between Robin's information and local news accounts. Ultimately, he accused her of being enthralled with a "celebrity defendant." To outsiders, it seemed the woman was fantasizing. Robin seemed to follow the case out of loneliness and boredom. Out in the hallways, people surmised that Robin Zygmont knew Della about as well as she knew O.J. Simpson. Local TV news carried quotations from her testimony, and viewers got a good laugh out of it.

Throughout the Robin Zygmont fiasco, one person who wasn't laughing was Della. She sat in the courtroom and didn't flinch. She maintained a look of innocence—the kind of look painted on the face of a Barbie doll—which was her stance throughout the trial.

Most of the time, Della kept a disinterested expression, one that indicated she was ready for all this to be over. She seemed to shun the spotlight. She had a superstar air about her, like she was tired of being hounded by cameras.

But secretly she was enjoying her celebrity. Nightly, prison guards caught Della watching glimpses of herself on TV.

CHAPTER | 84

GIVEN THE LITTLE POLKA-DOT APPEARANCE AROUND the edge of the wound, Dr. Carl Parrott, the coroner of Hamilton County, testified that the muzzle of the weapon was not in contact—not even in loose contact—with the skin when the shot was fired. The polka-dots meant there was soiling, which meant the gun was definitely not touching Darryl's head. Using his expert observations and citing a firearms analyst who reported that the gun was shot from a three-quarter-inch distance, Parrott discussed the results of the autopsy. He described the unusual angle of the bullet, which was "forward going," meaning it had been shot from behind his head. His findings were quite phenomenal.

Using a pointer and slides, Parrott was able to give precise suggestions about the significance of the bullet wound. In his lifelong career, he had never encountered a noncontact suicidal wound, nor had he encountered a forty-five-degree angle shot, a "front-to-back-type wound," in a suicide. In other words, people who shoot themselves in the head don't take chances. They put the gun to their skull, holding it directly to the side or front of the head. They don't shoot from behind, as was the case with Darryl Sutorius.

"Doctor, I have a question," Tolbert asked, pointing to a slide of Darryl's hand. "If this gun is in that hand as it's pulling the trigger, how is he going to get all that blood spray on the inside of his hands like that? Wouldn't the handle of the gun protect the inside of that hand from the spray?"

"Of course," Parrott confirmed, adding that there was a film of blood on Darryl's hand that had been "displaced."

As they moved away from autopsy slides and into the crime-scene photographs, Dr. Parrott pointed out a few other interesting facts. For one thing, the doctor had neatly placed his shoes under the coffee table; they were found side by side. Above them were his wallet, some loose change, his keys, and his pager. There was also a full glass of red wine. In Parrott's view, the victim had taken his shoes off, had tented the pillow under his head, had gotten himself into a comfortable position on the couch, and had taken maybe a sip of wine before he was shot. Behavior not quite consistent with a man about to kill himself.

The pictures detailed all the blood that was visible at the scene. Of particular note, there was a reddish film found on the handgrip of the gun, which divulged a partial fingerprint, meaning that the weapon had been handled by somebody with a bloody hand. Moreover, there was blood that had dripped down on the front of the sofa, and it had dripped in such a way as to defy gravity, because there was a clot of it stuck to the *underside* of the couch pillow.

"How did that get there?" Tolbert asked.

"I have no idea. I don't think it got there under its own influence. It's something that looks to be smeared," the coroner testified. "That's a smear. That's my opinion."

"So let's talk about these smears," Tolbert said, becoming animated. "Monday morning, February nineteenth, just before you arrive there, I run down to this couch and I start smearing my hand on this blood. I smear that blood on there, is that right, Doctor?"

"No. You can't have done that."

"Well, it's blood on there. Why couldn't I smear it Monday morning, let's say nine o'clock?"

"Because it's dried."

The encounter between Parrott and Tolbert was particularly amusing in light of Croswell's antics that had come before it. During his cross-examination of a prior witness, one of the sheriff's deputies, the defense attorney thought he was earning a lot of points by raising the possibility that any tampering at the scene could have happened during the time Della was left alone in the basement, in that sixty-second window when she ran downstairs and "found" Darryl. Croswell had even gone so far as to imply that Teddy, the dog, who had been sniffing around at that time, had possibly altered the blood patterns on the couch.

Now, confronted with expert testimony that Darryl had been dead for thirty-five to thirty-six hours by Monday morning, that the blood at the scene would have been "as dry as a chip," he looked rather foolish. Still, he seemed undaunted; he later tried to assert that the blood could have gotten there by way of Darryl having an involuntary seizure.

"When you observed the body of Dr. Sutorius on this couch Monday morning," Tolbert continued, walking over to the actual sofa, which the prosecutors had placed

313

in the middle of the courtroom, "looking at the pattern, the emerged blood that we have here, did it appear to you that this body had been moved?"

"His right arm was not in the same position that it had been in for some time, because at one point it had been in this position"—he bent his arm to demonstrate—"and now it was in this position."

Tolbert stood silent for a moment. Then, looking over at Della, he began an enactment for the court.

"Monday morning," he said, "while two deputy sheriffs are looking at a car in my garage, I run downstairs and I yell, 'wake up, wake up.' And I shake, and the arm flops over?"

"No."

"Why not, Dr. Parrott?" Tolbert asked, feigning amazement.

"The decedent was in full rigor mortis."

"On Monday morning at ten o'clock, what would it have taken for me to get that arm over like that? Like you found it?"

"A great deal of strength, and additionally, it would have caused what we refer to as 'breaking of rigor.' If I'm in rigor mortis and someone moves my arm, that breaks the rigor, and now my arm's loose."

"Was the arm hanging loose when you saw it?"

"No, the arm was rigid. Full rigor mortis had developed by six P.M Sunday night. That would be my expectation."

"And the blood. I run down," Tolbert began to shout. "I shake Dr. Sutorius. 'Please wake up! Please wake up!' Now I have this blood all over my hands. I pick up the gun and smear blood all over the gun and put the gun down. And the sheriff's come down. 'Oh, I'm sorry,'" he dramatized, "'I didn't mean to touch anything.'"

"You mean, that's not how it happened?" Tolbert asked.

"No, sir."

"Why not?"

"Because there's no fluid blood," Parrott said, pointing to the encrusted white couch they had in front of them. "The blood at the scene was as dry as it is right now."

By the time Steve Tolbert was finished, the coroner had testified that the blood on the trigger, the blood underneath the couch cushion, had gotten there within a couple hours of the death. Before he left the stand, Carl Parrott repeated his ruling that the death was a homicide.

CHAPTER | 85

DELLA'S ATTORNEY WAS GOOD. SO GOOD, HE TURNED Parrott's testimony around, getting the pathologist to admit that the blood smears could have been caused by Teddy, that they *could* have occurred during a seizure the doctor might have suffered as a result of the gunshot wound.

Even though the facts simply didn't fit, Parrott had to admit these things were theoretically possible. Parrott started to bring up the reality, mentioning that the couch had been examined by a nationally recognized expert in blood smears. Croswell cut him off, reminding him that *he* was not the blood splatter expert.

He grilled Parrott about why his team of crime-scene investigators hadn't searched the house for bloody clothes, hadn't looked through Della's closets, and hadn't checked the sinks and drains for blood. Croswell threw up enough smoke and mirrors to make people almost forget about the bloody fingerprint on the gun's handgrip.

Then he really landed on something when, during his cross-examination of the coroner, Croswell discovered that investigators just *assumed* the blood on the gun came from the hand of Della Sutorius, but they hadn't tested it. Since Ohio law dictates that a murder trial go to court within ninety days of the indictment, there wasn't enough time for DNA testing. The coroner testified that he'd discussed the matter with prosecutors, and the team didn't feel DNA testing was necessary.

"We know it's human blood," Parrott said, looking somewhat agitated.

"It's human blood, but you didn't get a scientific finding to determine if the blood on this gun matches the blood on the couch?" Croswell pressed.

"That is correct."

"Now, what I'm asking is, are there additional tests that could have been run, to match the blood on this gun with this couch pillow?"

"We could theoretically have attempted to do DNA testing, but we could not have done it in time for your discovery deadline."

"You entertained the idea of sending this gun out with blood from this pillow to see if DNA testing could match the two? You *entertained* that idea?"

"Yes."

Croswell used the point to imply that investigators left out a critical piece of evidence. Parrott insisted that it didn't matter whose blood was on the pillow, that it didn't matter whether it matched the gun or not, but Croswell had found a weak spot. He threw out the state's theory about Della's bloody fingerprint, arguing that the blood on the handgrip could belong to anybody.

"Is it Della Sutorius's fault that you don't know whose blood is on the gun?" Croswell ranted, his face reddening. "I mean, is that the way we're going to get into things? Is it Della's fault that you don't know whose blood this is? I want to get it straight. Did *Della* do anything to inhibit your ability to do a DNA test on the gun?"

"No, sir."

"Did *Scott Croswell* do anything to inhibit your ability to DNA-test this gun?" he asked, referring to himself in the third person, as was often his habit.

"We could not have gotten the results back by trial," Parrott told him, seeming somewhat ruffled.

"*I* had nothing to do with that, correct? Did you ever ask me to extend the trial date so that you could DNA-test this gun?"

"No, sir."

Because of this line of questioning, Croswell forced prosecutors to call in the original owner of the gun, as well as the Target World salesperson, both of whom testified as to the cleanliness of the used weapon at the time of sale. But it didn't deter Croswell. He continued to argue that since the amount of blood on the grip was so minuscule, since it was only detectable with a microscope, it could have easily been sold to Della in that condition.

End result: There was no way to prove whose blood was on the gun.

Croswell reminded the coroner about a comment Steve Tolbert made earlier involving "Della's gun, Della's bullet, and the two of them alone inside the house."

Under those conditions, if there were only two possibilities, Croswell asked Parrott, who shot the gun?

Carl Parrott could only say he did not believe it was Darryl.

CHAPTER | 86

*B*LOOD-SPLATTER TESTIMONY CONTINUED THE MORNING of June 3, 1996, and the jury was looking a bit weary, not too interested in the gory details. Even if Herbert MacDonell was one of the foremost consulting criminologists in the country, and one of the experts who testified in the O. J. Simpson trial, he still was rather formal and intellectual. But after he was sworn in and bid good morning, it didn't take long for Kunkel's questioning to get juicy, which mixed things up quite a bit.

One of the points MacDonell made evident was that the blood that landed underneath the couch cushion had been fresh blood, that it had been smeared there within three to six minutes of contact with the wound. It was a thin film of blood, and it wasn't something that happened as a natural flow.

Someone or something had to have done it, MacDonell testified, and in his inspection of the crime scene, he hadn't seen any paw prints. The smear was more consistent with someone's clothing rubbing up against fresh blood. It was probably something done accidentally. That was understood.

MacDonell discussed two different bloodstains at the scene: the one underneath the cushion, created with fresh blood; and another one, to the left of it, created with clotted blood.

As he spoke, the criminologist pointed to a slide of the two stains blown up larger than life. He couldn't really say what exact time sequence these stains occurred in, but one thing was certain: There had been a time interval between them. The fresh bloodstain had to occur within three to six minutes of the wound; the clotted blood stain had to occur later, perhaps an hour later, perhaps longer.

In answering Kunkel's questions about the body position shifting, about the possibility that the legs had been moved, MacDonell was willing to sit on the stained sofa to find out what would happen to the cushions with the shift in body weight. In front of the jury, he moved from one side of the couch to another, proving that the center pillow did lift up, exposing the area where blood had been smeared.

"In your opinion," Kunkel asked, "why would someone move his legs after that blood had been produced?"

"Simply to change the appearance of the scene," MacDonell said. "That's the only logical thing I can think of."

"Is that an attempt to make this look like a suicide?"

"That could be the reason. I can't think of another reason for moving the legs from horizontal to down in front of the center."

What the criminologist was saying was that someone had moved Darryl into a position where it would have looked like he was sitting up when he pulled the trigger.

Using his years of experience, his prestigious training, his scientific expertise, and after having reviewed all the evidence, Herbert MacDonell concluded that the shooting was not a suicide. Taking everything into account—the moved hand, the moved legs, the smeared blood, all they had discussed about bullet angles and trajectories—the world-renowned expert assured jurors that in his opinion, this death was a homicide.

When Croswell had his chance, he was incredibly polite to MacDonell, thanking him for the courtesies extended during discovery. It was a curious departure for a man who tended to berate witnesses.

In his softest tone, the defense attorney revisited the issue of the hands being moved, and brought up the possibility of convulsions. The expert had to agree that a convulsion was conceivable. When asked about the shot that had been fired into the couch, MacDonell conceded that could have been shot by someone contemplating suicide. Croswell got MacDonell to concede that nothing he had testified to was an absolute, hitting on every point Kunkel had covered. Of course it was unlikely that Darryl had flung blood under the couch pillow, but it *was* possible. There were a lot of options, Croswell pointed out. The partial fingerprint, for instance, could have been a palm- or footprint.

But by this time, many observers felt Croswell was stretching things too far, that he was too pushy with the witnesses. To make matters worse, he paraded around the courtroom like a peacock. Croswell was virtually taking over the courtroom with his vast list of hypotheticals, and even went so far as to suggest that the judge should break for lunch, certain that he would need another hour and a half with MacDonell before he was through.

But it didn't matter how many variables Croswell came up with. And it didn't matter that MacDonell agreed that certain opinions could be improper. On redirect, Kunkel went back to the slide photos of the partial fingerprint and the blood on the grip, and MacDonell testified that it was, indeed, made by a finger, that it had gotten there not as a direct result of the shooting, but by some other means. It got there later. Moreover, the blood expert testified that while it was physically possible for Darryl's blood to have smeared under the couch pillow during a seizure, it wasn't consistent with the evidence. Had he thrown clotted blood on the couch, there would have been clotted blood on his fingers, but photographs of his hands showed no blood on the doctor's fingers whatsoever.

Croswell came back and tried to stretch MacDonell's imagination. He even did an impression of a dog trying to cast something off its nose, using a full gulp of water to demonstrate his theory. But by insisting that MacDonell speculate on such far-out possibilities, he managed to exasperate the expert.

"I can logically conclude that someone put their hand underneath the victim for some reason," MacDonell insisted, "put the gun close to their hands and fired it, and transferred blood from the areas where it stained to the gun."

CHAPTER 87

THE MOTION TO KEEP THE TRANSCRIPTS OF THE TWO taped phone conversations between Cheryl Sullivan and Della out of court was denied. Cheryl was sworn in and asked to verify the contents of the two transcripts. As the jury followed along with typed handouts, the tapes were played.

A shy young woman, petite and thin, with the softest voice and a dimpled smile, Cheryl did not want to be photographed for television. She didn't like being associated with the highly publicized trial. Unlike Donna, who had flown in and held a press conference, Cheryl wanted nothing to do with publicity. It was clear she wasn't happy about her appearance there, and Della tried to stare her down, to intimidate her little sister, but Cheryl strained to look the other way.

It was extremely important that she testify, prosecutors made it known, especially since after all their arrangements, they never put Donna or Olga on the witness stand. With Olga, prosecutors never had a

chance to talk in person. The day before she was supposed to fly in to testify, her brother in England had
died, so she was out of the country, and unwilling to
make a special trip back. With Donna, it was a decision
based on her inability to focus when answering questions. In person, Donna drifted into stories about the
murdered dog and went on about the alleged murders
in California. Once they spent some time questioning
her, prosecutors determined they'd leave Donna out of
the trial. Still, she sat in the courtroom for a few days,
and her presence seemed to rattle Della; it was one of
the few times Della showed any kind of emotional
response.

As Cheryl focused on the jury, she took comfort in the
support of her husband, Gary, who sat directly behind
prosecutors in the crowded courtroom. She acknowl-
edged taping two phone calls in February 1996, because
she was concerned Della might try to use her "as an
alibi," and also because she was hoping Della might
"admit something" to her. At the request of police, she
turned the two tapes over.

The jury listened to the phone ringing, then heard
both sides of the conversation start; it was eerie to eavesdrop on Della's conversation. Della was denying to
Cheryl any involvement with drugs, was quite confident
she'd get out of that charge, and was claiming she really
didn't know what had happened to Darryl. The police
showed up, she said, and had she put out the kitchen
trash that morning, she would have known Darryl's car
was in the garage. As it was, she had no idea he'd been
home the whole time, dead in the basement.

She complained to Cheryl about how mean the police
were, questioning her for hours and not letting her go,
even though her back hurt and she was in so much pain.
She thought it was 10:00 A.M. Sunday morning when
Darryl killed himself, she wasn't sure. Throughout the
taped call, Della didn't seem to be thinking logically or

rationally. She was fuzzy about the details of the weekend Darryl was shot.

Next, jurors heard a tape already in progress; it was the sisters' conversation, February 24, 1996, in which Della was insisting she wasn't a bad person, that she just needed someone to love her. She talked about Beth calling the cops the day she was ready to commit suicide, and mentioned the old woman down the block who had just been murdered. It was creepy, Cheryl thought, and Della agreed. Maybe there was a killer loose.

Della complained about how the media was mistreating her—making her out to be some kind of monster for no reason. She ranted about Olga calling the police, asking Cheryl to keep their mother away—wondering why Olga hated her so much.

"My attorney thinks my family is a normal family," Della's voice whispered, "and I told him they're not going to help me. They're all lined up to flip the electric switch. They don't care if I'm dead or alive."

"What are you goin' to do, then?" Cheryl's voice trailed off.

"Well, if you're not a menace to society, I mean, obviously I'm not a serial killer," Della said. "I haven't hurt a child, you know what I'm saying. Basically, I guess they just say I did it. But I'm not a danger to society, the fact that you've killed your husband doesn't mean you're going to go start robbing banks and killing people. If they think I killed my husband, they pretty much better stop it right there. They're not going to say that I'm a serial killer, hopefully."

"Well, you haven't been charged."

"Well, you know, all day I've been in a daze, thinking, God, I came so close to killing me, too. I had started. I had taken the first two pills. You know I wouldn't be sitting right here talking to you. I would be dead."

"Is this *Olga* who interrupted you on one of these calls?" Croswell asked on cross, his voice gruff.

"Yes," Cheryl said.

"So let me get this straight. You and your mother decide between the two of you that your sister's committed a crime, is that right?"

"No, we did not decide that."

"So you casually hooked up the recorder to your machine?"

"No."

"This mother of yours is the same mother, apparently, who was calling Dr. Sutorius, right?"

"I believe *he* was calling her."

"Yeah. This mother of yours operates on a lunatic fringe. Doesn't she?"

"I don't think so."

"So she's calling up, having conversations with Dr. Sutorius and tells him God knows what, right?"

"I wasn't there. I don't know."

"What was that sister's name of yours? That was giving TV interviews the other day? Is she back in here now? That nasty-looking one with the long hair. What is her name?"

"Donna."

"Donna. She flew in from California to give TV interviews, right?"

"I don't know. You have to ask her."

"I have to ask her." Croswell snorted. "And where is that mother of yours?"

"She is in England."

"When she was calling and wanted to know what Della had to say on the phone, where was she calling from?"

"Her home in Florida."

"Florida. So in other words, this mother of yours, that operates on a lunatic fringe, lives in Florida, but decides for this trial she is going to blast out to England, right?"

"Wrong."

"What is she doing there? I bet she is being

knighted," he sneered. "She is going to get some kind of reward from the king, right?"

"Her brother died. She is at his funeral."

"Her brother died. We have got your word for that, right? And what kind of crap did she fill Dr. Sutorius full of?"

"I don't know."

"She was calling and saying there were twenty-five dead bodies or whatever, telling him he better watch himself. And you know what I'll bet? I'll bet if Della couldn't put Dr. Sutorius over the edge, your *mother* sure could."

Scott Croswell reviewed the taped conversations in detail and asked Cheryl to explain each statement, describing the context for the comment about "killing me, too" as being Della's identification with Darryl's suicide. Croswell's interpretation of the line was that Darryl killed himself, and now Della might kill herself, too. But it didn't fly with Cheryl.

He tried to put Olga on trial, tried to put Cheryl on trial, but she wasn't about to defend herself. This was Della's day in court. Her answers were curt—and she was cool, calm, and collected, no matter how demeaning Croswell became.

On redirect, Kunkel asked Cheryl about Della's compassion for her husband's death. Cheryl said her sister didn't seem to think of Darryl's death at all; she was more concerned about brushing her teeth.

CHAPTER | 88

*T*HE PROCESS OF JUSTICE, BEING FULLY CAPTURED BY Court TV and its team of eager analysts, did not take long in the case of the State vs. Della Dante Sutorius. In between the flashes of coverage from the war crimes tribunal in Bosnia, in between the sound bites of commercials for Dirt Devil and Red Lobster, the commentators on Court TV were simply amazed at how quickly the state rested its case. With their authoritative voices, they speculated on the tack the prosecution was taking, and pinpointed the strengths of Croswell's battle to raise reasonable doubt.

Even before the case was fully heard, a national jury of sorts had been set up, with viewers calling in from around the country to offer their opinions. One woman phoned from Michigan to say Darryl seemed to have so much dysfunction around him, it was possible the doctor might have "done himself in," making it look like a murder, "just to make Della suffer."

The clips on television were a virtual show and tell—there was Croswell pounding on the couch, taking off his coat to mimic a cloth smearing against it. There was Longano, his handsome face and deep-set eyes looking as serious as a Roman statue, silent behind the prosecutor's table. And, of course, there was Della, with closeups of her perfectly made-up face, her dark roots showing but every strand of hair in place.

In the backdrop were the curious onlookers, the people filling the court benches, the families, the friends, and the thrill seekers. The main action focused on the people in dark suits—the prosecution team on one end, Croswell and his cocounsel on the other. With him were Don Richardson, an attorney who sat next to Della throughout the proceedings, primarily to hold her hand, and Elizabeth Agar, Croswell's partner—neither of whom left the defense table.

It was a case filled with passion, with attorneys hot under the collar, some using extremely sarcastic and patronizing tones. Reporters noted it was a rare case, that the coroner's testimony was pivotal.

But the most amusing thing about it all was Della's narcissism. At the request of her attorney, she had been granted a special motion to wear her makeup and street clothes, and each day seemed to amount to yet another fashion opportunity for the petite blonde.

She changed her appearance almost as much as Madonna, at first donning granny glasses, then opting for a childish look in flowers and lace. On the day Cheryl testified, Della's outfit made her look like she was ready for a toga party—some kind of draped white tunic that was far too large for her. She looked out of place, like a child playing dress-up in adult clothes.

But if Della seemed a bit unreadable, a bit naive, her attorney was the one who most definitely orchestrated it. Scott Croswell was a highly polished showman, and he knew just the right buttons to press to get the jury's sympathy. And he made sure she looked innocent.

Before he began his case for the defense, Croswell motioned for an acquittal under Criminal Rule 29 and was overruled, Judge Neihaus having decided that the state had provided enough evidence as to all the essential elements of the crimes charged in the indictment.

Croswell's strongest line of attack would be the mental state of Dr. Sutorius at the time of his death, and to that end he brought in Dr. Ronald Maris, a "suicidologist" who had flown in from the University of South Carolina, where, as the director of the Center for the Study of Suicide and Life Threatening Behavior, he taught courses in "death and dying" and had published the "bible" on the subject of suicide.

Croswell gleefully brandished Dr. Maris's scientific journal, *Suicide and Life Threatening Behavior,* the only journal of its kind, which Dr. Maris had long produced as editor-in-chief. Croswell took his time with the expert, making sure he covered every bit of Dr. Maris's international and national achievements in the field of suicidology. He wanted the jury to know just what weight this expert's opinion would bear.

"It's a fairly new science," Dr. Maris testified, as he continued to elaborate on his curriculum vitae, mentioning his latest book, *Assessment and Prediction of Suicide,* which Croswell held up for everyone to see.

Before he got to the meat of the questioning, the defense attorney insisted that he had *not* told Dr. Maris anything about the personal life of Darryl Sutorius, that he had *not* told him anything about the facts of the case. Whatever opinion Dr. Maris fashioned, jurors could be sure, would be entirely of his own accord.

With the help of a chart and an easel, Dr. Maris detailed the "fifteen common single predictors of suicide." He testified that Darryl exhibited the following twelve: depressive illness, alcohol abuse, suicide ideation, isolation, hopelessness, occupation problems, economic problems, marital problems, family pathology, stressful life events, nagging physical problems, and anger.

As Croswell led him through the list, Dr. Maris became quite good at relating the various predictors directly to Darryl Sutorius's life. Dr. Maris mentioned Darryl's troubled first divorce and the talk of suicide in 1991. He touched on Darryl's financial problems, exacerbated by the alimony he paid his first wife, and the difficulties he was experiencing in his profession. He discussed Darryl's family history regarding his kids, which was shaky, and moved to the problems Darryl faced in the marriage with Della, pointing out that he struggled with impotence.

By the time Dr. Maris was done assessing Darryl, it was clear the surgeon had a diminished quality of life. Darryl had many persistent problems, it seemed, and with no friends to turn to, he was just angry at the world. A man in his shape was at the highest possible risk for suicide, the expert testified. In his view, the combination of all these problems had finally taken their toll.

"We have to remember, even today in enlightened times," Dr. Maris said, "that suicide is still a highly stigmatized event. It's something you would like to avoid. I mean, there are suicide exclusion clauses in life insurance policies. There's a lot of people who would want to disguise a suicide and make it look like something else."

Wisely, Croswell elicited testimony from the expert that explained Darryl's upbeat behavior in the last days of his life. According to Dr. Maris, once a suicidal person has formulated a plan to kill himself, he often feels better. People about to commit suicide feel relief; they no longer have to face their problems.

"If we could assume that he had resolved to do this," Dr. Maris testified, "he would clearly look upbeat. He wouldn't have to do anything with an impending divorce, or his future practice, or better relations with the family."

Based on his thirty-five years of education and training, and on his experience in death scene investigations and suicide, Dr. Ronald Maris stated "with a reasonable degree of scientific certainty" that Darryl Sutorius "could well have committed suicide."

CHAPTER | 89

*T*HE FIREWORKS STARTED THE MINUTE LONGANO started his cross, and TV stations carried the bombastic moment when the prosecutor walked over and removed the "suicide predictor" chart, tossing it aside.

"Are you telling us that if someone exhibits these predictors that they will, in fact, commit suicide?" Longano wanted to know.

"No, sir, I am not saying that."

"I guess, then, that someone could show each and every one of these fifteen predictors and still never commit suicide?"

"That is correct."

Longano mentioned how impressed he was with Dr. Maris's book—he was up until 4:00 A.M. reading it the night before—but what he really wanted to find out was what, *exactly*, did Dr. Ronald Maris know about Dr. Sutorius's life? After all, Dr. Maris hadn't dealt with Darryl directly; he had knowledge of him strictly through court transcripts, which was a pretty narrow window.

But Dr. Maris didn't agree; he became defensive. Even though he never met Darryl face-to-face, even though he had only had a small amount of experience testifying in criminal cases, he wanted to spar.

But the questions Longano started to pose quickly undercut Dr. Maris's testimony. Dr. Maris was forced to defend his opinions about Darryl, without having sufficient facts to back anything up. When the prosecutor asked him to justify his claim that Darryl was a heavy drinker, all the expert could do was point to the testimony from Beth Evans, in which she mentioned he was at her house drinking on Christmas Eve.

"How many drinks did he have?" the prosecutor pressed.

"Two or three scotches, as I understand."

"And that's evidence of *heavy drinking?*"

"I'm saying that was one concrete incident where I know that he was a drinker," Dr. Maris replied. "Apparently in the transcript his wife had talked about her telling his colleagues he was an alcoholic. There were some scattered references, more than one, to his alcohol."

"So that's *Della* saying he's an alcoholic. That's no one else saying he's an alcoholic."

"I'm saying that there's three instances in the record where there was mention of drinking," he argued. "I'm just saying there was alcohol present in his life."

Every red flag Dr. Maris pointed out was like waving a cloth in front of a bull. Longano discarded each suicide factor, and by the time he was through, Dr. Maris seemed visibly unnerved. The more Longano picked on the expert's predictors, the more he was able to show jurors the expert's unfamiliarity with the real facts about Darryl. It was devastating to the defense.

"Where is the evidence of Dr. Sutorius's plan to commit a suicide?"

"Did I say that he had a plan?" Dr. Maris chided.

"Did he have a plan?"

"I don't know."

"Was he planning on committing suicide a week before the day he was murdered?"

"I have no way to know that."

The two of them got into a heated battle about the profession Dr. Maris was in, Longano having deemed it "not nearly as scientific as, say, forensic pathology."

Dr. Maris didn't agree. He argued that the opinion of a forensic pathologist was not superior to his as a psychologist, stating for the record that all the evidence in the case was inconclusive, specifically the physical evidence.

With that, Tom Longano just blew up.

The prosecutor had to remind him that bullet trajectories and contact wounds were not subjective, that the findings of Dr. Carl Parrott were not open to interpretation.

"Are you aware in this case that Dr. Parrott was able to do an autopsy and determine that the cause of Dr. Sutorius's death was a bullet through his head?"

"Yes."

"Yet *you* can't sit here today and tell us one hundred percent that Dr. Sutorius committed suicide?"

"Neither can Dr. Parrott."

Before they moved off Dr. Parrott, Dr. Maris talked about the specific wound on Darryl's head being "very close to where suicide wounds are." He was adamant that in his view this *could* have been a suicide, even though Dr. Parrott's opinion was virtually uncontroverted. There was no physical evidence to point to anything other than the fact that this was a homicide *made to look like* a suicide.

But Dr. Maris still wanted his say. Even though he wasn't a medical doctor, even though he had performed *zero* autopsies, Dr. Maris criticized the coroner's findings but was quickly put in his place when he determined that Della was not Darryl's problem, that Darryl caused his own problems. For one thing, Longano asked him about the .22-caliber handgun, wondering why Darryl had brought it to police. Dr. Maris had no response. When asked about the .38 Della brought in the house, the expert said it was *their* gun, not just Della's.

"Did you read the part where she goes and buys some ammunition, and she tells the sales clerk, 'My husband found the first gun, he isn't going to find the second one, I'm going to hide it'?" Longano ridiculed. "Now, this is what you call *their* gun? You still want to stick with that, or you want to change it?"

"It is in their house," Dr. Maris testified. "Either one of them could have access to it."

"There's no evidence in the transcript that Dr. Sutorius knew that there was a .38 in the house, right?"

"As far as I understand, there is not."

"As far as you understand it. *You* read the transcripts. *You* are the one testifying as an expert. Do you know, *yes or no?*"

CHAPTER | 90

"ON FEBRUARY EIGHTEENTH, 1996, AT TWO-THIRTY in the morning, as Darryl Sutorius lay sleeping on this very couch," Jerry Kunkel told the jury, "Della Sutorius put a bullet in the back of his head, ending his life, and then tried to make it look like a suicide."

The prosecutor had a little bit of Larry King about him. Maybe it was just the suspenders, but he seemed to lull the courtroom audience, and there was something about his voice that made you believe him. He was entirely credible without being arrogant.

In the closing statement, Kunkel talked about motive, about the letter addressed to Darryl marked "personal and confidential" which was found among Della's things. It was her copy of the request to waive her rights to his pension funds—so she knew what she was doing.

He mentioned opportunity, reminding everyone that while Darryl was filling out divorce papers, she was out buying a gun. As he pieced together every thread of evidence, he drew a diagram of "Della's Web." The evidence stacked up nicely. Particularly effective was Darryl's dying declaration, the answering machine tape, which was played again.

It was like the movie *Black Widow*, where the woman killed for money without remorse, he said; Della was cold, she was calculating, and Kunkel fit all the pieces of the jigsaw together. He brought out the Target World practice sheet, the black silhouette showing Della's marksmanship. Not only was she capable of it, she savored it. She hit the bull's-eye from twenty-one feet.

The partial fingerprint on the gun was Darryl's, he said. Della wanted it there; she had put his hand around the gun and fired the second shot.

"That woman is the most dangerous person you will ever see in your life," he told jurors, "and you know *why*? Because she doesn't look it."

Epilogue

THE SORDID SAGA OF DELLA DANTE FAYE HALL HOEFfer Beyer Bassett Britteen Sutorius ended on June 7, 1996. A tear rolled down her face as she listened to closing arguments, then Della collapsed in her chair as the jury announced the verdict: Guilty of aggravated murder in the death of her husband.

Deborah Sutorius leaned forward in sobs of relief, her trembling hands covering her face, while deputies placed handcuffs on Della's pale arms. It was the overwhelming physical evidence that had convinced them, jurors said afterward.

Two weeks later, Della was given the maximum sentence by Judge Richard Neihaus, who deemed her "beyond hope of rehabilitation." For the aggravated murder, she would be required to serve the maximum twenty years; for the related weapons charge, she would serve three years; for the drug possession, another eighteen months was tacked on. Della Dante Sutorius would be seventy years old before she'd even be eligible for parole, required to serve at least twenty-four years of her sentence.

"You have now earned something probably for the first time in your life," Judge Neihaus told her. "This sentence is inherently fair because of your lifelong history of aberrant behavior. It's not fair to compare you to a black widow spider," he continued, "because a black widow does not disguise itself. I believe you are more suitably compared to a creature called the lionfish. The outward appearance of the creature completely belies its deadly, poisonous, aggressive nature. The lionfish attracts its prey through its appearance, and then consumes all that comes close to it. That creature is you."

As Della was led from the courtroom, Shawn stood in the hallway, her face filled with tears. She had been to see her mom in the Justice Center, Della swore she was innocent, and there was a part of Shawn that believed her. She remembered the phone conversation the two of them had on February 19, that Sunday afternoon when Della was talking about going to the movies with Darryl. It just didn't seem possible that her mother could have done this.

As Della caught a glimpse of Shawn, she mouthed, "Don't cry." She was certain she would win the appeal, but on June 25, 1997, a panel of three judges at the First District Court of Appeals upheld the conviction. Her right to appeal to the Supreme Court of Ohio would not be automatic. The chances of her case being heard a third time would be slim.

A happily married mother of three, Shawn went back to her home in Indiana, hoping to help Della in any way possible. She changed her mind, however, when Della started calling from the Marysville Correctional Center for Women, somehow managing to reach Shawn without calling collect. She was calling to harass. She accused Shawn of stealing her diamond tennis bracelet and was insisting she gain entry to the Symmesridge house to demand certain items from the Sutorius clan. Della wanted Shawn to sell off the Victoria's Secret chandelier and some other items, her fur coats among them. She badgered Shawn with constant calls and letters.

When they had been brought in before the grand jury, all of her former husbands and boyfriends had met and compared stories. None, with the exception of Grant Bassett, had anything to say to the media. They were thrilled not to have to testify—David Britteon was the only one with that distinction—and all of them wanted their lives to go back to normal, thankful to never think about Della's vengeful ways again.

Although Jerry Springer publicly denied knowing the "notorious Sutorius," his name popped up in the press multiple times, along with mention of the scandal he had been involved in once before—back in 1974, Councilman Springer resigned from office, admitting that he had engaged in an "act of prostitution" when he wrote a $25 check to a woman identified as Norma Jean Hall.

With a single bullet, Cincinnati would never be the same. Deadly Della took her place next to Marge Schott as one of the leading ladies who managed to tarnish the image of the Queen City.

A year after her sentencing, the county auctioned off her jewelry to help defray the taxpayer money spent on the trial. But eleven pieces of her gold ornaments fetched a mere $5,100 from the buyer, who later said he was "told by an angel" to purchase everything in one lump. An editorial in the *Cincinnati Enquirer* teasingly likened the sale and viewing of Della's "described chattels" to the auction of the estate of Jackie O. Tongue in cheek, people teased about a catalogue being issued.

One of her hairdressers remembered Della's claim that, through her English bloodline, she was distantly related to the Royal Family. Another spoke of her as a "working" girl, turning tricks in the Omni Netherland Hotel, obsessed with the smell of her fake nails.

In spite of everything, Deborah Sutorius was happily wed "in a ceremony of Christian love" on October 5, 1996; she had married into one of the most prosperous families in Ohio, and held a reception at her in-laws' gigantic estate. At the small church ceremony, Deborah walked down the same aisle she'd walked for her dad's memorial—this time wearing white, with a penny from her dad's belongings in her satin shoe.

"There's no way you can put the impact of this into words. It's not over for us," the beautiful bride confided. "It'll never be over for us until she's dead."

Sitting in prison, Della has fantasies about her own TV movie. She told Shawn that Sally Field would be a good pick, but changed her mind about the prospect when her attorney informed her about the "Son of Sam" law. Having learned she couldn't gain any profit whatsoever, she remembered the appeal she'd intended to fight for. A silly movie could ruin her chances, and besides, cooperating with something like that was beneath her, really.

So far, Della has yet to comment to TV reporters, though they have tried repeatedly to bring cameras around. Not that she would allow audiences to see her wearing drab prison garb, especially with her gray roots showing and her face-lifts coming undone.

The word is, she has been put on dishwashing duty, and her back is killing her. She has tried like hell to get

a doctor's note to excuse her, but apparently her warden
has been in no mood to listen.

The last person to have heard from her was Beth.
Dante called to request that her furry little pet be sold.
If she couldn't have him, then she wanted the *cash*.
Teddy, at least, would get her a couple hundred.